HOTELS OF CHARACTER
AND CHARM IN SPAIN

While every care has been taken to ensure the accuracy of the information in this guide, time brings change, and consequently the publisher cannot accept responsibility for errors that may occur. Prudent travelers will therefore want to call ahead to verify prices and other perishable information.

Published in the United States by Fodor's Travel Publications, Inc.
Published in France by Payot/Rivages

Fodor's is a registered trademark of Fodor's Travel Publications, Inc.

ISBN 0-679-00210-3
Second Edition

Hotels of Character and Charm in Spain

Translators: Anne Norris, Derry Hall
Rewriting: Marie Gastaut
Cover design: Fabrizio La Rocca
Front cover photograph: Parador de Oropesa (Castilla Manche)
Back cover: Cortijo Torre de la Reina (Andalusia)

Special Sales

Fodor's Travel Publications are available at special discounts for bulk purchases for sales promotions or premiums. Special editions, including personalized covers, excerpts of existing guides, and corporate imprints, can be created in large quantities for special needs. For more information, contact your local bookseller or Special Markets, Fodor's Travel Publications, 201 E. 50th Street, New York, NY 10022.

Printed in Italy by Litho Service
10 9 8 7 6 5 4 3 2 1

Fodor's RIVAGES

HOTELS
of Character
and Charm
IN SPAIN

Conceived by
Michelle Gastaut and Fabrice Camoin

Project editor
Michelle Gastaut

Fodor's Travel Publications, Inc.
New York • Toronto • London • Sydney • Auckland
www.fodors.com/

This new 1998 edition details 240 hotels, and the inns and hotels selected are in different categories ranging from simple comfort to 'grande luxe'. We have insisted that our readers can always easily identify the category of each inn or hotel, independently even of its star rating.

You should also note that the prices quoted are those in force at end–1997 and naturally some of them may since have changed. The paradors notably, adjust their prices in the month of March.

As a result all prices quoted should be treated as indicative and when making your reservation by phone or fax, you should ask for the latest detailed rates–also because most hotels quote rates to us **without including VAT (value-added tax), which is 7% or 15% depending on hotel category.** You should also understand that rates quoted for half board and full board are often to be added to the room rates given.

In this new edition we have also given a selection of restaurants and cafés grouped by the major tourist areas, as a complement to your travels and to better appreciate the life of the country. The range of prices given is for a full meal, but excludes drinks.

How to use this guide

We have classified hotels by regions in alphabetical order, and within each region by town or locality in alphabetical order. The number of the hotel page corresponds to the hotel number used on the regional maps, in the Contents pages and in the index of hotel names.

Practical information

All such information (airports, phone & fax numbering system, and exchange rates) is given on page 20.

Please let us know...

If you are attracted by an inn or small hotel not listed in our 1997 guide, and you think it worthy of selection, please tell us about it so that the author may visit it. In like manner, if you are disappointed by any of our selection, please also let us know about it.

EDITIONS RIVAGES
Michelle Gastaut
10, rue Fortia
13001 Marseilles
France

CONTENTS LIST

CONTENTS RESTAURANTS

CONTENTS

In Spain the I.V.A. (7 %) will be added to these prices

A N D A L U S I A

A R A G O N

A S T U R I A S - C A N T A B R I A

B A L E A R I C   I S L A N D S

C A S T I L L A M A N C H A

C A T A L U N Y A

E X T R E M A D U R A

G A L I C I A

M A D R I D

N A V A R R A

P A I S   V A S C O

PRINCIPALITY OF ANDORRA

V A L E N C I A

*Prices shown in brackets are prices for a double room, sometimes with half board or full board. For precise details, go to the page mentioned.

ESSENTIAL INFORMATION

TIME DIFFERENCES

Spain: 6 hours after EST; 1 hours after GMT

TELEPHONE/FAX

To contact your correspondent in Spain from USA:
International 00-34 – Town code ★ – Number wanted (★ but omitting the first number between brackets, used only in internal communications).

LODGING

Paradores: You can contact the central reservation office in Madrid Tel. (9)1-435 9700; fax (9)1-435 9944.

GETTING AROUND BY PLANE

Iberia: Spain's major national airline, flied out of hubs Madrid and Barcelona on both international and domestic routes. In Madrid Tel. (9)1-587 81 56. In Barcelona Tel. (9)3-412 56 67. Aviaco, a subsidiary of Iberia, covers only domestic routes.

WEIGHTS AND MESURES

1 meter (m) = 1.09 yards	1 yards = 0.92 m
1 kilometer (km) = 0.62 mile	1 mile = 1.61km
1 gram (g) = 0.04 ounce	1 ounce = 25g
1 liter = 1.6 quarts	1 quart = 0.94 liter

AIRPORTS

ANDALUSIA
– **Almeria**: Tel. (951) 22 19 54 - 12km.
– **Gibraltar**: 2.5km.
– **Granada**: Tel. (956) 27 33 22 - 17km.
– **Jerez de la Frontera**: Tel. (956) 33 42 32 - 11km.
– **Málaga**: Tel. (952) 32 20 00 - 9km.
– **Melilla**: Tel. (952) 68 35 64 - 4km.
– **Sevilla-San Pablo**: Tel. (95) 451 61 11 - 14km.

ARAGON
– **Saragosa**: Tel. (976) 32 62 62 - 9km.

ASTURIAS CATABRIA
– **Bilbao - Sondica**: Tel. (94) 453 06 40 - 11km.
– **Fuentarrabia**: Tel. (943) 42 35 86
– **San Sebastian - Fuentarrabia**: Tel. (943) 64 21 67 - 20km.
– **Santander**: Tel. (942) 25 10 09 - 7km.
– **Vitoria**: Tcl. (945) 27 00 00 - 8km.

BALEARIC ISLANDS
– **Ibiza**: Tel. (911) 30 03 00 - 9km.
– **Menorca - San Clemente in Mahón:** Tel. (971) 36 15 77 - 5km.
– **Palma de Mallorca**: Tel. (971) 26 42 12 - 11km

CASTILLA-LEÓN
– **Valladolid Airport**: Tel. (983) 56 01 62 - 14km.

CATALUNYA
– **Barcelona**: Tel. (93) 317 10 11 - 12km.

ESTREMADURA
– **Badajoj**: Tel. (924) 44 00 16 - 16km.

GALICIA
– **Coruña - Alvedro:** Tel. (981) 23 35 84 - 10km.

MADRID
– **Madrid - Barajas**: Tel. (91) 205 40 90 - 13km.

NAVARRA
– **Pamplona**: Tel. (948) 31 72 02 - 7km.
– **Reus**: Tel. (977) 30 37 90 - 3km.

VALENCIA
– **Alicante**: Tel. (96) 528 50 11 - 12km.
– **Murcia - San Javier**: Tel. (968) 57 00 73 - 50km.
– **Manises**: Tel. (96) 379 08 50 - 12km.

CALENDAR OF FESTIVALS, 'CORRIDAS' AND FAIRS ★

March
- 'Fallas' Festival of bonfires at Valencia
- 'Semana Santa' (Holy Week). The best-known are those of Seville, Valladolid, Toledo, Murcia, Lorca and Cuenca

April
- Seville fair

May
- Horse Fair at Jerez de la Frontera
- Festival of 'Córdoban patios' at Córdoba
- Fair of San Isidro at Madrid
- 'Romerio de Rocio' (Gipsy festival) at Huelva (no 'Corrida')

June
- Corpus Christi (Catholic festival celebrated throughout Spain). The best-known are those of Granada, Toledo, Málaga - and others.
- 'Hogueras' of San Juan, Burgos fair

July
- Pamplona fair ('Encierro' (Bull-running) and 'Corrida')
- San Jaíme fair at Valencia (Second week of July)

August
- Málaga fair (end-July, early-August)
- Burgos fair
- Flamenco festival at Jerez de la Frontera

September
- 'Corridas' of Valencia
- Salamanca fair
- Grape harvest fair of Logroño
- 'Corridas' of Barcelona

October
- Fair of the feast of the 'Virgen del Pilar', closing the 'Corridas' season

★ This list naturally cannot be exhaustive and only mentions the major events in Spain. Verify dates with the Spanish tourism office, which can also give you a copy of its complete listing of hundreds of local events.

MAPS

KEY TO THE MAPS

Scale : 1:1.120.000

MOTORWAYS

A9 - L'Océane

Under construction
projected

ROADS
Highway
Dual carriageway
Four lanes road
Major road
Secondary road

TRAFFIC
National
Regional
Local

JUNCTIONS
Complete
Limited

DISTANCES IN KILOMETRES
On motorway   10
On other road   10

BOUNDARIES
National boundary
Region area
Department area

URBAIN AREA

Town
Big city
Important city
Medium city
Little city

AIRPORTS

FORESTS

PARKS
Limit
Center

Cartography by

90, rue Nationale
75 013 PARIS
01 45 84 30 84

MAR CANTABRICO

Cabo de Ajo

sta

Noja

Santoña

Escalante

Cabo Machichaco

Laredo

Colindos

225

226

Limpias

Castro-
Urdiales

Plentzia

Bakio

Bermeo
Mundaka

230 ▸ 232

El Puente

Amuero

Las Arenas

Getxo

Algorta

Mungia

Ea

Lekeitio

Ramales
de la Victoria

N634

Santurtzi
Portugalete

Gernika
de Arteaga

BI638

Ondarroa

San Sebastián

Barakaldo

BILBAO

Gernika-
Lumo

Mutriku

Zarautz

Hern

Carranza

Sodupe

Deba
Zumaia

Usurbil

Lasarte

Balmaseda

Güeñes

223

Arrigorriaga

Amorebieta

Markina-
Xemein

Eibar

Cestona

Azkoitia

Azpeitia

Andoai

227

233

Villasante

Artziniega

Respaldiza

Llodio

Cebério

Durango

Axpe

Placencia
de las Armas

Tolosa

C6318

Villasana
de Mena

Amurrio

Orozco

GI2632

Bergara

Zúmarraga

Medina
de Pomar

Quincoces
de Yuzo

Ciorroga

224

Arrasate-
Mondragon

Oñati

Beasain

Betelu

Quintanilla
la Ojeda

Orduña

Legutiano

Aránzazu

4

Berberana

Murguia

Arroyabe

Audicana

Etxarri-
Aranatz

Trespaderne

Barcina
del Barco

Gasteiz
Vitoria

Argomaniz

Salvatierra-
Aguráin

Olazagutia

Alsasua

Oña

Salas de B.

Subijana

222

Arraia Maeztu

Zudaire

N232

Puentelarra

Treviño

NA132

Sta Maria
de Ribarredondo

Miranda
de Ebro

75

Peñacerrada

Acedo

Estella

Pancorbo

117

Bernedo

Sta Cruz
de Campezo

Briviesca

Haro

Samaniego

Lapoblación

Los Arcos

Allo

Monasterio
de Rodilla

N1

N232

Laguardia

A124

Cenicero

N111

Viana

Mendavia

Le

Villafranca-
Montes de Oca

Belorado

Santo Domingo
de la Calzada

San Asensio

Fuenmayor

Oyón

Logroño

Lodosa

Alcanadre

Andosilla

N120

Santurdejo

Nájera

Navarrete

N120

A68

N232

El Villar
de Arnedo

S. Adrián

Calahorra

Pradoluengo

Badarán

Ezcaray

C113

Arnedo

116

Villorobe

Islallana

N111

LR115

Autol

LR11

Pineda
de la Sierra

Anguiano

Torrecilla
en Cameros

Pradillo

Arnedillo

Que

Barbadillo de H.

115

C115

Vizcainos

C113

Villavelayo

Neila

Montenegro
de Cameros

Lumbreras

Diustes

Yangas

Ortigüela

Sales de
los Infantes

Quintanar
de la Sierra

Duruelo
de la Sierra

La Póveda
de Soria

Huérteles

San Pedro
Manrique

Cervera del
Rio Alhama

sto Domingo
e Silos

13

Vinuesa

14

Aguilar
Rio Alha

C111

Huerta
del Rey

S. Leonardo
de Yagüe

N734

La Gallega

Terra

La Rubia

Magaña

HOTELS

Hotel Reina Cristina

11200 Algeciras (Cádiz)
Paseo de la Conferencia
Tel. (9)56-60 26 22 - Fax (9)56-60 33 23
Sr Gonzalez

Category ★★★★ **Rooms** 140 with air-conditioning, telephone, bath, WC and TV.
Price Single 9,000-11,500Pts, double 15,500-20,000Pts, suite 23,000-23,200Pts.
Meals Breakfast 1,750Pts, served 7:15-10:30; half board + 4,500Pts, full board
+ 6,000Pts. (per pers.). **Restaurant** Service 13:00-15:30; menu 3,000Pts, also à la
carte. Specialties: regional and international cooking. **Credit cards** All major. **Pets**
Small dogs allowed in the rooms. **Facilities** Swimming pool, tennis, minigolf, sauna,
parking. **Nearby** Beaches of Getares, Chaparral, Los Ladrillos, El Rinconcillo -
Ceuta - The road from Algeciras to Ronda. **Open** All year.

This hotel is haunted with memories. Its history began in 1890
when the government commissioned a British company to build
the railway from Bobadilla to Gibraltar. Lodging in Algeciras during
the work, the director was so attracted by the region that he decided
to build a hotel here. The setting for the Algeciras Conference in
1906 and a haunt of spies during the war, it has now recovered all its
old peace and quiet. Large gardens planted with pine and cypress
trees surround the hotel, which has retained its comfortable, rather
British style. Its principal charm is in the fact that it is a haven in an
all too touristic region.

How to get there *(Map 24): 124km southeast of Cádiz via N430; 200 meters
from the port.*

Parador Casa del Corregidor

11630 Arcos de la Frontera (Cádiz)
Plaza de Espana
Tel. (9)56-70 05 00 - Fax (9)56-70 11 16
D. Perez Moneo

Category ★★★ **Rooms** 20 with air-conditioning, telephone, bath, WC, satellite TV and minibar. **Price** Double 17,500Pts. **Meals** Breakfast 1,300Pts, served 8:00-11:00. **Restaurant** Service 13:00-15:30, 20:00-22:30; menu 3,500Pts, also à la carte. Specialties: regional cooking. **Credit cards** All major. **Pets** Dogs not allowed. **Facilities** Parking. **Nearby** Church of Santa Maria in Arcos de la Frontera - Jerez de la Frontera - Bornos - Monastery of the Cartuja - Villamartin (wine cellars of Pajarete) - Càdix. **Open** All year.

Arcos de la Frontera is on the summit of a granite promontory surrounded by the Guadalete River, in the midst of a Mediterranean landscape of vines, orange and olive trees. The hotel is in town but thanks to its location on the edge of a cliff, it forms a natural balcony with a superb view. It is a very old building but has been sumptuously reconstructed while retaining its original architecture. The panorama can be enjoyed from the lounges, bar, dining room, and the best rooms which have terraces. Close to Jerez de la Frontera, this is a good center for visiting the bodegas and sherry wine cellars of the region.

How to get there (Map 24): 65km northeast of Cádiz via A4, exit Jerez de la Frontera, then N342; opposite the Ayuntamiento (town hall).

Cortijo Fain

11630 Arcos de la Frontera (Cádiz)
Caret. Algar, km 3
Tel. (9)56-23 13 96 – Fax (9)56- 23 13 96
Sr Jose Luis Jimenez

Category ★★★ **Rooms** 10 with with air-conditioning, bath and WC. **Price** Double 10,000Pts, suite 15,000Pts. **Meals** Breakfast 1,000Pts, served 8:00-11:00. **Restaurant** Service 13:30-15:30, 20:00-23:00; menu 4,000Pts. Specialties: regional cooking. **Credit cards** All major. **Pets** Dogs allowed. **Facilities** Swimming pool, parking. **Nearby** Church of Santa Maria in Arcos de la Frontera - Jerez de la Frontera - Bornos - Monastery of the Cartuja - Villamartin (wine cellars of Pajarete Càdix). **Open** All year except for Christmas and New Year.

This large property situated 3km from Arcos de la Frontera is not a typical hotel, but ten rooms have been opened in this beautiful 17th-century farm for the use of guests, who can also take part in the daily life of the estate. The rooms are very large and each has a lounge and open fireplace, and all are comfortably arranged and decorated in the best Andalusian style. Two have their own private terraces. Guests can also avail of the library, which, with its 10,000 volumes, is one of the finest private collections in Spain. The house, with its white-walled setting covered with bougainvillea, is surrounded by olive trees which make for very pleasant walk's. In summer the swimming pool can also be used while horse riding is available in the Campos Andalus throughout the year.

How to get there *(Map 24): 68km northeast of Cádiz via A4, exit Jerez de la Frontera, then N342 and Algar road for 3km.*

Los Olivos

11630 Arcos de la Frontera (Cádiz)
Paseo de Boliches, 30
Tel. (9)56-70 08 11 - Fax (9)56-70 20 18
Sr J. A. Roldan

Category ★★★ Rooms 19 with air-conditioning, telephone, bath or shower, WC, TV and minibar. **Price** Single 4,000-5,000Pts, double 7,000-9,000Pts, suite 9,000-11,000Pts, + 2,000Pts (extra bed). **Meals** Breakfast 600Pts, served 8:00-11:00. **Restaurant** See p. 240. **Credit cards** Amex, Visa, Eurocard, MasterCard. **Pets** Dogs not allowed. **Nearby** Church of Santa Maria in Arcos de la Frontera - Jerez de la Frontera - Bornos - Monastery of the Cartuja - Villamartin (wine cellars of Pajarete) - Càdix. **Open** All year.

An astonishing small Andalusian town, Arcos de la Frontera aligns its white houses on the crest of the plateau overlooking the Guadalete River. The town has conserved some beautiful remnants of its Moorish past and its magnificent church in the flamboyant Gothic style (Santa Maria de la Asunción) is well worth a visit. The hotel is simple but all is arranged in good taste: cane furniture in the lounge-gallery that surrounds the interior patio, and rather monastic rooms that very well maintained. Some rooms overlook the river. Prices are reasonable.

How to get there *(Map 24): 65km northeast of Cádiz via A4, exit Jerez de la Frontera, then N342.*

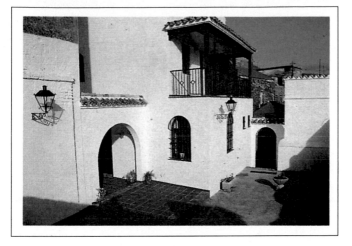

Hotel El Convento

11630 Arcos de la Frontera (Cádiz)
Maldonado, 2
Tel. (9)56-70 23 33 – Fax (9)56-70 23 33
Sra Moreno

Category ★ **Rooms** 11 with air-conditioning, telephone, bath, WC, and TV. **Price** Single 4,280-5,350Pts, double 7,490-10,700Pts. **Meals** Breakfast 300-700Pts, served 8:30-10:30. **Restaurant** Service 13:00-16:00, 19:00-22:30 (winter) or 20:00-23:00 (sommer); menu 2,500Pts, also à la carte. Specialties: Ajo a la comendadora - Sopa de clausura - Pierna de cordero. **Credit cards** All major. **Pets** Dogs not allowed. **Nearby** Church of Santa Maria in Arcos de la Frontera - Jerez de la Frontera - Bornos - Monastery of the Cartuja - Villamartin (wine cellars of Pajarete) - Càdix. **Open** All year.

The Hotel El Convento occupies part of the convent of Monjas de Clausuras Mercedarias Descalzas, built in the 17th century. A small hotel with only ten bedrooms in a typically Andalusian style, a simple family atmosphere is found here, along with excellent home cooking. Moreover, recent improvements have further enhanced the comfort. In a historically classified village and completely free from cars, it is just a few paces from several listed national historical monuments. The village is full of charm and the hotel is one of those that one dreams of finding on a journey in southern Spain. Seville is just 70km away !

How to get there *(Map 24): 59km northeast of Cádiz via A4, exit Jerez de la Frontera, then N342 to Antequera.*

Cortijo Barranco

1998

El Bosque km 8,2 11630 Arcos de la Frontera (Cádiz)
Molino Ntra Sra de la Luz
Tel. (9)56-23 14 02 - Fax (9)56-23 14 02
Sr José Gil Amián

Rooms 8 with bath. **Price** Double 7,000-8,000Pts – 70,000-80,000Pts (apart. for 1 week). **Meals** Breakfast included, served 8:00-11:00. **Restaurant** Service 13:30-15:30, 20:00-23:00; menu 2,500Pts. Specialties: regional cooking. **Credit cards** Not accepted. **Pets** Dogs allowed. **Facilities** Swimming pool, parking. **Nearby** Jerez de la Frontera - Bornos - Monastery of the Cartuja - Villamartin (wine cellars of Pajarete). **Open** All year.

You leave the road to Arcos and continue for three kilometers through fields of sunflowers and olive trees before arriving at an attractive white farm house nestling on the hillside. An impressive wooden gate opens and you discover a courtyard resplendent with geraniums, rambling roses and lemon trees where swallows have taken up residence. If a fine collection of popular art is displayed on the walls to remind you that you are in a center of "rural tourism", the rest of the place is no less elegant. The rooms, while not particularly large, are pleasantly decorated with regional furniture including wrought-iron beds and colorful printed fabrics. Every room has a view of the sunflowers and there is an apartment for those who prefer a little more privacy. The lounge and billiard room are at your disposal, along with a magnificent swimming pool with an exceptional view overlooking the valley.

How to get there *(Map 24): 3km from Arcos de la Frontera on C-344 towards Embalse de Arcos. The dirt road is marked camino privado.*

Casa Convento la Almoraima

11350 Castellar de la Frontera (Cádiz)
Tel. (9)56-69 30 50 – Fax (9)56-69 32 14
Sr Montoya

Category ★★★★ **Rooms** 11 with telephone, bath, and WC. **Price** Single 8,000Pts, double 10,000-13,000Pts. **Meals** Breakfast 750Pts, served until 11:00; half board + 3,000Pts, full board + 6,000Pts. (per pers.). **Restaurant** Service 13:30-17:00, 21:00; menu 3,000Pts. Specialties: game. **Credit cards** All major. **Pets** Dogs allowed. **Facilities** Swimming pool, minigolf, hunting, fishing, riding (1,700Pts), parking. **Nearby** Medina Sidonia - Benalup de Sidonia - Costa de la Luz from Càdiz to Tarifa - Algeciras - Gibraltar. **Open** All year.

This ancient convent founded in 1603 has had a rather disturbed past. In the 19th century the Spanish government sold all the possessions of the Friars and it became a private estate. In 1972 it became the hunting lodge of a leading Spanish citizen, from whom it was expropriated in 1982. Nevertheless, a very special atmosphere reigns in this house where everything has been maintained in its original state. Very well equiped to receive its guests, it has a swimming pool, tennis court, billiard room, and a music lounge. Horses and a Land Rover are at your disposal to discover the 16,000 hectares (62 square miles) of the largest 'latifundium' (landed property) in Europe, where deer, stags and wild sheep roam in full freedom, while one can also fish and hunt. On your holiday road in Andalusia, this is an ideal staging post to relax for a few days.

How to get there *(Map 24): 145km southeast of Cádiz via N340 to Algeciras, then after 12km towards Jimena de la Frontera for 9km; opposite the Factoria de Corcho (cork factory).*

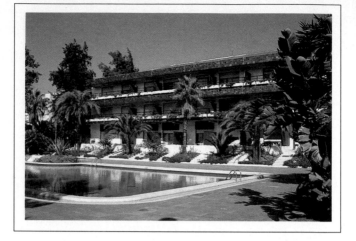

Hotel Jerez

11400 Jerez de la Frontera (Cádiz)
Avenida Alcalde Alvaro Domecq, 35
Tel. (9)56–30 06 00 – Fax (9)56–30 50 01/31 95 43
E-mail: jerez@travelcom.es - Web: http://www.travelcom.es/jerez

Category ★★★★ Rooms 121 with air-conditioning, telephone, bath, WC, satellite TV, minibar; elevator. **Price** Single 12,600-14,000Pts, double 15,800-18,900Pts, suite 26,200-31,500Pts. **Meals** Breakfast 1,400Pts, served 7:15-12:00; full board + 6,500Pts. (per pers.). **Restaurant** Service 13:00-16:00, 20:30-23:30; à la carte. Specialties: fish - shellfish. **Credit cards** All major. **Pets** Small dogs allowed. **Facilities** Swimming pool, tennis, parking. **Nearby** Real Escuela Andaluza del Arte Ecuestre (Royal Andalusian School of Equestrian Art) de Jerez de la Frontera; Jerez's wine cellars (Bodegas de Xéres de Gonzalez Byass, Pedro Domecq, Williams Humbert); Feria del Caballo (Horse Fair 4/6 May); Flamenco Festival in August; Vintage Festival in September- Càdiz - Arcos de la Frontera - Bornos - La Cartuja - Sanlúcar de Barrameda. **Open** All year.

Only 4km from the town center in a modern building in the residential area, this hotel in the Ciga chain enjoys a wonderfully calm setting. The bedrooms are luxurious and all have a balcony, most of which look onto the garden and its beautiful lawns, palm trees and exuberant plants, all protected from the road by thick hedges. You can also enjoy the large swimming pool at your leisure. The restaurant offers excellent seafood dishes, accompanied by the well known wines of the area, world-renowned cellars. Service and comfort are very high quality, but one should remember that prices/rates are marked up by 30% during the Feria.

How to get there *(Map 24): 35km northeast of Cádiz via A4, exit Jerez de la Frontera; 4km from town center.*

Hotel Serit

11400 Jerez de la Frontera (Cádiz)
Avenida Higueras, 7
Tel. (9)56-34 07 00 - Fax (9)56-34 07 16 - Sra Acosta Jimenez

Category ★★★ **Rooms** 29 with air-conditioning, telephone, bath, WC, satellite TV, safe; elevator - 1 room for disabled persons. **Price** Single 5,000-8,000Pts, double 7,000-12,000Pts. **Meals** Breakfast 400Pts, served 8:00-11:00. **Restaurant** See p. 241. **Credit cards** All major. **Pets** Dogs allowed. **Facilities** Parking (1,000Pts). **Nearby** Real Escuela Andaluza del Arte Ecuestre (Royal Andalusian School of Equestrian Art) of Jerez de la Frontera; Jerez's wine cellars (Bodegas de Xéres de Gonzalez Byass, Pedro Domecq, Williams Humbert); Feria del Caballo (Horse Fair 4/6 May); Flamenco Festival in August; Vintage Festival in September - Càdiz - Arcos de la Frontera - Bornos - La Cartuja - Sanlúcar de Barrameda. **Open** All year.

Jerez is a town made famous by the wine carrying its name: 'sherry' (slightly deformed by the British because of its impossible pronunciation). It also boasts a riding school with a great reputation, as well as the attractions of the vine. The annual Feria in honor of the horse is one of the most important in Andalusia. In a small street close to the center, the Serit is one of those hotels with a discreet facade but whose appeal is evident once the front door is opened. The comfort, calm and the reasonable rates all appeal. Although rather standardized, the rooms are agreeable and all have a small antichamber separating them from the bathroom. A corner lounge on the ground floor has comfortable sofas and a marble floor, while beautiful photographs on the walls recall different aspects of Jerez life.

How to get there *(Map 24): 35km northeast of Cádiz via A4, exit Jerez de la Frontera; next door to La Plaza de las Angustias.*

Posada de Palacio

11540 Sanlúcar de Barrameda (Cádiz)
Calla Caballeros, 11
Tel. (9)56-36 48 40 – Fax (9)56-36 50 60
Sr Navarrete

Category ★★★ **Rooms** 13 with telephone, bath and WC. **Price** Double 6,000-8,000Pts, suite 10,000Pts. **Meals** Breakfast 800Pts, served 8:30-11:30. **Restaurant** See p. 242. **Credit cards** Diners, Visa, Eurocard, MasterCard. **Pets** Small dogs allowed. **Nearby** Bodegas (Hijos de A. Pérez, Meijía, Manuel Garcia Monje, Rafael Reig y Cia) in Sanlúcar; Feria of the Manzanilla in May - Jerez de la Frontera - Monastery of Nuesta Señora de Regla close Chipiona - Beaches of Rota - Bornos - La Cartuja - Sanlúcar de Barrameda. **Open** All year.

Sanlúcar de Barrameda is an aristocratic town whose reputation is due to its churches and excellent cellars, as well as its very beautiful houses. One of these houses has been converted into a posada with a great deal of love and taste by a very attractive young couple, who have respected the original architecture of the house. You are immediately won over by the patio and one feels comfortable in the welcoming rooms, even though their comfort does vary. The best, strangely, is on the ground floor with a large window onto the street. And as this is a region of cellars, there is a bar of course with a few tables in the white and flowered courtyard.

How to get there *(Map 23): 121km south of Seville via A4, to Jerez de la Frontera, then C440.*

Hotel La Solana

11360 San Roque (Cádiz)
Ctra. Cádiz-Málaga, km 116,450
Tel. (9)56-78 02 36 - Fax (9)56-78 02 36 - M. José A. Ceballos

Rooms 13 and 7 suites with bath, TV and minibar. **Price** Single 8,000Pts, double 12,000Pts, suite 14,000Pts. **Meals** Breakfast included, served 9:00-11:00. **Restaurant** Only for residents. Service 14:00-16:00, 21:00-23:00; menu 2,500Pts. **Credit cards** All major. **Pets** Small dogs allowed. **Facilities** Swimming pool (July-Aug), parking. **Nearby** Mediterranean and Atlantic beaches - Castellar - Sierra of Cádiz - Toros road- Tarifa andt Sotogrande - Alcaidesa and San Roque golf course (18-Hole). **Open** All year.

A painter and sculptor of talent, José Cetallos has transformed this beautiful country residence into a hotel, whose 20 hectares of land are situated in the center of the Campo de Gibraltar. One is first attracted by the quality of the decoration, a skilful mix of 'High Period' furniture, magnificent carpets, paintings and bronzes by the master of the house, along with the numerous personal acquisitions that make a fine collection. The interior patio is exquisite with its jacarandas and daturas in superb colors. A little further away is the swimming pool near the cork-oak and eucalyptus trees. Whether on the ground floor, on the patio or on the second floor, all the rooms are attractive. At La Solana there is a particularly calm atmosphere reflected in the owner's personality. In this region of sometimes excessive temperatures and grandiose landscapes (Gibraltar and the African coast), you will feel sheltered here in a refreshing and cultivated environment.

How to get there *(Map 24): 15km from Algeciras towards Málaga-Cádiz. Via N340 exit at km 116.5, on right you find immediately the way of the hotel. From the other direction, at km 117, take the motorway in the reverse direction and then exit.*

Hotel Convento de San Francisco

11150 Vejer de la Frontera (Cádiz)
La Plazuela, 6
Tel. (9)56-45 10 01/02/03 - Fax (9)56-45 10 04
Sr Antonio Bonilla Gerena

Category ★★★ Rooms 25 with telephone, bath and WC. **Price** Single 6,600Pts, double 8,800Pts, extra bed 1,700Pts. **Meals** Breakfast 525Pts, served 8:00-11:30; half board + 2,185Pts, full board + 3,950Pts. (per pers.). **Restaurant** Service 13:00-15:30, 20:30-23:30; closed Tues; menu 2,205Pts, also à la carte. Specialties: Cocina de mercado. **Credit cards** All major. **Pets** Dogs not allowed. **Nearby** Medina Sidonia - Benalup de Sidonia - Costa de la Luz from Càdiz to Tarifa - Càdix; Campo San Andrès golf course (18-Hole). **Open** All year.

On a steep hill stands an old 17th-century Franciscan convent now transformed into a hotel. One is first of all impressed by the entrance which happily has conserved its multicolored mosaics. The lounges have kept their grandiose aspect, even if the furniture has. Particular care has however been taken with the vast bedrooms, where simplicity and the rustic have been melded together, notably with the usage of open stonework. The small town of Vejer is classified as a 'historical-artistic monument' and has a rather wild charm with its windmills. To lovers of folklore it offers a full calendar of fêtes and fairs.

How to get there (Map 24): 53km southeast of Cádiz via N430.

Hotel Alfaros

14001 Córdoba
Calle Alfaros, 18
Tel. (9)57-49 19 20 - Fax (9)57-49 22 10
M. David Madrigal

Category ★★★★ Rooms 133 with air-conditioning, telephone, bath, WC, satellite TV, safe and minibar; elevator - Wheelchair access. **Price** Single 9,500-12,200Pts, double 11,900-15,800Pts, suite 16,500-19,500Pts. **Meals** Breakfast 1,100Pts (Buffet), served 9:00-11:00. **Restaurant** Service 13:30-15:30, 20:30-23:00; menu 2,000Pts, also à la carte. **Credit cards** All major. **Pets** Dogs not allowed. **Facilities** Swimming pool, parking (1,400Pts). **Nearby** Córdoba: Fiesta de los Patios (5-15 May); Feria de Nuestra Señora de Fuensanta (Sept.) - Medina Azahara(6km) - Monastery of San Jerónimo - Las Ermitas de Córdoba (13km) - Sanctuary of Santo Domingo de Scala Dei - Los Villares golf course (18-Hole). **Open** All year.

One can only know Spain and Andalusia well by visiting Córdoba, the former capital of the Moslems whose cultural and spiritual empire stretched from Rome to Africa, and further to the west. The mosque-cathedral is alone worth the journey but the town with its flowered patios, wrought ironwork and 'azuleros' also has a lot of charm. The Alfaros Hotel has sought to transpose all such influences into a modern decor, which has created a luxurious and theatrical hotel. Great comfort reigns throughout the hotel which also offers all the latest technology: fax connection, TV satellite dish and magnetic card access to rooms, etc.. All rooms are spacious and light. The swimming pool is worthy of an Arabian Gulf palace. Along with the full-time service, this is a great hotel.

How to get there *(Map 25): in the center of town.*

1998

Hotel Al-Mihrab

14012 Córdoba
Avenida del Brillante, km 5
Tel. (9)57-27 21 88– Fax (9)57-27 12 80

Category ★★★ **Rooms** 29 with air-conditioning, telephone, shower, WC, satellite TV.
Price Single 6,000Pts, double 7,000-11,000Pts. **Meals** Breakfast 500Pts, served
7:30-10:00. **Restaurant** 13:30-15:30, 20:30-23:00; menu 1,650Pts, also à la carte.
Credit cards All major. **Pets** Dogs allowed. **Facilities** Parking. **Nearby** Medina
Azahara - Monastery of San Jerónimo - Las Ermitas de Córdoba - Sanctuary of Santo
Domingo de Scala Dei - Córdoba: Fiesta de los Patios (5-15 May) - Feria de Nuestra
Señora de Fuensanta (Sept.) - Los Villares golf course (18-Hole). **Open** All year.

The name of the hotel plainly evokes the period of wealth and
splendor this city experienced during its occupation by the
Moors. It was at that time that the Great Mosque was built and its
presence explains why Cordoba has been classified part of Humanity's
Legacy. The Mirhab in a mosque is the holiest of places, the one
where the Koran is kept. This Cordoban-style residence dating from
the latter half of the 19th century has recently been renovated and
transformed into a very pleasant hotel. Located in a residential
neighborhood and away from the center of the city, it offers a garden
with small palm trees brought from the Canary Islands. The interior is
uncluttered and gets its decorative effect from fabrics with brightly
colored geometric patterns. The rooms are large and comfortable, the
lounge has a fine view of the sierra and the city, and the restaurant,
reserved for the hotel's guests, gives you an excellent opportunity to
try the region's specialties. A truly charming hotel.

How to get there *(Map 25): 140km of Sevilla. 5km from the city center, to
Plaza de Colón and avenida del Brillante.*

Hotel Conquistador

14003 Córdoba
Calle Magistral González Frances, 15/17
Tel. (9)57-48 11 02 - Fax (9)57-47 46 77
Sr P. Albujer

Category ★★★★ **Rooms** 102 with air-conditioning, telephone, bath, WC, TV and room-service. **Price** Single 10,700-12,300Pts, double 13,375-16,585Pts, suite 19,000-23,000Pts. **Meals** Breakfast 1,000Pts, served 7:00-10:30. **Restaurant** See p. 240. **Credit cards** Diners, Visa, Eurocard, MasterCard. **Pets** Dogs not allowed. **Facilities** Sauna (1,500Pts), parking (1,200Pts). **Nearby** Córdoba: Fiesta de los Patios (5-15 May); Feria de Nuestra Señora de Fuensanta (Sept.) - Medina Azahara (6km) - Monastery of San Jerónimo - Las Ermitas de Córdoba (13km) - Sanctuary of Santo Domingo de Scala Dei - Los Villares golf course (18-Hole). **Open** All year.

This is the former Hotel Adarve which the new owners have baptized as the Conquistador. All the amenities however remain the same while the prices, in contrast, have been lowered a little. Adjoining the mosque, this modern hotel was nevertheless built in an Andalusian Moorish style using both mosaics and marquetry to a very successful effect. All the reception rooms give onto a charming patio where there are columns, a fountain and luxurious vegetation. The rooms are designed with elegance and some, such as Numbers 110, 210 and 310, are very luxurious with marble bathrooms, and a view onto the patio. Those on the facade have a view of the mosque that is illuminated at night-time.

How to get there (Map 25): in the old town.

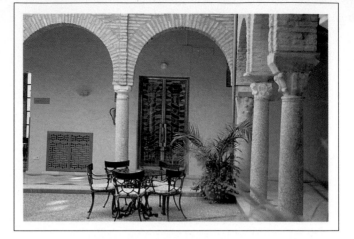

Hotel Amistád Córdoba

14004 Córdoba
Plaza de Maimónides, 3
Tel. (9)57-42 03 35 - Fax (9)57-42 03 65 - Sr. Billagran

Category ★★★★ **Rooms** 69 with air-conditioning, telephone, bath, WC, TV and minibar; elevator. **Price** Single 12,300Pts, double 15,000Pts. **Meals** Breakfast 1,200Pts, served 7:30-11:30. **Restaurant** Service 12:00-16:30, 20:30-23:30; à la carte. **Credit cards** All major. **Pets** Dogs not allowed. **Facilities** Garage (1,000Pts). **Nearby** Córdoba: Fiesta de los Patios (5-15 May); Feria de Nuestra Señora de Fuensanta (Sept.) - Medina az Zahara (6km) - Monastery of San Jerónimo - Las Ermitas de Córdoba (13km) - Sanctuary of Santo Domingo de Scala Dei - Los Villares golf course (18-Hole). **Open** All year.

The Amistàd of Córdoba is a very new hotel in the Barrio dela Judería, the former Jewish ghetto with its white and flowery narrow streets, giving on to the famous Córdoban patios. Do not fail to visit the well-known Mezquita (cathedral-mosque) in this quarter, and also the synagogue, one of the most celebrated in Europe (along with that of Toledo). The hotel is close by and even if the buildings are 18th-century, entry is still made via an arch pierced in the ancient Moorish wall. To shelter the hotel, two former residences have been joined but the interior mudejar patio has been preserved. All amenities are resolutely contemporary but with some references to local style, as with the suite of arcades in the main lounge. The decor is contemporary, elegant and very sober. The rooms are much warmer, spacious and just as refined. Comfort and personalized services are the main priorities, and this is one of the best hotels in Córdoba.

How to get there *(Map 25): in the old town.*

16

Hostal Séneca

14003 Córdoba
Calle Conde y Luque, 7
Tel. (9)57-47 32 34 - Fax (9)57-47 32 34- Sra Peignier

Category ★ **Rooms** 7 with basin and 5 with bath (some with air-conditionning with extra charge) **Price** Single 4,000-4,300Pts, double 5,100-5,400Pts, triple 7,400-7,650Pts. **Meals** Breakfast included, served 9:00-11:00. **Restaurant** See p. 240. **Credit cards** Not accepted. **Pets** Dogs allowed. **Facilities** Parking (1,500Pts). **Nearby** Córdoba: Fiesta de los Patios (May 5-15); Feria de Nuestra Señora de Fuensanta (Sept.) - Medina az Zahara (6km) - Monastery of San Jerónimo - Las Ermitas de Córdoba (13km) - Sanctuary of Santo Domingo de Scala Dei - Los Villares golf course (18-Hole). **Open** Jan 15 - Dec 15.

In the heart of old city, this small hotel is run by a very attractive French woman who, came here more than ten years ago after falling in love with Córdoba. Each year she sees the return of a loyal band of devotees won over by the atmosphere of calm and studied simplicity reigning here. Even if the comfort is less than perfect, you will feel relaxed and at ease in the nicely personalized rooms. Number 14 is recommended for its access to the terrace with its view over the roofs and minaret of the Mezquita close by. There is no restaurant but Number 8 on the same street is strongly recommended by the owner. A warm and relaxing ambiance is assured in this house with a soul all of its own.

How to get there *(Map 25): in the old town. Put your car aside at the parking Mezquita, the hotel is at 100 meters.*

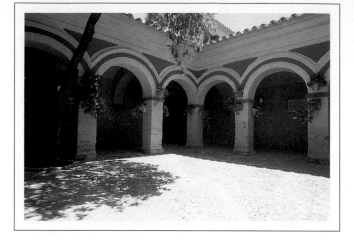

Hospedería de San Francisco

14100 Palma de Rio (Córdoba)
Avenida Pio XIII, 35
Tel. (9)57-71 01 83 - Fax (9)57-71 01 83/71 05 32
Sr Martinez

Category ★★★ **Rooms** 22 with air-conditioning, telephone, bath, WC and TV. **Price** Single 7,500Pts, double 11,000Pts. **Meals** Breakfast 750Pts, served 8:00-11:00; half board + 2,185Pts, full board + 3,950Pts. **Restaurant** "El Refectorio". Service 13:00-15:30, 20:30-22:30; menu 3,00-3,600Pts, also à la carte. Specialties: regional cooking. **Credit cards** Visa, Eurocard, MasterCard. **Pets** Dogs allowed. **Facilities** Parking. **Nearby** Medina Azahara - Monastery of San Jerónimo - Las Ermitages de Córdoba - Sanctuary of Santo Domingo de Scala Dei - Córdoba (May 5-15) - Feria d'automne (Sept 25-27) - Los Villars golf course (18-Hole). **Open** All year.

Palma del Rio is an interesting stop located between Seville and Cordoba with a number of small and pretty churches and archeological remains. The hotel was once a monastery and has managed to keep the atmosphere of its earlier days. The open-air cloister is painted in shades of yellow and bordeau, the rooms, formerly monks' cells, retain their attractive entrances with reinforced arches. Each one is decorated with antique furniture and religious engravings. The restaurant is in what was once the dining hall, and the manager, who is also the chef, is a Basque who skillfully combines the art of Basque cuisine with that of Andalusia. A very friendly welcome awaits his guests.

How to get there *(Map 24): 92km northwest of Seville towards Carmona and Palma del Rio.*

Hotel la Bobadilla

18300 Loja (Granada)
Finca La Bobadilla - Apartado, 144
Tel. (9)58-32 18 61 - Fax. (9)58-32 18 10
Sr Klaudiuj Heckh

Category ★★★★★ **Rooms** 60 with air-conditioning, telephone, bath, WC, satellite TV and minibar; elevator. **Price** Single 22,700-28,200Pts, double 32,200 36,500Pts, suite 38,600-59,800Pts. **Meals** Breakfast included, served 8:00-11:00; half board + 5,500Pts, full board + 11,000Pts. (per pers.). **Restaurant** Service 13:30-15:30, 20:30-23:00; "La Finca": à la carte 4,900-6,500Pts - "El Cortijo": à la carte 2,100-4,600Pts. Specialties: regional and international cooking. **Credit cards** All major. **Pets** Dogs allowed except in the restaurant. **Facilities** Swimming pools, tennis, riding, sauna, health center, bikes, garage. **Nearby** Loja - Los Infiernos de Lojas - Santa Fe - Granada. **Open** All year.

The Bobadilla is a 'grand luxe' hotel in a very beautiful residence built in the best Andalusian style, with succeeding patios, flowered terraces, gardens and fountains. The rooms are very comfortable and exquisitely decorated. The two restaurants serve a cuisine of quality. This hotel attracts with all that it offers for a truly relaxing stay: tennis court, swimming pool, horse riding and a fitness center. All this is in a region not lacking in tourist interest, and note that very interesting reduced rates are available in the winter months (Christmas excepted), depending on length of stay.

How to get there (Map 25): 76km east of Granada via A 92 (Granada/Sevilla); exit number 175: Villanueva, Iznájar, Salinas.

Alhambra Palace

18009 Granada
Peña Partida 2, 4
Tel. (9)58-22 14 66/67/68 - Fax (9)58-22 64 04
Sr Hernandez Medina

Category ★★★★ Rooms 136 with air-conditioning, telephone, bath, WC, TV, room-service and minibar; elevator. **Price** Single 16,000Pts, double 20,500Pts, triple 27,675Pts. **Meals** Breakfast 1,300 Pts, served 7:30-10:00; half board + 4,400, full board 9,600Pts. (per pers., 3 days min.). **Restaurant** Service 13:00-15:30, 20:30-23:30; menu 4,400Pts, also à la carte. **Credit cards** All major. **Pets** Dogs allowed. **Facilities** Parking. **Nearby** Villages of Santa Fe, Fuentevaqueros, Valderrubio, Viznar (Federico Garcia Lorca National Park) - Guadix cathedral - Sierra Nevada. **Open** All year.

At the top of a small hill inside the Alhambra Gardens, the towers and minaret of this immense building dominate Granada and have a magnificent view from the terraces over the city and the year-round snow on the Sierra Nevada. The decoration of the entrance hall and the living room are new. In addition to confortable rooms there are some luxurious suites, which enjoy the superb panorama. We also appreciated the availability of room service until 11 p.m., the attention of the personnel and the private parking in a city with an almost full-time tourist presence. This is a good and beautiful hotel.

How to get there (Maps 25 and 26): inside the Alhambra Gardens.

Hotel America

18009 Granada
Real de la Alhambra, 53
Tel. (9)58-22 74 71 – Fax (9)58-22 74 70
Sr Garzón

Category ★ **Rooms** 13 with air-conditioning, telephone, bath or shower, and WC. **Price** Single 7,900Pts, double 11,900Pts, suite 14,000Pts. **Meals** Breakfast 900Pts, served 8:00-10:00; half board + 2,000Pts, full board + 4,000 Pts (per pers. 3 days min.). **Restaurant** Service 13:00-15:00, 20:00-22:00; menu 2,200Pts, also à la carte. Specialties: Potajes al pujarreño - Cocidos - Platos de jamon - Serrano - Quesos manchegos. **Credit cards** All major. **Pets** Dogs not allowed. **Nearby** Villages of Santa Fe, Fuentevaqueros, Valderrubio, Viznar (Federico Garcia Lorca National Park) - Guadix cathedral - Sierra Nevada. **Open** Mar 1 - Nov 30.

It is inside the Real of the Alhambra that you will find the pretty white facade and flowered windows of the Hostal America. This modest but attractive place with its fourteen rooms has become a really charming hotel thanks to the care and talents of the owner. One is above all attracted by the relaxed atmosphere reigning here, and the place soon becomes intimate and almost familiar. The small size of the hotel, its simple but personalized decoration, the family cuisine and the warm welcome all mean a lot here and give its clients the impression of being guests in a friend's house. In summer meals are taken under the trellis in the green cool courtyard. One will always return here with pleasure.

How to get there (Maps 25 and 26): inside the Alhambra.

Parador San Francisco

18009 Granada
Real de la Alhambra
Tel. (9)58-22 14 40 - Fax (9)58-22 22 64
Sr Gianello Louro

Category ★★★★ **Rooms** 38 with air-conditioning, telephone, bath, WC, TV and minibar. **Price** Single and double 29,500-33,000Pts. **Meals** Breakfast 1,300 Pts, served 8:00-11:00. **Restaurant** Service 13:00-16:00, 20:30-22:30; menu 3,700Pts, also à la carte. Specialties: Gazpacho - Tortilla de Sacramonte - Choto a l'alpurrena. **Credit cards** All major. **Pets** Dogs not allowed. **Facilities** Parking. **Nearby** Villages of Santa Fe, Fuentevaqueros, Valderrubio, Viznar (Federico Garcia Lorca National Park) - Guadix cathedral - Sierra Nevada. **Open** All year.

Set within the walls of the Alhambra, close to the Arab Alcazar and the palace of Charles V, the parador is housed in a former Franciscan convent founded by the Catholic Kings after the reconquest of the town. In the midst of the famous Alhambra Gardens, there is a superb view over the Generalife, the Albaicin and the Sierra Nevada. One has to wander through the galleries decorated with old Spanish furniture, in the patio and the chapel to be imbued with the serenity and beauty of this unique site. Ideal for idleness, a small Arab lounge recalls the origins of this site. Perfect for relaxation, the convent rooms are comfortable, while Numbers 205, 206 and 207 have terraces opening onto the Generalife. This Truly is a real "plus" in your discovery of Grenada; but be warned: 6-months advance reservation's are required in high season.

How to get there *(Maps 25 and 26): inside the Gardens of the Alhambra.*

Finca Buen Vino

21293 Los Marines (Huelva)
Tel. (9)59-12 40 34 – Fax (9)59-50 19 29
Sr and Sra Chesterton

Rooms 4 with bath (2 in the room) and WC. **Price** Half board (1 pers.) 12,000-15,000Pts, double (per pers.) 11,000-13,000Pts. **Meals** Breakfast included. **Evening meals** Menu. Speciallies: Spanish and international cooking. **Credit cards** Visa, Eurocard, MasterCard. **Pets** Dogs not allowed. **Facilities** Swimming pool (June-Sept), parking. **Nearby** Gruta de las Maravillas in Aracena (cave of Marvels) - Almonaster la Real - Church of the convent of Santa Clara in Moguer - Almonte - Isla Cristina - El Romero del Rocio of Huelva (May). **Open** Jan 15 - Dec 15.

At equal distance from Lisbon and Gibraltar, and 50km from the border with Portugal, the Finca Buen Vino will prove a charming stopover for you. A residential hotel, you must reserve in advance if you wish to enjoy this pretty house with only three rooms open to visitors. The traditional Hispano-Moorish facade is overrun by roses and clematis. Bought a few years ago by an English couple, you will find full British charm and comfort in the interior: old furniture, chintzes, pot-pourri, souvenirs of the Empire, and so on. The same refinement is found around the guests' tables: linen napkins, silverware, crystal; all of it however arranged with a certain simplicity – even if correct dress is required for dinner. Midday meals are served on the terrace in summer. The kitchen garden, mixing flowers, vegetables and fruit supplies the house recipes. The welcome is cordial.

How to get there *(Map 17): 100km west of Seville via N433 (km 95).*

Parador Castillo de Santa Catalina

Oeste 23001 Jaén
Tel. (9)53-23 00 00 – Fax (9)53-23 09 30
Sr Huete

Category ★★★★ **Rooms** 45 with air-conditioning, telephone, bath, WC, satellite TV and minibar; elevator. **Price** Double 17,500Pts. **Meals** Breakfast 1,300Pts, served 8:00-10:30; full board + 6,375Pts. (per pers. 2 days min.). **Restaurant** Service 13:00-16:00, 20:30-23:00; menu 3,500Pts, also à la carte. Specialties: regional cooking. **Credit cards** All major. **Pets** Dogs not allowed. **Facilities** Swimming pool. **Nearby** In Jaén Feria de San Lucas (Oct) - Baeza - Ubeda - Martos. **Open** All year.

Attached to the impressive fortress built at the same period and in the same style as the Alhambra at Grenada, the Parador Santa Catalina has the severe appearance of a fortified castle with its stone outworks and the tiny apertures of its facade. The view however is superb over a valley scattered with olive groves. Most of the rooms have balconies and you can enjoy such a view at your leisure. The reception rooms are very spacious and have been arranged with furniture sometimes very much in the 1960's 'designer' style, and decorated with tapestries and canvasses on loan from various national museums. Do not miss the dining room with its lamps created in the spirit of Moorish–Arabic art.

How to get there (Map 25): 4,5km west of Jaén.

Hotel de la Perdíz

23200 La Carolina (Jaén)
Carret. N IV
Tel. (9)53-66 03 00 - Fax (9)53-68 13 62
Sr Francisco Javier Muñoz

Category ★★★★ **Rooms** 95 with air-conditioning, telephone, bath and WC; elevator. **Price** Single 7,200 Pts, double 10,000Pts. **Meals** Breakfast included, served 7:30-11:00; half board + 5,000Pts, full board + 6,300Pts. (per pers.). **Restaurant** Service 13:30-15:45, 20:45-23:15; menu 3,000Pts, also à la carte. Specialties: game. **Credit cards** All major. **Pets** Dogs allowed (except in restaurant). **Facilities** Swimming pool, garage, parking. **Nearby** Convento de la Sierra Morena and Palacio de la Carolina - Feria (May). **Open** All year.

There is a very 'hunting lodge' ambiance in this hotel that owes its name to the park close by renowned for its abundant game. The large fireplaces, the hunting trophies and arms collections on the walls, the impressive beams of the ceiling and beautiful old Spanish furniture, all contribute to the warm and rustic atmosphere of the lounges. The bedrooms are more simple but are all carefully maintained and pleasant. At the heart of the building is a small enclosed garden planted with palm trees, scented cypresses and fig trees, which form a small haven of cool and peace. Most of the rooms have a view of the garden while others have terraces. If you cannot get one of these, go for those looking over the olive groves and the village.

How to get there *(Map 19): 44km north of Linares via N322 to Bailén, then N4.*

Parador de Cazorla

Sacejo
23470 Cazorla (Jaén)
Tel. (9)53-72 70 75 - Fax (9)53-72 70 77

Category ★★★ **Rooms** 33 with telephone, bath, WC and TV. **Price** Double 12,500-15,000Pts. **Meals** Breakfast 1,200Pts, served 8:00-10:30. **Restaurant** Service 13:00-16:00, 20:30-22:30; menu 3,200Pts. Specialties: game, trouts. **Credit cards** All major. **Pets** Dogs not allowed. **Facilities** Swimming pool, parking. **Nearby** Ubeda - Nature Park of Sierra de Cazorla: Embalse del Tranco and shores of the Guadalquivir - Quesada - Villages of the Sierra de Segura "Valle del Paraiso": Orcera, Beas de Segura and Segura de la Sierra. **Open** All year.

Arrival at the parador is possible only after quite an expedition up the mountain road at Cazorla leading to Sacejo. The trip is however worthwhile, both for the wild and wooded site and the picturesque villages that you drive through. One comes here above all for the walking, fishing or to hunting. The source of the Guadalquivir river is close by, and the Sierra de Cazorla is a very beautiful nature park scented by pines, oaktrees and junipers–the home of stags, deer and wild boar. The hotel architecture is inspired by the Andalusian 'cortijos', with care taken to look out over the surrounding nature as much as possible. It is better to go for the rooms looking over the swimming pool side, they have the best view. The decor is sober but comfortable and very well maintained. In the restaurant, a cuisine favoring game, the specialty of the region, is served. To better profit from your stay do not hesitate to take part in the excursions (free) organized by the hotel for clients: cultural visits, horse riding and mountain bike trips, all to the natural sites of Andalusia.

How to get there *(Map 26): 25km east of Cazorla.*

Parador Condestable Davalos

23400 Úbeda (Jaén)
Plaza Vasquez de Molina, 1
Tel. (9)53-75 03 45 – Fax (9)53-75 12 59
Sr Mumoz

Category ★★★★ **Rooms** 31 with air-conditioning, telephone, bath, WC, satellite TV and minibar. **Price** Double 16,500-18,500Pts. **Meals** Breakfast 1,300Pts, scrved 8:00-10:30. **Restaurant** Service 13:00-16:00, 21:00-23:00; menu 3,700Pts, also à la carte. Specialties: Ajo blanco - Espiñacas al estilo Jaén - Pimientos rellenos de perdíz - Natillas con borrachuelos. **Credit cards** All major. **Pets** Dogs not allowed. **Nearby** Sabiote - Nature Park of Sierra de Cazorla: Embalse del Tranco and shores of the Guadalquivir - Villanueva del Arrobispo - Jaén - Segura de la Sierra. **Open** All year.

This 16th-century palace boasts a long, Greco-Roman style facade in the historical part of the town, where a number of monuments from the Renaissance period rival its beauty. Renovated in the 18th century, it was converted into a hotel in 1942. The long glazed galleries, a dream patio where in summer a canopy is put up to create some cool, and bedrooms with a postcard view, all contribute to its delightful charm! To note: The suite on the facade forming the corner is very beautiful, and reasonably priced, while a 'taverne' on the ground floor will delight all lovers of good wines.

How to get there (Map 19): 24km east of Linares via N322; nearby the Salvador church and the Ayuntamiento (town hall).

Parador del Golf

29080 Málaga
Tel. (9)5-238 12 55 - Fax (9)5-238 21 41
Sr Garcia Alonso

Category ★★★★ **Rooms** 56 and 4 suites with air-conditioning, telephone, bath, WC, satellite TV and minibar. **Price** Double 17,500Pts. **Meals** Breakfast 1,300Pts, served 8:00-10:30. **Restaurant** Service 13:30-16:00, 20:30-23:00; menu 3,500Pts. **Credit cards** All major. **Pets** Dogs not allowed. **Facilities** Swimming pool, tennis, golf, parking. **Nearby** Beaches of Torremolinos - Cártama - Alora and Convento de Nuestra Señora Flores - Tropical gardens of the Hacienda de la Concepción (7km) - El Chorro and the Garganta del Chorro - Club Campo de Málaga golf course (18-Hole). **Open** All year.

1 4km west of Málaga, the Parador del Golf will prove a stopping place particularly appreciated by adepts of this sport. On the golf course, the hotel is thus protected from the galloping urbanization that is ravaging the Costa del Sol. Access to the course is free for hotel guests from November 1 to June 30. Those not playing the game can always play tennis or unwind beside the large swimming pool or on the beach close by. The architecture is without much personality but has the merit of being discreet. The bedrooms are quiet and decorated with care. The service is irreproachable. Rather than a hotel of charm, here we have a 'de luxe' hotel to spoil all golfers.

How to get there (Map 25): 6km west of Málaga towards Torremolinos.

Parador Gibralfaro

Gibralfaro
29016 Málaga
Tel. (9)5-222 19 03 - Fax (9)5-222 19 04
Sr Juan Carlo Garcia Alonso

Category ★★★ **Rooms** 12 with air-conditioning, telephone, bath, WC, satellite TV and minibar. **Price** Double 17,500-19,000Pts. **Meals** Breakfast 1,300Pts, served 8:00-10:30. **Restaurant** Service 13:00-16:00, 20:30-23:00; menu 3,700Pts. **Credit cards** All major. **Pets** Dogs not allowed. **Facilities** Parking. **Nearby** Beaches of Torremolinos - Cártama - Alora and Convento de Nuestra Señora Flores - Tropical gardens of the Hacienda de la Concepción (7km) - El Chorro and the Garganta del Chorro - Club Campo de Málaga golf course (18-Hole). **Open** All year.

Situated on the Gibralfaro hill, the parador enjoys an uninterrupted view over the town and commercial port. The hotel has just a few comfortable and air-conditioned rooms, which is a considerable advantage in this part of Spain. Each room has its own terrace while the restaurant also has one, from which one can see the Malagueta quarter and the bullring. On a summer evening it is fun to linger at the bar and have a drink, while watching the lighted ships pass by. One also appreciates the beautiful walks in the gardens of the ancient fortress close to the hotel.

How to get there (Map 25): 3km from the center of Màlaga.

La Fonda

29639 Benalmádena Pueblo (Málaga)
C/. Santo Domingo, 7
Tel. (9)5-256 82 73 – Fax (9)5-256 82 73
Sr José Antonio Garcia

Category ★★★ **Rooms** 28 with air-conditioning, telephone, bath, WC, TV and minibar. **Price** Single 5,150-8,300Pts, double 7,300-11,500Pts, triple 8,400-13,650Pts. **Meals** Breakfast included. **Restaurant** Service 13:00-15:00, closed Saturday, Sunday and National Holidays; menus and also à la carte. Specialties: regional and international cooking. **Credit cards** All major. **Pets** Dogs not allowed. **Facilities** Heated swimming pool, parking. **Nearby** Beaches of Marbella - Màlaga - Cártama - Alora and Convento de Nuestra Señora Flores - Tropical gardens of the Hacienda de la Concepción (7km) - El Chorro and the Garganta del Chorro - Club Campo de Málaga golf course (18-Hole). **Open** All year.

Impossible to resist its charm, this hotel is located a few paces from the ravishing little square of Benalmádena, where it is delightful to linger among the orange trees. Despite its proximity to the tourist-magnet coast, only 4km away, the village has been preserved by some miracle. Built out of earlier houses, one is surprised to find no less than three different patios, one of them boasting a swimming pool. The purest Andalusian style, with the white of the walls set off by prettily arranged green plants and flowers, is highly attractive, while the superb view of the sea further emphasizes the architecture of the hotel. The most pleasant bedrooms are those enjoying this view.

How to get there (Map 25): 20km south of Málaga, on the highway Málaga-Cádiz, exit Benalmádena.

Hotel Husa Mijas

29650 Mijas (Málaga)
Urbanizacion Tamisa, 2
Tel. (9)5-248 58 00 – Fax (9)5-248 58 25
Sr Martinez

Category ★★★ Rooms 91 and 3 suites with telephone, bath, WC and satellite TV.
Price Single 8,000-12,000Pts, double 10,000-14,000Pts, suite 20,000-28,000Pts.
Meals Breakfast 1,350Pts, served 7:30-10:30; half board + 4,150Pts, full board
+ 6,950Pts. (per pers.). **Restaurant** With air-conditioning. Service 13:00-15:30,
20:00-22:30; menu 2,800Pts, also à la carte. **Credit cards** All major. **Pets** Dogs not
allowed. **Facilities** Swimming pool, tennis, sauna (1,500Pts), parking. **Nearby** Costa
del Sol - Málaga - Benalmàdena - Marbella - Club Campo de Málaga and Mijas golf
course (18-Hole). **Open** All year.

If you are afraid of the crowds on the over-visited Costa del Sol, but
adore its sunshine and tanning all year round, you must make a trip
up to the village of Mijas. Here on the small hills between Málaga and
Marbella, among the pines and palm trees, with a view that cannot be
taken away, is located the Mijas Hotel with a typically Andalusian
character and a certain English spirit. The public rooms are sober but
very comfortable, while the terraces promise delicious breakfasts in the
shade of the olive trees, and are the ideal setting for summer dinners.
The Mijas offers comfortable bedrooms but the suites are the most
comfortable aven though only three have the best views. Two beautiful
swimming pools, one heated throughout the year, a tennis court and a
health center add to the attractions of this hotel.

How to get there *(Map 25): 30km southwest of Málaga via N340 towards
Cádiz; at Fuengirola take small road for Mijas.*

Parador de Nerja

29780 Nerja (Málaga)
Playa de Burriana
Tel. (9)5-252 00 50 - Fax (9)5-252 19 97
Sr Embiz Fabregas

Category ★★★★ **Rooms** 73 with air-conditioning, telephone, bath, WC, satellite TV, minibar. **Price** Double 15,000-19,000Pts. **Meals** Breakfast 1,300Pts, served 8:00-10:00. **Restaurant** Service 13:00-15:30, 20:00-22:30; menus 3,500Pts, also à la carte. Specialties: Gazpacho - Frituras de pescados. **Credit cards** All major. **Pets** Dogs not allowed. **Facilities** Swimming pool, tennis, parking. **Nearby** Caverns of Nerja - Costa del Sol - Màlaga - Club Campo de Málaga golf course (18-Hole). **Open** All year.

Nerja is a tourist town on a high cliff overlooking the Costa del Sol, at the foot of which stretch away beaches of fine sand. This is said to be 'the balcony of Europe' from where one can enjoy a splendid panorama of the sea and the high sierras surrounding it. The parador can also be proud of its superb view. It dominates the beach of Burriana which can be reached directly by elevator. In the bedrooms offer excellent comfort, and almost all of them have balconies and are fitted with beautiful bathrooms. One rather regrets however a somewhat impersonal decor that deserves more care. In the lawned garden are the bar and swimming pool. Here you can enjoy the calm of the site in the shade of the Bella Sombra, some very beautiful trees that serve as sun-umbrellas. For a more pleasant stay, come here out of season.

How to get there *(Map 25): 51km east of Málaga via N340.*

Refugio de Juanar

29610 Ojén (Málaga)
Tel. (9)5-288 10 00 – Fax (9)5-288 10 01
Sr Gomez Avila

Category ★★★ **Rooms** 25 with telephone, bath, WC, TV and minibar. **Price** Single 7,200-7,700Pts, double 8,800-14,200Pts, suite 11,000-18,000Pts., apart. for 6 pers. 24,000-27,000Pts. **Meals** Breakfast 875Pts, served 8:30-11:00; half board + 3,200Pts, full board + 7,400-7,850Pts. (per pers.). **Restaurant** Service 13:00-16:00, 20:00-22:30; menu 2,900Pts, also à la carte. Specialties: game. **Credit cards** All major. **Pets** Dogs not allowed. **Facilities** Swimming pool, tennis, parking. **Nearby** Marbella Coìn - Alozaina - Ronda. **Open** All year.

A parador in other times, this hotel has now been taken over by its employees. Starting from Ojen, take a small mountain road leading to the Sierra de Ronda, a major center for hunting the 'capra hispanica', as well as smaller game (partridges, rabbits, etc.). Hidden in this superb countryside is this former property of the Marquis de Tarios, a favorite hunting ground of King Alfonso XVIII. This is a comfortable mountain hotel where an ambiance of warmth reigns, and where a good cuisine based on game is available. For the bedrooms, our favorite is Number 3, in which General de Gaulle completed the writing of his memoirs !

How to get there *(Map 25): 65km southwest of Málaga via N340 to Marbella, then continue via C337; 10km after Ojén.*

Marbella Club Hotel

29600 Marbella (Málaga)
Bd. Principe Alfonso Von Hohenlohe
Tel. (9)5-282 22 11 – Fax (9)5-282 98 84 – Sr Erik Jansen
E-mail: mchotel@wcostasol.es

Category ★★★★ Rooms 100 with air-conditioning, telephone, bath, WC, satellite TV, safe and minibar. **Price** Single 22,500-43,000Pts, double 26,000-51,500Pts, suite 42,500-115,000Pts. **Meals** Breakfast 2,600Pts (buffet), served 8:30-11:00; half board + 8,500Pts, full board + 12,500Pts. (per pers.). **Restaurant** Service from 13:30 and 20:30; menu 6,000Pts, also à la carte. Specialties: international cooking. **Credit cards** All major. **Pets** Dogs not allowed. **Facilities** Heated swimming pool, beach, tennis, sauna, parking. **Nearby** Costa del Sol - Ojén - Coìn - Rio Real los Monteros golf course (18-Hole), Nueva Andalucia golf course (18-Hole). **Open** All year.

In a magnificent and faultlessly maintained garden, the Marbella Club Hotel's bungalows assure complete privacy and unmatched comfort. The impeccable decor matches the image of the place, luxurious and refined. Bathrooms in marble, coordinated printed fabrics—nothing is left to chance. Those Hollywood stars coming here to find relaxation in line with their standing will not be disappointed. Besides the fully equiped beach and the beautiful swimming pool, all the services you could wish for are assured, to guarantee a 'de luxe' and charming stay.

How to get there (Map 25): 56km southwest of Málaga via N340.

Puente Romano

29600 Marbella (Málaga)
Tel. (9)5-282 09 00 - Fax (9)5-277 57 66
Sr Giloas Renaux

Category ★★★★★ **Rooms** 226 with air-conditioning, telephone, bath, WC, satellite TV, safe and minibar. **Price** Single 21,500-36,300Pts, double 24,200-49,500Pts, suite 30,500-160,000Pts. **Meals** Breakfast 2,000-2,600Pts (buffet), served 8:00-11:00; half board + 7,3000Pts, full board + 10,900Pts. (per pers.). **Restaurant** Service 13:00-16:00, 20:00-24:00; à la carte 6,700Pts. Specialties: international cooking. **Credit cards** All major. **Pets** Small dogs allowed in the room and in the garden. **Facilities** Swimming pools, tennis, fitness center, sauna, parking. **Nearby** Costa del Sol - Ojén - Coìn - Rio Real los Monteros golf course (18-Hole), Nueva Andalucia golf course (18-Hole). **Open** All year.

A 'grande luxe' hotel, the Puente Romano sports its five stars with serenity and without ostentation. With its elegant Andalusian architecture (unfortunately beside a busy national road), the hotel is made up of small bungalows in an admirable garden of exquisite freshness. The contemporary decor is luxurious but in good taste and the super-abundance of equipment of all sorts (3 swimming pools, a gym, 3 restaurants, private beach, etc.), and the quality of service will satisfy even the most demanding. Situated in the «Milla d'Oro», the nicest district between Marbella and Puerto Banus, the hotel is a true oasis in an extremely builtup region.

How to get there *(Map 25): 56km southwest of Málaga via N340.*

Hotel Reina Victoria

29400 Ronda (Málaga)
Tel. (9)5-287 12 40 - Fax (9)5-287 10 75
Sra Caballero

Category ★★★★ **Rooms** 87 and 2 suites with air-conditioning, telephone, bath or shower, WC, TV and 2 with minibar; elevator. **Price** Single 9,975-13,450Pts, double 13,650-16,800Pts, suite 20,000-23,000Pts, extra bed 2,300-2,500Pts. **Meals** Breakfast 1,450Pts (buffet), served 7:45-10:45. **Restaurant** Service 13:00-15:30, 19:30-22:30; menu 3,500Pts, also à la carte. Specialties: regional and international cooking. **Credit cards** All major. **Pets** Small dogs allowed. **Facilities** Swimming pool, parking. **Nearby** Setenil - Alozaina - Serriana de Ronda via San Pedro de Alcántara - Grazalema - Road from Ronda to Ubrique - Feria of Ronda (May). **Open** All year.

One can understand why the Austrian poet made the Hotel Reina Victoria his favorite vacation resort. This spot is romantic to excess and has everything to exalt even the most blasé personalities. The town is perched on a rocky spur traversed by the spectacular gorges of the Rio Tajo, and has several architectural treasures. The traditional habitat of chalk-whited houses has been preserved with great care. As for the surrounding country environment, it is quite simply superb. The ultimate of superlatives, opt for a 'room with a view' from Numbers 105 to 124, or 205 to 222, or—even better—305 to 307, and enjoy the magic of the site and splendor of the panorama. The decoration is still a bit old-fashioned, with spacious rooms furnished with copies of antiques. They are all very quiet. The amenities have been improved by renovations, while the gardens are still being re-done. The only problem is the hotel is used by too many tour groups.

How to get there *(Map 24): 96km north of Algeciras.*

Hotel Alfonso XIII

41004 Sevilla
San Fernando, 2
Tel. (9)5-422 28 50 – Fax (9)5-421 60 33
Sra Pilar Monzón

Category ★★★★★ **Rooms** 149 with air-conditioning, telephone, bath, WC, satellite TV and minibar; elevator. **Price** Single 31,000-52,000Pts, double 40,000-64,000Pts, triple 50,000-74,000Pts, suite 75,000-110,000Pts. **Meals** Breakfast 2,500Pts (buffet), served 7:00-12:00; half board + 9,400Pts (per pers.). **Restaurant** Service 13:00-15:30, 20:30-23:30; menu 7,000Pts, also à la carte. Specialties: regional and international cooking. **Credit cards** All major. **Pets** Dogs not allowed. **Facilities** Schwimmb., parking, garage (2,000Pts). **Nearby** Cantillana - Carmona - Alcala de Guadaira - Sanlúcar la Mayor - Convento de San Isidoro del Campo in Santiponce and ruins of the Roman colony of Itàlica - Romero de Rocio of Huelva (May) - Semana Santa (Holy week in March) and the April Fair (May) ; Golf e Hipodromo del Club Pineda golf course (9-Hole). **Open** All year.

The Alfonso XIII was built to receive leading visitors to the Hispano-American Exhibition in 1929, and since then it has continued as a luxury hotel linked to the very history of Seville. The work of the architect Espinau-Munoz, who insisted that the hotel should truly represent the city, he designed it as a major Hispano-Moorish palace. The building is set around a large central patio surrounded by a glazed gallery, with arches deployed above white marble columns. Gardens planted with tropical vegetation surround the four facades of the palace. Sumptuous lounges follow each other in succession; while the bedrooms are perfect, we would have preferred if they gave onto the garden.

How to get there (Map 24): *alongside the cathedral.*

Hotel Tryp Colon

41001 Sevilla
Canalejas, 1
Tel. (9)5 422 29 00 – Fax (9)5 422 09 38

Category ★★★★★ **Rooms** 218 with air-conditioning, telephone, bath, WC, satellite TV, minibar; elevator; rooms for disabled persons. **Price** Double 23,150-42,000Pts. **Meals** 1,650Pts, served 7:00-12:00; half board + 5,700 Pts, full board + 7,840 Pts (per pers.). **Restaurant** 13:00-15:30, 20:30-23:30; menu 4,100Pts, also à la carte. Specialties: regional and international cooking. **Credit cards** All major. **Pets** Dogs not allowed. **Facilities** Fitness room, sauna, parking and garage (2,200Pts). **Nearby** Cantillana - Carmona - Alcala de Guadaira - Sanlúcar la Mayor - Convento de San Isidoro del Campo in Santiponce and ruins of the Roman colony of Itàlica - El Rocio of Huelva - Semana Santa (Holy week in March) and the April Fair (May) - Golf e Hipodromo del Club Pineda golf course (9-Hole). **Open** All year.

The Tryp Colon was built on the edge of Seville's historic center for the Exposition of 1929 and its architecture is an authentic reflection of the style of the period. Its imposing facade gives way to a majestic circular reception area and large salon with a lovely Art-Deco stained-glass ceiling. It is truly luxurious hotel and offers all the comfort and service that one may expect in a hotel of this category.

How to get there *(Map 24): near the Museo of Bellas Artes.*

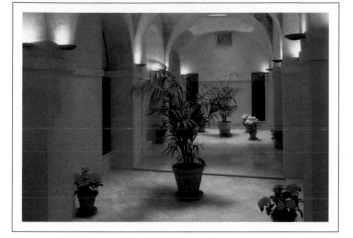

Hotel Los Seises

41004 Seville
Calle Segovias, 6
Tel. (9)5-422 94 95 - Fax. (9)5-422 43 34 - Sr Reinoso

Category ★★★★ Rooms 43 with air-conditioning, telephone, bath, WC, satellite TV, safe and minibar; elevator. **Price** Single 13,000-25,000Pts, double 16,000-35,000Pts. **Meals** Breakfast 1,500Pts, served 8:00-10:30; half board + 6,600Pts, full board + 10,000Pts (per pers., 2 days min.). **Restaurant** Service 13:30-15:30, 20:30-23:00; à la carte. **Credit cards** All major. **Pets** Dogs not allowed. **Facilities** Swimming pool, parking. **Nearby** Cantillana - Carmona - Alcala de Guadaira - Sanlúcar la Mayor - Convento de San Isidoro del Campo in Santiponce and ruins of the Roman colony of Itàlica - Romero de Rocio of Huelva (May) - Semana Santa (Holy week in March) and the April Fair (May); Golf e Hipodromo del Club Pineda golf course, (9-Hole). **Open** All year.

L os Seises is a 'de luxe' hotel of very unique design in the heart of Seville. By adapting a 16th-century palace into a hotel, numerous ancient remnants were found and conserved in this 'neo-Art Deco'-style, with its very pure lines. Thus one comes across a Roman mosaic, an Arab well and 16th-century marble columns, among other discoveries. The bedrooms are very elegant with their beds harmonizing with the light-colored walls and terra-cotta tiled floors. Without useless knick-knacks, one easily feels at home, while certain rooms can be surprising–such as Number 219, traversed by an ancient stone arch that creates an astonishing contrast. The last surprise is the hotel roof, which has been transformed into a large terrace with a view of the roofs of the town; it also has a swimming pool, an inestimable attraction in Seville. At weekends, the hotel offers very interesting rates.

How to get there *(Map 24): near to the Giralda.*

Taberna del Alabadero

41001 Seville
Zaragozas, 20
Tel. (9)5-456 06 37 - Fax (9)5-456 36 66
Sr Luis Lazana

Category ★★★★ **Rooms** 7 with air-conditioning, telephone, bath, WC, satellite TV, safe and minibar; elevator. **Price** Single 12,000Pts, double 15,000Pts. **Meals** Breakfast included, served 8:00-10:30. **Restaurant** Service 13:00-16:00, 21:00-24:00; à la carte 4,100-7,000Pts. Specialties: Basque and Andalusian cooking. **Credit cards** All major. **Pets** Dogs not allowed. **Facilities** Garage (1,900Pts). **Nearby** Cantillana - Carmona - Alcala de Guadaira - Sanlúcar la Mayor - Convento de San Isidoro del Campo in Santiponce and ruins of the Roman colony of Itàlica - Romero de Rocio of Huelva (May) - Semana Santa (Holy week in March) and the April Fair (May); Golf e Hipodromo del Club Pineda golf course (9-Hole). **Open** All year except in Aug.

Right in the heart of the Andalusian capital, close to the famous Real Maestranza bullring and the Santa Cruz quarter, here is found the Taberna del Alabadero. This 19th-century house formerly belonged to the Spanish poet José Antoine Cavestany, before becoming a well-known restaurant famed for its Basque-Andalusian cuisine. To add perfection to all this, a few bedrooms have been opened, all luxurious, very refined and very comfortable. Some look onto the typical Sevillian narrow streets, others onto the patio. As so often, everything radiates out from the large hallway on the ground floor, filled with the splashing sounds from the refreshing fountain and lit by a large glazed roof. This is the heart of the house and it is here that one can take a meal or a glass at the bar, as this is a beautiful address.

How to get there *(Map 24): in the Arenal district.*

Hotel San Gil

41002 Seville
C/. Parras, 28
Tel. (9)5-490 68 11 - Fax (9)5-490 69 39

Category ★★★ **Rooms** 39 with air-conditioning, telephone, bath, WC, TV and minibar. **Price** Single 11,500-14,200Pts, double-duplex 13,900-17,100Pts, suite (4 pers.) 20,100-24,000Pts. **Meals** Breakfast included, served 7:00-11:00. **Restaurant** See pp.242-243. **Credit cards** All major. **Pets** Dogs not allowed. **Facilities** Swimming pool. **Nearby** Cantillana - Carmona - Alcala de Guadaira - Sanlúcar la Mayor - Convento de San Isidoro del Campo in Santiponce and ruins of the Roman colony of Itàlica - Romero de Rocio of Huelva (May) - Semana Santa (Holy week in Mar) and the April Fair (May) ; Golf e Hipodromo del Club Pineda golf course (9-Hole). **Open** All year.

The Hotel San Gil has only recently opened in the center of Seville, in an old building with a loggia and balconies in wrought iron, framed by two more recent wings that respect the traditional architecture. The entry, reception and elevator areas are abundantly decorated with a patchwork of colored ceramics in the Moorish style, and the lounges are in this older part of the building. The bedrooms are in the windowed building surrounding the interior garden with its inevitable fountain. Most are in duplex-style or apartments with well-equipped kitchens for a longer stay. One finds pastel colors with a mix of modern and older-style furniture, along with well-appointed bathrooms, and all ensure full comfort. The swimming pool on the roof is also a major attraction for those visiting southern Spain in the summer. This is definitely 'algo mas que un hotel" ("more than just a hotel"), as the brochure tells us.

How to get there *(Map 24): near the Arco de Macapena.*

Hotel Ciudad de Sevilla

41013 Sevilla
Avenida Manuel Siurot, 25
Tel. (9)5 423 05 05 – Fax (9)5 423 85 39

Category ★★★★★ **Rooms** 90 with air-conditioning, telephone, bath, WC, satellite TV, minibar, safe; elevator. **Price** Double 13,800-32,000Pts, duplex 20,000-30,000Pts. **Meals** Breakfast 1,500Pts, served 7:30-11:30. **Restaurant** Service 13:30-15:30, 20:30-23:00; à la carte 4,000-4,500Pts. Specialties: Basque and Andalusian cooking. **Credit cards** All major. **Pets** Dogs not allowed. **Facilities** Swimming pool, garage. **Nearby** Cantillana - Carmona - Alcala de Guadaira - Sanlúcar la Mayor - Convento de San Isidoro del Campo in Santiponce and ruins of the Roman colony of Itàlica - El Rocio of Huelva - Semana Santa and the April Fair - Golf e Hipodromo del Club Pineda golf course (9-Hole). **Open** All year.

This hotel, built for the Exposition of 1927, is in a comfortable residential district, close to the Plaza de Espad ruins of the Roman colony of Itálica – El Rocio de Huelva – Week Santa and the April Fair; Golf e Hipodromo del Club Pineda golf course (9-Htine columns and coats of arms along with works in varnished terra cotta and even an exquisite little bell tower at the far end of the building. The interior is truly contemporary, even if the patio is surrounded with ungainly gangways leading to the rooms which are spacious and furnished with attractive modern furniture and stunning modern paintings reminiscent of the finest works of Tapiès. Our first choice would be the duplex with its own living room. From the roof, you look down on the swimming pool and the luxurious greenery on the Avenida de la Palmera.

How to get there (Map 24): near the María Luisa Park.

Patios de la Cartuja

41002 Sevilla
Lumbrera, 8-10
Tel. (9)5-490 02 00- Fax (9)5-490 20 56
Myria Ortis

Apartments 34 with air-conditioning, kitchen, 1 room, 1 lounge, telephone, bath, WC, satellite TV, safe; elevator. **Price** 6,400-13,600Pts (1 pers.), 8,000-17,000Pts (2 pers.), + 2000Pts (3nd pers.), + 2000Pts (4nd pers.). **Meals** Breakfast 600Pts, served 8:00-11:00. **No restaurant** See pp. 242-243. **Credit cards** All major. **Pets** Dogs not allowed. **Facilities** Garage (500Pts). **Nearby** Cantillana - Carmona - Alcala de Guadaira - Sanlúcar la Mayor - Convento de San Isidoro del Campo in Santiponce and ruins of the Roman colony of Itàlica - El Rocio of Huelva - Semana Santa and the April Fair - Golf e Hipodromo del Club Pineda golf course (9-Hole). **Open** All year

Two residential hotels, under the joint name of Patios de Sevilla, have opened here in the center of Seville with an excellent quality/price ratio. The apartments are for two people including a well-equipped kitchen, a bedroom, a bathroom and a lounge with a fold-up bed making it possible to accommodate three or even four. Both hotels are virtually identical in their furnishings but we prefer the Patio de Cartuja for its charm as it is a long building with balconies decked with hundreds of small geranium pots surrounding a superb patio. The apartments are in a somewhat standardized Sevillian style but the atmosphere is a very comfortable one and the service very efficient. This is an especially good choice for a stay in Seville at the best possible price as lodging in this city is particularly expensive.

How to get there *(Map 24): via the Plaza Duque de la Victoria and Calle Jésus del Grand Poder.*

Patios de Alameda

41002 Sevilla
Alameda de Hércules, 56
Tel. (9)5-490 49 99- Fax (9)5-490 02 26
Myria Ortis

Apartments 22 with air-conditioning, kitchen, 1 room, 1 lounge, telephone, bath, WC, satellite TV, safe; elevator. **Price** 6,400-13,600Pts (1 pers.), 8,000-17,000Pts (2 pers.), + 2,000Pts (3nd pers.), + 2000Pts (4nd pers.). **Meals** Breakfast 600Pts, served 8:00-11:00. **No restaurant** See pp. 242-243. **Credit cards** All major. **Pets** Dogs not allowed. **Facilities** Garage (500Pts). **Nearby** Cantillana - Carmona - Alcala de Guadaira - Sanlúcar la Mayor - Convento of San Isidoro del Campo in Santiponce and ruins d'Italica - El Rocio de Huelva - Semana Santa and the April Fair (2 weeks after the Holy week) - Golf e Hipodromo del Club Pineda (9-Hole). **Open** All year.

In the same direction and with the same concept is the Patio de Alameda, located on a large square frequented by people of the neighborhood because of the numerous small bars and restaurants nearby. Here again are apartments with well-equipped kitchens that can accommodate up to four people, even if this causes slightly crowded conditions. The cleaning is done daily and the reception desk is open 24 hours. We expect the Patio de Alameda to attract an increasing number of faithful clients.

How to get there *(Map 24): via the Plaza Duque de la Victoria and Calle Jésus del Grand Poder.*

Hotel Doña Maria

41004 Sevilla
Don Remondo, 19
Tel. (9)5-422 49 90 – Fax (9)5-421 95 46
Sr Rodriguez Andrade

Category ★★★★ **Rooms** 61 with air-conditioning, telephone, bath, WC, TV, safe and 20 with minibar; elevator. **Price** Single 8,000-17,000Pts, double 13,000-28,000Pts, triple 18,200-39,200Pts. **Meals** Breakfast 1,500Pts, served 8:00-11:00. **Restaurant** See pp. 242-243. **Credit cards** All major. **Pets** Dogs not allowed. **Facilities** Swimming pool on the roof, parking. **Nearby** Cantillana - Carmona - Alcala de Guadaira - Sanlúcar la Mayor - Convento de San Isidoro del Campo in Santiponce and ruins of the Roman colony of Itàlica - Romero de Rocio of Huelva (May) - Semana Santa (Holy week in March) and the April Fair (May); Golf e Hipodromo del Club Pineda golf course (9-Hole). **Open** All year.

In the heart of the city, the Hotel Doña Maria is newly constructed. Nonetheless, the arcades of the interior architecture, the wrought iron work, the old furniture and the ravishing patio with its exuberant and exotic plants, all give it a very Andalusian character. The bedrooms are all personalized and beautiful, but Room 310, all white with lace and a canopied bed, gets our top vote; it also has a balcony opening onto the square, the orange trees and the cathedral. However, the supreme luxury of this hotel is the swimming pool on the roof, with the tower of the Giralda rising beside it just a few meters away. Lately, the hotel has been less well-kept, the breakfasts unremarkable, and the hospitality cooler than in the past.

How to get there *(Map 24): next to the cathedral, facing the Giralda.*

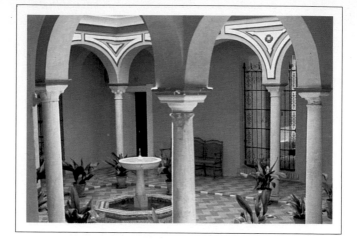

Las Casas de la Juderia

41004 Seville
Callejon de dos Hermanas, 7
Tel. (9)5-441 51 50 – Fax (9)5-442 21 70

Category ★★★ **Apartments** 57 with air-conditioning, telephone, bath, WC and kitchen. **Price** Single 7,500-20,000Pts, double 24,000-46,000Pts, double with Lounge 28,000-52,000Pts, suite with 2 rooms 40,000-70,000Pts. **Meals** Breakfast 1,200Pts (buffet), served 7:30-11:30. **Restaurant** See pp. 242-243. **Credit cards** All major. **Pets** Dogs not allowed. **Facilities** Garage (500-1,000Pts). **Nearby** Cantillana - Carmona - Alcala de Guadaira - Sanlúcar la Mayor - Convento de San Isidoro del Campo in Santiponce and ruins of the Roman colony of Itàlica - Romero de Rocio of Huelva (May) - Semana Santa (Holy week in March) and the April Fair (May); Golf e Hipodromo del Club Pineda golf course (9-Hole). **Open** All year.

In the real heart of historic Seville, Las Casas de la Juderia is a very old private hotel transformed into suites of one, two or three rooms. Long stays are possible here as most suites have a kitchen. The architecture of the place is really exceptional, with numerous flowered patios made pleasant by fountains, so that one can enjoy some peace and quiet in the shade of the arcades. The quality refurbishing of this house does not stop at the exterior and a real effort has been made to decorate the rooms (all different) with old furniture or quality reproductions. Finally, you can go up on the terraces with their view over the city roofs. The personnel are friendly and this is a stopping place of real charm.

How to get there *(Map 24): in the historic center of the town.*

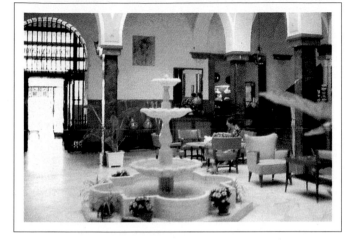

La Rábida

41001 Seville
Castelar, 24
Tel. (9)5-422 09 60 - Fax (9)5-422 43 75

Category ★★**Rooms** 100 with air-conditioning, telephone, bath or shower, WC, satellite TV; elevator. **Price** Single 4,700-5,500Pts, double 7,500-8,500Pts. **Meals** Breakfast 400Pts, served 8:00-10:30; half board + 2,400Pts, full board + 3,600Pts (per pers., 3 days min.). **Restaurant** Service 13:00-15:00, 20:00-22:00; menu 1,925Pts. **Credit cards** All major. **Pets** Dogs not allowed. **Nearby** Cantillana - Carmona - Alcala de Guadaira - Sanlúcar la Mayor - Convento de San Isidoro del Campo in Santiponce and ruins of the Roman colony of Itàlica - Romero de Rocio of Huelva (May) - Semana Santa (Holy week in Mar) and the April Fair (May) ; Golf e Hipodromo del Club Pineda golf course (9-Hole). **Open** All year.

Even though it is in the historic center of Seville, close to the cathedral, La Rábida is a comfortable hotel; the reception is welcoming and the rooms are well furnished. The welcome and service are efficient. Apart from the historical and artistic interest of the city itself, the capital of Andalusia, Seville organizes each year two major events, Holy Week and 'La Feria', which attract a large number of tourists from around the world. This is why it is so difficult to find lodgings and one can only recommend that reservations be made as soon as possible.

How to get there (Map 24): in the city center.

Hotel Residencia Sevilla

41003 Seville
Calle Daóiz, 5
Tel. (9)5-438 41 61 - Fax (9)5-490 21 60
M. José Arenas

Category ★★ **Rooms** 38 with air-conditioning, telephone, bath or shower, WC; elevator. **Price** Single 3,200-6,500Pts, double 5,350-9,500Pts. **Meals** No breakfast. **Restaurant** See pp. 242-243. **Credit cards** Amex, Visa, Eurocard, MasterCard. **Pets** Dogs allowed. **Facilities** Parking (1,000-1,500Pts). **Nearby** Cantillana - Carmona - Alcala de Guadaira - Sanlúcar la Mayor - Convento de San Isidoro del Campo in Santiponce and ruins of the Roman colony of Itàlica - Romero de Rocio of Huelva (May) - Semana Santa (Holy week in Mar) and the April Fair (May); Golf e Hipodromo del Club Pineda golf course (9-Hole). **Open** All year.

This is a small and unpretentious hotel, a very precious staging post in Seville. The hotel is on a charming and very quiet square scented by the orange trees lining it. The hotel offers a pretty flowered patio and simple but comfortable rooms, and a central location that speaks in its own favor. No breakfast is served but the attractive bar opposite will make it their pleasure to welcome you.

How to get there (Map 24): in the city center via Sierpes street.

Hotel Oromana

41500 Alcala de Guadaira (Seville)
Avenida de Portugal
Tel. (9)5-568 64 00 – Fax (9)5-568 64 00
Clara Campoamor

Category ★★★ **Rooms** 30 with air-conditioning, telephone, bath, WC and TV. **Price** Single 7,700-14,200Pts, double 10,200-14,200Pts. **Meals** Breakfast included, served 8:00-11:00. **Restaurant** Service 13:30-15:30, 20:00-23:00; à la carte 2,000-3,000Pts. Specialties: Croquelos de Ave - Arroz caldoso con Gambas. **Credit cards** All major. **Pets** Dogs not allowed. **Facilities** Swimming pool, parking. **Nearby** Gandul - Seville - Carmona - Sanlùcar la Mayor ; Convento de San Isidoro del Campo in Santiponce and ruins of the Roman colony of Itàlica - Romero de Rocio of Huelva (May) - Semana Santa of Sevilla (Holy week in Mar) and the April Fair (May); Golf e Hipodromo del Club Pineda golf course (9-Hole). **Open** All year.

A group of very attractive Andalusian women have just taken over the hotel and have doted it with a shared name: Clara Campoamor. Nobody doubts that they will succeed in their undertaking, and at 14km from Seville this hotel will well suit those looking for some peace, and the cool and fresh air of the evening. The Hotel Oromana is in fact in a wooded park not far from the river Guadaira which is lined with old Arab mills. A real example of Andalusian architecture, it attracts from the very first view. Inside its intimate decoration gives it the air of a family home, and all the rooms are attractive with their comfort and view of the countryside. The special gentleness of the welcome, the very reasonable prices and the ease of parking will perhaps make you prefer this hotel.

How to get there *(Map 24): 14km southeast of Seville via N334; in the pine woods of Oromana.*

Hotel Hacienda San Ygnacio

41950 Castilleja de la Cuesta (Seville)
Calle Real, 190
Tel. (9)5-416 04 30 – Fax (9)5-416 14 37
E-mail : sygnacio@arrakis.es - Web : www.arrakis.es/~sygnacio/index.htm

Category ★★★★ **Rooms** 16 with air-conditioning, telephone, bath, WC, satellite TV and minibar. **Price** Single 7,000-14,000Pts, double 10,000-19,000Pts, suite 45,000-65,000Pts. **Meals** Breakfast 1,100Pts, served 8:00-11:00. **Restaurant** "Almazara" Service 13:30-15:30, 20:00-23:00; closed Sun and Mon; menu 2,500-3,000Pts, also à la carte. **Credit cards** All major. **Pets** Dogs not allowed. **Facilities** Swimming pool, parking. **Nearby** Gandul - Seville - Carmona - Sanlúcar la Mayor - Golf e Hipodromo del Club Pineda golf course (9-Hole). **Open** All year.

Only 6 kilometers from Seville, this is a good bet for those bold enough to visit southern Spain in summertime. They will find peace and quiet here and can pass the hottest hours of the day beside the swimming pool, before setting off on an excursion. The hotel is a former 'hacienda' that has retained its architecture intact – a variety of buildings with a mixture of roofs, chimneys, terraces, bell-towers, all enclosing a large central courtyard planted with four superb palm trees. The large dining room of the 'Almazara', in the former mill of the 'hacienda' gives straight onto this beautiful patio. There are not many rooms and they are sober, decorated with wrought iron beds and rustic furniture, but all are spacious and comfortable. The swimming pool is in a green corner of the garden, surrounded by palm and orange trees.

How to get there *(Map 24): 6km northwest of Seville via A49, towards Huelva, exit 3.*

Cortijo Torre de la Reina

41209 Torre de la Reina (Sevilla)
C/. Paseo de la Alameda
Tel. (9)5-578 01 36– Fax (9)5-578 01 22 – Sra Paz Medina

Rooms 6 and 8 suites with air-conditioning, telephone, bath, WC, satellite TV. **Price** Single 13,500-17,000Pts, double 16,500-21,500Pts, suite 20,500-26,000Pts. **Meals** Breakfast 1,300Pts, served 8:30-11:30; half board + 4,500 Pts, full board + 8,000Pts (per pers.). **Restaurant** Service 13:00-16:00, 20:30-23:00; menu 3,500Pts. **Credit cards** All major. **Pets** Small dogs allowed on request. **Facilities** Swimming pool, parking. **Nearby** Cantillana - Carmona - Alcala de Guadaira - Sanlúcar la Mayor - Romero de Rocio of Huelva (May) - Semana Santa (Holy week in Mar) and the April Fair (May); Golf e Hipodromo del Club Pineda golf course (9-Hole). **Open** All year.

Ascant fifteen kilometers from Seville, this superb and historic property was occupied successively during the 13th and 14th centuries by King Fernando III during the conquest of Seville, and later by the queen Do in Seville at the best possible price as restored and as a result has been classified as a National Monument. Today, it receives essentially wealthy guests. Its gorgeous garden surrounds a series of buildings connected by arcades and patios, all bearing the marks of both Arab and Andalousian architecture. The interior is intimate and luxurious, creating an atmosphere reminiscent of a private home, one having changed very little over the years; there are rugs, furniture and old paintings as well as books and photographs, all seeming part of a carefully-kept personal collection. The rooms are very comfortable, matching the high standard of their decoration. It should be noted, however, that noisy events in the reception room may disturb other guests.

How to get there *(Map 24): 12km North Sevilla via SE30 towards Merida. Junction for La Algaba and Torre de la Reina.*

Trasierra

41370 Cazalla de la Sierra (Seville)
Tel. (9)54-88 43 24 – Fax (9)54-88 33 05
Sra Charlotte Scott

Rooms 6 with bath and lounge. **Price** Double 12,000Pts (per pers.). **Meals** Breakfast included. **Restaurant** Evening meals by reservation. Service 13:00-16:00, 20:30-22:00; menu 3,500Pts. Specialties: regional cooking. **Credit cards** Amex, Visa, Eurocard, MasterCard. **Pets** Dogs allowed on request. **Facilities** Swimming pool, parking. **Nearby** Seville, Còrdoba. **Open** All year on request.

Residential hotels are not very common in Spain and the rare examples we have found are always homes opened by foreigners in love with this country. This is the case with Charlotte and Nick Scott who have restored a large olive oil mill and its outhouses in the Sierra Morena, about one hundred kilometers from Seville. This was a sizeable job and needed all the passion of the owners and skills of the local workers to restore the spirit of the property. The bedrooms are vast and sober, decorated with travel souvenirs or traditional articles reworked in the neighboring village, which are also sold in the hotel's small boutique. The wild environment of the Sierra Morena is superb and your very welcoming hosts will be your best guides.

How to get there (Maps 18 and 24): 100km north of Seville.

La Cartuja de Cazalla

41370 Cazalla de la Sierra (Sevilla)
A-455, km 3
Tel. (9)5 488 45 16 - Fax (9)5-488 35 15

Rooms 8 with bath. **Price** Single 8,000Pts, double 12,000Pts, triple 15,000Pts.
Restaurant Menu: 2,500Pts. **Credit cards** Visa, Eurocard, MasterCard. **Pets** Dogs
allowed. **Facilities** Swimming pool, parking. **Nearby** Constantina - Sevilla. **Open** All
year.

Cazalla de la Sierra is known not only for its Stone Age relics and
the restoration of a statue of Marcus Aurelius but also for its
outstanding anisette and eau de vie. Here, you can visit several lovely
churches in 'mudéjar' style and the romantic ruins of the old charter
house. Carmen Ladròn de Guevara bought them all with an eye to
restoring them. So far, work on several buildings has been completed
and some offer rooms and small apartments, others have large
exhibition halls for artists who come here seeking the calm necessary
for their work. Let's wish her the best of luck on her courageous
undertaking as the village is a particularly friendly one.

How to get there *(Map 18): 85km north of Seville, C431 to Cantillana,*
Pedroso and Cazalla.

Casa de Carmona

41410 Carmona (Seville)
Plaza de Lasso
Tel. (9)5-419 10 00 – Fax (9)5-419-01 89 – Sr Schwabach

Category ★★★★★ **Rooms** 30 with air-conditioning, telephone, bath, WC, satellite TV, safe and minibar; elevator. **Price** Single 17,000-29,000Pts, double 18,000-39,000Pts, 3 pers. 29,000-45,000Pts. **Meals** Breakfast 1,500Pts, served from 8:00-11:00; half board + 4,000Pts, full board + 8,000Pts (per Pers.). **Restaurant** Service 12:30-16:00, 20:30-24:00; menu 4,000Pts, also à la carte. Specialties: regional cooking. **Credit cards** All major. **Pets** Dogs allowed. **Facilities** Swimming pool, fitness club, sauna, parking. **Nearby** Church Santa Maria, Roman Necropolis (Elephant Vault, Servilia Tomb...), in Carmona - Fuentes de Andalucia - Seville; Golf e Hipodromo del Club Pineda golf course (9-Hole). **Open** All year.

Just a few kilometers from Seville, the ancient Andalusian city of Carmona shelters one of the most luxurious hotels of charm in Spain. Opened in 1991, the Casa de Carmona is a former palace furbished with a luxury of refinements. The public rooms are remarkable; the admirable patio with its flowery pot plants gives a tone to the entrance; and two lounge–conference rooms decorated with portraits of aristocrats and ancient livery all give you the impression of being received by some Spanish grandee. The small swimming pool is ravishing and allows you to freshen up in the shade of the marble columns. All the rooms are different and each has its own personality via a subtle mix of old furniture and coordinated pastel shades and fabrics. We recommend Number 6 for its admirable ceiling of Andalusian caissons, but also Numbers 14 and 18 for their views over the town. With the new management, the maintenance of the hotel should be better.

How to get there *(Map 24): 33km east of Seville via N4, towards Córdoba.*

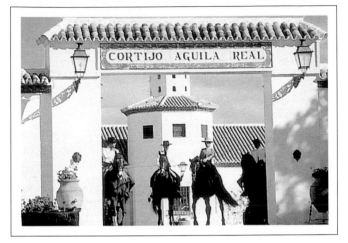

Hotel Cortijo Aguila Real

41210 Guillena (Seville)
Tel. (9)55-578 50 06 - Fax (9)55-578 43 30
Sra Martinez

Category ★★★★ **Rooms** 8 and 3 suites with air-conditioning, telephone, bath, WC, TV. **Price** Single 15,000Pts, double 20,000Pts. **Meals** Breakfast 1,500Pts, served 9:00-11:00; half board + 4,500Pts, full board + 7,000Pts (per pers.). **Restaurant** Service 13.15-16:00, 20:15-22:30; menu 3,500Pts, also à la carte. Specialties: game. **Credit cards** All major. **Pets** Dogs not allowed. **Facilities** Swimming pool, parking. **Nearby** Seville - Satiponce - Itàlica - Alcala del Rio - Cantillana - Carmona. **Open** All year.

At some twenty kilometers from Seville one arrives at Cortigo Aguila Real via a road lined with fields of wheat and sunflowers, and arid land. Little by little, like some oasis in the desert, one begins to see the Cortigo on the summit of its hill. It is a former farm and the farm buildings surrounding the large courtyard have been arranged to give great independence to visitors. The rooms are very spacious and fitted with regional furniture, while three also have open fireplaces. All are perfectly comfortable and impeccably maintained. Meals can be taken either in the dining room, on the terrace or in the shade of the pine trees beside the swimming pool, from where one has a very splendid view over the plain with Seville in the distance. A same flexibility with the menus, which you can amend as you wish. Game, fresh and natural produce are the basics of the cuisine served. The hotel organizes bullfighting demonstrations in the ring on the property, as well as horse riding trips or tourist visits. Peace and quiet and a very warm welcome make this hotel an admirable address.

How to get there *(Map 24): 20km north of Seville via E803, to Merida; at Guillena (after the Itàlica ruins, road to the right between tow gas station), then to Burguillos.*

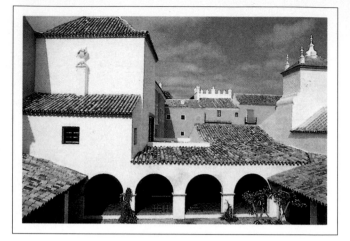

Hacienda Benazuza

41800 Sanlùcar La Mayor (Seville)
Tel. (9)55-70 33 44 - Fax (9)55-70 34 10 - Sr Elejabeitia - Sr Wyss

Category ★★★★ **Rooms** 44 suites with air-conditioning, telephone, bath, WC, satellite TV, safe and minibar. **Price** Single 28,000-42,000Pts, double 35,000-52,000Pts, suite 47,000-135,000Pts. **Meals** Breakfast 1,500-2,050Pts, served 7:00-12:00; half board + 5,500Pts, full board + 12,500Pts (per pers.). **Restaurant** "La Alqueira" service 14:00-16:00, 21:00-24:00; à la carte 6,000Pts, "La Alberca" (swimming pool) à la carte 7,000Pts. **Credit cards** All major. **Pets** Dogs allowed. **Facilities** Swimming pool, tennis, paddle tennis, putting green, parking. **Nearby** Seville - Cantillana - Carmona - Alcala de Guadaira. **Open** Oct - July 14.

Hacienda Benazuza is a large hotel of charm in the Aljarafe (highlands) of Seville. Arabo-Andalusian in style, it is a collection of buildings assembled in the course of centuries. The surrounding wall reminds one of its Saracen origins in the 10th century, while the tower above the entry postern carries the coat of arms granted to the Counts of Benazuza in the 16th century. Most careful work in the archives has given its original splendor back to the Hacienda. The walls have refound their ocre, red, yellow and orange colors, the lounges their mudejar ceilings and the floorings of terra-cotta and enamelled tiles. The rooms and their bathrooms are superb even though one would have preferred that they continue in the Hispano-Moorish style. In the restaurants one discovers both Mediterranean and Oriental flavors. The small Hacienda chapel plays an active part in Holy Week and the 'Rocio de Sanlucar La Mayor': you will be well placed to enjoy these events, some of the most important in Andalusian culture.

How to get there (Map 24): 33km west of Seville via N431, towards Huelva.

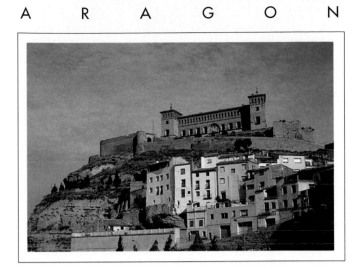

Parador La Concordia

44600 Alcañiz (Teruel)
Castillo de los Calatravos
Tel. (9)78-83 04 00 – Fax (9)78-83 03 66
Sr Cruz Sanchez

Category ★★★ **Rooms** 12 with air-conditioning, telephone, shower, WC, TV and minibar; elevator. **Price** Double 15,000-17,500Pts. **Meals** Breakfast 1,300Pts, served 8:30-11:00. **Restaurant** Service 13:00-16:30, 20:30-23:00, menu 3,500Pts, also à la carte. Specialties: Ternasco asado - Costilletas a la baturra - Dulces tipicos. **Credit cards** All major. **Pets** Dogs not allowed. **Nearby** Calaceite (Plaza Mayor) - Gretas - Valderrobres - Monastery of Rueda in Escatrón - Morella. **Open** Feb 1 - Dec 18.

At the summit of a hill dominating Alcañiz, the present chateau dates mainly from the 18th century and was converted into a parador in 1968. Today it is the ideal setting for a romantic stay and everything helps make this hotel such a charming place. The decor is sober but in good taste: white walls, Spanish furniture and polished floors. The rooms on the courtyard are rather small and a bit sober: those looking over the town and the River Guadalupe are much lighter. The bathrooms are spacious and attractive. The menu allows one to appreciate specialties of Aragonese cuisine, and certainly do not leave without trying the Almendrades (confectionery of almond paste), a specialty of Alcañiz.

How to get there (Map 15): 103km southeast of Zaragoza via N232.

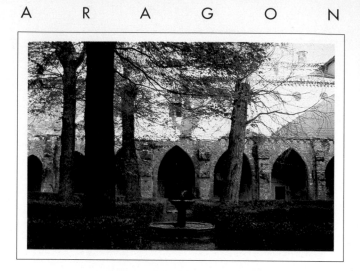

Hotel Monasterio de Piedra

50210 Nuévalos (Zaragoza)
Tel. (9)76-84 90 11 – Fax (9)76-84 90 54
Sr Montaner
Web: http://www.zar;hnet.es/monastpiedra

Category ★★★ Rooms 61 with telephone, bath, WC and TV. **Price** Single 7,000Pts, double 10,000Pts. **Meals** Breakfast 500Pts, served 8:00-10.30, half board + 3,100Pts, full board + 5,250Pts (per pers., 2 days min.). **Restaurant** Service 13:00-17:00, 21:00-23:00; menu 2,600Pts, also à la carte. Specialties: Migas - Trucha del monasterio - Ternasco de Aragón. **Credit cards** All major. **Pets** Dogs allowed (except in restaurant). **Facilities** Swimming-pool, tennis. **Nearby** Alhama de Aragon - Jaraba - Cetina - Ariza - Catalayud. **Open** All year.

Founded in the 12th century by Cistercian monks, this remarkably well-conserved monastery has a great beauty. This is an astonishing site and a real and fresh oasis, full of greenery and rising right out of the Meseta, a dry and rugged region surrounded by steep sierras. Here the genius of man has associated with the genius of nature. One should for example note the monumental staircase, illuminated by opaque alabaster windows to give a dream-like light. The rooms are simple in the former monks' cells, with access via long and vaulted galleries. Some have terraces, others are located around the cloisters, yet others surround the entrance courtyard with its elm tree planted in 1681. Certainly do not leave the hotel without having visited the other parts of the monastery, and having walked in the woods with the many lakes, waterfalls and caves.

How to get there *(Map 14): 30km southwest of Catalayud via C202 to Nuévalos, then follow the signs for Monasterio de Piedra.*

Parador Fernando de Aragón

50680 Sos del Rey Católico (Zaragoza)
Arquitecto Sainz de Vicuña, 1
Tel. (9)48-88 80 11 - Fax (9)48-88 81 00
Sr Rizos Garrido

Category ★★★ **Rooms** 65 with air-conditioning, telephone, bath, WC, TV and minibar; elevator. **Price** Double 12,500-15,000Pts. **Meals** Breakfast 1,300Pts, served 8:00-11:00; half board + 4,300Pts, full board + 6,375Pts. **Restaurant** Service 13:00-15:30, 20:30-22:30, menu 3,500Pts, also à la carte. Specialties: regional cooking. **Credit cards** All major. **Pets** Dogs not allowed. **Facilities** Parking. **Nearby** Uncastillo (Santa Maria Church and the Casa Consistorial) - Longas road. **Open** Feb 22 - Jan 11.

Situated in the historically classified village of Sos, the Parador Fernando de Aragón was built a few years ago by one of the best Spanish architects, with respect for just one rule: the Aragonese style. Thus the craftsman's finish has been conserved and the stone already seems to have several centuries behind it. The rooms are very large with polished floor-tiles and beds of copper. Those on the second floor have a gallery, while the rooms on the third have balconies. The bathrooms are successfully realized and not short of practical fittings. The dining room on the fourth floor, with its massive pillars, overlooks the valley, and the restaurant is one of the best in the region.

How to get there *(Map 6): 63km southeast of Pamplona via N240 towards Jaca, then C127.*

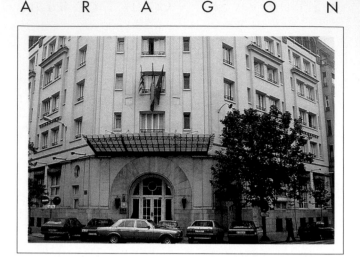

Gran Hotel

50001 Zaragoza
Calle Joaquin Costa, 5
Tel. (9)76-22 19 01 – Fax (9)76-23 67 13
Sra G. Elizaga

Category ★★★★ **Rooms** 140 with air-conditioning, telephone, bath, WC, satellite TV and minibar; elevator. **Price** Double 10,000 (weekend)-14,000Pts, junior suite 16,000 (weekend)-18,000Pts. **Meals** Breakfast 1,350Pts, served 7:00-11:00. **Restaurant** Service 13:00-15:30, 20:00-23:00; menu 3,500Pts, also à la carte. Specialties: meats. **Credit cards** All major. **Pets** Small dogs allowed. **Facilities** Parking (1,700Pts). **Nearby** Basilica de Nuestra Señora del Pilar, La Seo, Palacio de la Aljaferta - Churches in Utebo, Alagon, San Mateo de Gàllego, Zuera - Cartuja Aula Dei - Pina. **Open** All year.

Opened in 1929 by King Alfonso XIII and recently restored, this hotel has known how to keep its class, delightful atmosphere and refinement, in a town where any establishment of character is sadly rare. The rather luxurious ambiance is not at all starchy. The large round lounge with its glazed roof is a good example of the elegant decor. The bedrooms are spacious and very comfortable, and decorated with taste, each with its own functional and very neat bathroom. For preference you can take the suite in which King Juan Carlos lived when a student at the Zaragoza military academy. A good welcome, an excellent quality-price ratio, and private parking are further reasons for choosing this hotel sited right in the town center.

How to get there *(Map 15): near the Plaza del Dragón.*

Hotel La Casona de Amandi

Amandi
33311 Villaviciosa (Asturias)
Tel. (9)8-589 01 30 – Fax (9)8-589 01 29
Sr R. Fernandez

Category ★★★ Rooms 9 with telephone, bath, WC and TV. **Price** Double 10,900Pts. **Meals** Breakfast 850Pts. **No Restaurant. Credit cards** All major. **Pets** Dogs not allowed. **Facilities** Parking. **Nearby** In Amandi: Church of San Juan; Fiesta de la Virgen del Protal (Sept) - Oviedo - Tazones - Roman church of Priesca - Villabona - Monastery San Salvador of Valdedios. **Open** All year (except in Jan).

Very well situated between sea and mountains, the little village of Amandi is a real refuge of tranquility at the foot of the first peaks of the Asturias, and yet only 15 kilometers from the beaches. The 'casa' is a marvellous little house from the 19th century that has kept all the atmosphere of a private home, surrounded by a vast very green and flowery garden. The beautiful rustic wooden planking has been retained, as have the thick slats of wood in the very large bedrooms, all personalized with antique furniture. In the very well equiped bathrooms, the original ceramics have been restored. Various small lounges allow one to read, just rest or have breakfast provided one does not prefer the winter garden arranged on the first floor. In the fine weather one can then appreciate the large garden planted with magnolias and other handsome trees. All the comforts and good taste are to be found here, to ensure a most enjoyable stay.

How to get there *(Map 3): 30 km east of Gijón, towards Villaviciosa.*

1998

La Casona de Pío

33150 Cudillero (Asturias)
Riofrío, 3
Tel. (9)8-559 15 12 - Fax (9)8-559 15 19

Category ★★ Rooms 11 with telephone, bath, WC and TV. **Price** Double 6,000-8,000Pts. **Meals** Breakfast 850Pts, served 8:00-10:30. **Restaurant** Service 13:00-14:30, 20:30-22:30; à la carte. Specialties: Almejas a la marinera - Pixín amariscado - Merluza del "pincho" de Cudillero rellena de marisco - Fideos con bogavante. **Credit cards** Visa, Eurocard, MasterCard. **Pets** Dogs not allowed. **Nearby** El Pito - Beaches of Concha de Artedo - San Martín de Luiña and Soto de Luiña. **Open** All year.

The small village of Cudillero is nestled by a creek at the foot of two green hills. The houses are tightly clustered around the square where the town hall, the church and the port are located. In an old and elegant residence which has been very carefully restored you find one of the most charming small hotels on the Asturian coast. The rooms have attractive regional furniture and are extremely comfortable; there is even hydro-massage in the bathtubs. The delightful dining room is a fine setting in which to enjoy meals of a very high quality that include traditional dishes of fish and seafood from the Cantabrian Sea. The welcome you receive here is incredibly friendly, and the management offers everything from light lunches prepared to your order to the organization of excursions in the region. The Casona de Pío is truly a tiny patch of Asturian paradise.

How to get there (Map 3): 61km northwest of Oviedo, 54km west of Gijón.

Palacio de Vallados

33330 Lastrcs (Asturias)
Pedro Villarta
Tel. (9)8-585 04 44 - Fax (9)8-585 05 17
M. Ernesto Seijas

Category ★★★ **Rooms** 28 with tel., bath, WC, satellite TV and minibar; elevator. **Price** Single 5,800-8,000Pts, double 7,250-10,000Pts. **Meals** Breakfast 600Pts, served 8:00-11:00, half board + 2,600 Pts, full board + 4,600Pts. **Restaurants** Service 13:00-16:00, 20:30-23:30; menu 2,600Pts. Specialties: regional cooking.**Credit cards** All major. **Pets** Dogs not allowed. **Facilities** Garage and parking. **Nearby** Ribadesella - Colunga - Caravia - Cueva de la Moria. **Open** All year (except in Feb).

In this charming village where all the white houses with their red tile roofs seem to straddle the port, the Palacio de Vallados assumes the character of a 'grand hotel.' It is a residence once belonging to nobles and well up on a hill which means most of its rooms have a view of the sea. The subtly-lighted interior is of a lovely pink, although the decor is perhaps a little too functional despite the quality of the comfort of its rooms. The view, however, is nothing less than picture-perfect.

How to get there *(Map 3): 46km east of Gijón.*

Hotel La Arquera

La Arquera 33500 Llanes (Asturias)
Tel. (9)8-540 24 24 - Fax (9)8-540 01 75

Category ★★★ **Rooms** 12 with telephone, bath, WC, TV, minibar and kitchen. **Price** Double 7,000-10,500Pts, triple 8,500-12,500Pts, 4 pers. 10,000-15,000Pts. **Meals** Breakfast 800Pts. **No restaurant. Credit cards** Visa, Eurocard, MasterCard. **Pets** Dogs not allowed. **Facilities** Garage and parking. **Nearby** Vidiago - Cave of Pindal in Pimiango - Beaches of Celorio and Nueva. **Open** All year.

At the foot of the Sierra de Cuera, Llanes is an attractive little port with a very picturesque old town quarter. Numerous beaches such as the 'Playa de Toro' and 'Playa del Sablon' have made its tourist reputation. The Spanish also come here to celebrate the local feasts, giving the 'Llaniscos' every occasion to remember all their traditions in a colorful manner. The hotel occupies a country house typical of this region, and has retained its grain store. 2 kilometers from the village, the hotel is well protected by its little garden. The glazed lounges have a wonderful view onto the mountains, while the bedrooms are large and well equiped for long stays, since as well as the traditional comforts, they also have small kitchens fitted with cookers, fridges, etc. Some rooms cater for up to four people. Besides the pleasures of the beach, do not miss those of the small village of Celorio and ay Nueva, and the 'Playa del Mar'—the region is rich in prehistoric sites that are all of interest.

How to get there *(Map 4): 96km from Santander and 2km south of Llanes.*

La Posada de Babel

La Pereda
33509 Llanes (Asturias)
Tel. (9)8-540 25 25 - Fax (9)8-540 26 22

Category ★★★ **Rooms** 11 with air-conditioning, telephone, bath, WC and TV. **Price** Double 8,400-11,000Pts. **Meals** Breakfast 850Pts. **Restaurant** Closed Tues and Feb; à la carte 3,000-4,500Pts. Specialties: regional cooking. **Credit cards** Amex, Visa, Eurocard, MasterCard. **Pets** Dogs allowed. **Facilities** Bikes, practise golf, parking. **Nearby** Vidiago - Cave of Pindal in Pimiango - Beaches of Celorio and Nueva. **Open** All year.

In this beautiful region of the Asturias, La Posada de Babel offers a quality retreat for those appreciating the serenity of an all calming nature, but also with the possibility-less than 3 kilometers away-of plunging into the more lively ambiance of the beaches. The hotel enjoys a superb site looking over fields and woods, surrounded by a park of more than 1 hectare, planted with magnolias, apple trees and camelias. The house is a beautiful modern construction in the spirit of Le Corbusier. The ground floor shelters the lounge, library and dining room, and via a large glazed gallery directly communes with nature. The more traditional interior has kept a very warm ambiance: classical furniture in good taste, beautiful canvasses and lithographs on the walls and an open fire in season. The same cosy atmosphere is in the bedrooms, and five of them have terraces. Our preference is for No. 8, a tiny little house on two floors in the garden, but always with the same charming decoration, both simple but carefully chosen. The restaurant is excellent and along with the daily market, it lets you try the specialties of the region. To better appreciate the surroundings, the hotel has bikes available and can also organize horse riding, or 4x4 outings.

How to get there *(Map 4): 96 km from Santander and 4 km south of Llanes.*

Hotel de la Reconquista

33004 Oviedo (Asturias)
Calle Gil de Jaz, 16
Tel. (9)8-524 11 00 – Fax (9)8-524 11 66
Sr Don ramon Felip

Category ★★★★★ **Rooms** 142 with air-conditioning, telephone, bath, WC, TV and minibar; elevator. **Price** Single 18,750-23,200Pts, double 23,500-29,000Pts, suite 42,000-67,000Pts. **Meals** Breakfast 1,950Pts, served 7:00-10:30; half board + 7,600Pts, full board + 11,250Pts (per pers.). **Restaurant** Service 13:30-16:00, 21:00-23:30; menu 5,650Pts, also à la carte. Specialties: Fabada. **Credit cards** All major. **Pets** Dogs not allowed. **Facilities** Sauna (1,200Pts), garage. **Nearby** Cathedral of Oviedo - Church of Santa Maria del Naranco - San Claudio; Club Deportivo la Bargariza golf course (9-hole). **Open** All year.

This former hospice-hospital was built in the 18th century by the renowned architect P. A. Menendez. The building has only two floors but is dominated by a huge Spanish coat of arms in the center, a remarkable example of baroque sculpture. Having traversed the porch, you find yourself in a vast rectangular lounge lit by a glazed roof. A mezzanine runs all around and is supported by a double stone colonnade. The hotel offers exceptional facilities: a gym, a sauna, conference rooms, and also a concert hall set out in the very beautiful chapel, with an octagonal plan and two tiers of superposed seating. The bedrooms and service are those of a real palace.

How to get there *(Map 3): in the town center near the San Francisco Park.*

Hotel Casa del Busto

33120 Pravia (Asturias)
C/ Rey Don Silo, 1
Tel. (9)8-582 27 71 - Fax (9)8-582 27 72
Sr Mencos

Category ★★★ **Rooms** 27 with telephone, bath or shower, WC, TV. **Price** Single 4,500-6,500Pts, double 6,500-8,500Pts. **Meals** Breakfast 500-750Pts, served 9:00-11:00. **Restaurant** Service 13:30-15:30, 21:00-23:00; menu 1,200Pts, also à la carte. Specialties: Fabes - Arroz con leche. **Credit cards** Amex, Visa, Eurocard, MasterCard. **Pets** Dogs allowed. **Nearby** Beaches of Aguilar, Santa and Maria del Mar - Cudillero - El Pito - Cabo de Vidio - Catedral of Oviedo. **Open** All year.

Only a few kilometers inland from the charming village of Cudillero and the beautiful Concha de Artado beach is an old caseròn dating from the 16th century that has been converted into a hotel. The sobriety of its exterior is particularly noteworthy. Inside, its furniture and regional fabrics harmonize nicely with the rustic architecture. In the large outdoor patio with its traditional overhead glass-enclosed gallery, you can enjoy a coffee, a drink or a snack as well as a view of the mountainous surroundings. There is an interior patio with a pleasant decor of stone columns and an intimate restaurant. The rooms are in attractive provincial style and very comfortable. This is a very well placed hotel in the triangle formed by Ovido, Gijon and Aviles.

How to get there (Map 3): 55km from Oviedo on the Oviedo-Pravia highway. Take the Barco-Pravia exit; Asturias-Pravia airport.

Hotel Marina

33056 Ribadesella (Asturias)
Tel. (9)8-586 00 50 - Fax (9)8-586 01 57
Mme Anesada Lidu

Category ★★ **Rooms** 46 with telephone, bath, WC and satellite TV; elevator. **Price** Double 6,000-8,500Pts. **Meals** Breakfast 500Pts, served 7:00-11:00. **Restaurant** Service 12:30-15:00- 20:30-23:30; menu 1,200Pts. Specialties: regional cooking. **Credit cards** All major. **Pets** Dogs not allowed. **Nearby** Ribadesella: the old town, cave of Tito Bustillo - Cueva de la Moria - San Estebán de Leces - Carvia - Colunga - Lastres. **Open** All year (except Jan and Feb).

Ribadesella is one of the seaside resorts on the Asturian coast known for the kayak run stretching from Arriondas to the port which spectators can watch from the small train that runs parallel to the river. This small fishing port does not have the charm of nearby Llanes or San Vicente, but it has a lovely setting at the mouth of the Sella River. This historical town has some attractive 17th- and 18th-century palaces which are totally unlike the Hotel Marina which is noteworthy for the use of the color green in its architecture which is not unlike that of Vienna or Prague. The interior seems a bit dated with lamps from the 50s and sofas from the 70s, all contributing to an amusing and faintly kitsch ambiance. We recommend the rooms offering balconies with view. This hotel can nicely break up the trip from Santander to Gijon.

How to get there (Map 3): 67km east of Gijón.

La Rectoral

33775 Taramundi-La Villa (Asturias)
Tel. (9)8-564 67 67 - Fax (9)8-564 67 77
Sr Barrenechea

Category ★★★★ **Rooms** 18 with air-conditioning, telephone, bath, WC, TV and minibar. **Price** Single 10,000-12,000Pts, double 12,000-15,000Pts, 3 pers. 15,000-18,000Pts. **Meals** Breakfast 950Pts; half board 16,500Pts (per pers.). **Restaurant** Service 13:00-15:00, 21:00-22:00; menu 2,200Pts. **Credit cards** All major. **Pets** Dogs not allowed. **Facilities** Sauna, garage. **Nearby** Mazo de Meredo - Tapia de Casariego - Castropol - Figueras. **Open** All year.

This is one of the most charming of Spanish inns, in the heart of deepest Spain in a tiny village on the frontier between the Asturias and Galicia—and so the local reputation is based not on its cutlery alone! This former 18th-century presbytery has been transformed into a comfortable hotel. The barn has become the lounge, and next to it a bar (where the bartender will let you taste the local liqueurs), and then the dining room. The bedrooms have been decorated in the traditional style of the Asturias, and are welcoming, opening onto a small private terrace with a superb view over the gentle green hills. Everything here is simple, very authentic and top quality. A good halting place for discovering a different Spain.

How to get there *(Map 2): 65km northeast of Lugo, via N640 to Vilaodriz; then take the small road on the right.*

Palacete Peñalba

42100 Figueras del Mar (Asturias)
El Cotarelo
Tel. (9)8-563 61 25 – Fax (9)8 563 62 47

Category ★★★ Rooms 12 with telephone, bath, WC and TV. **Price** Single 8,000Pts, double 10,500Pts, suite 14,500Pts. **Meals** Breakfast 700Pts, served at any time. **Restaurant** "Peñalba", av. Trenor-Puerto, service 13:00-15:00, 20:00-22:00; à la carte 4,500-5,800Pts. Specialties: regional cooking and fish. **Credit cards** Amex, Visa, Eurocard, MasterCard. **Pets** Small dogs allowed. **Facilities** Parking. **Nearby** Beaches - Valley of Masma via N634 from Barreiros (Lourenza, Lindin). **Open** All year.

Built in 1912 by a disciple of Gaudi, the Palacete Peñalba is about to be classified a historic monument. Converted into a hotel five years ago, it has a rather faded charm, an impression given by the colors and furnishings, but not at all by the irreproachable amenities and comfort. The bedrooms will delight any lover of big spaces, while Numbers 12, 14 and 15 have large terraces. In the suites, the bathrooms are set in a veranda. Very peaceful, the house is surrounded by a garden planted with various species of pine trees, along with a superb palm tree. There is no restaurant in the hotel but in the little port of Figueras, just 200 meters away, the same proprietor also owns a restaurant whose renown has spread beyond the frontier of the Asturias and even of Spain, due in large part to the excellent fish dishes.

How to get there (Map 2): 150km northeast of Oviedo, on the coast and 3km from Ribadeo.

Hotel Asturias

33201 Gijón (Asturias)
Plaza Mayor, 11
Tel. (9)8-535-06 00/01/02 – Fax (9)8-534-68 72
M. Juan Luis Alfonso

Category ★★ **Rooms** 65 with Telelephone, bath, WC and TV. **Price** Single 6,000Pts, double 8,000Pts. **Meals** Breakfast 350Pts, served 7:30-11:00. **Restaurant** Service 12:30-15:00, 20:30-23:30; menu 1,200Pts. Specialties: regional cooking. **Credit cards** All major. **Pets** Dogs not allowed. **Nearby** Castiello golf course (18-Hole). **Open** All year.

The Hotel Asturias is the only hotel on the Plaza Mayor in the heart of this city on the Cantabrian coast. It is very close to the attractive port and the large and well-maintained San Lorenzo Beach. The entrance way with its elliptical glass roof suggests a 19th-century bodega rather than a hotel. The lobby is spacious with ample facilities for quiet conversations. The comfortable and classically decorated rooms are upstairs, the best among them giving on the square, but you should bear in mind, especially in the summer, that the cafés, the bars and the fishermen's restaurants in the port stay open all night.

How to get there *(Map 3): 29km Northeast of Oviedo.*

Casal del Castro

39520 Comillas (Cantabria)
San Jerónimo
Tel. (9)42-72 00 36/ 72 23 91 – Fax (9)42-72 00 61
Sr Angel Gonzalez Mirones

Category ★★★ **Rooms** 43 with telephone, bath, WC. and satellite TV; elevator.
Price Single 5,200-8,300Pts, double 8,500-11,500Pts, suite 13,500-18,600Pts.
Meals Breakfast included, served 7:00-11:00. **Restaurant** Service 13:30-16:00,
21:00-23:30; menu 2,100Pts; also à la carte. Specialties: fish.**Credit cards** Visa,
Eurocard, MasterCard. **Pets** Dogs not allowed. **Facilities** Parking. **Nearby** Santillana
del Mar (Collegiale), cave of Altamira. **Open** All year.

Comillas is a very charming seaside resort, once the royal
residence of King Alphonso XII. What remains from the date of
his reign are the palace and, in the garden, a pavilion he
commissioned Gaudí to design. Today, that is where you will find a
fine, elegant restaurant called *El Caprichio de Gaudí*. The hotel itself
occupies part of the casona, a noble residence dating from the 17th
century and typical of the region. The ground-floor lounges still
reflect some of the magnificence of that period. The best rooms are
in this older part and some of them have a view of the village. A
more recent addition, extending from the old white building, has far
less charm although it lacks nothing in terms of comfort. The
restaurant features a great deal of fish dishes and offers a very pleasant
terrace. And should you choose to try something a little different, we
recommend the very pleasant *El Molino*, a restaurant in Puente Arce
on the road to Santander.

How to get there *(Map 4): 49km west of Santander.*

Hotel del Oso

39539 Coscaya (Cantabria)
Tél. (9)42-73 30 18 – Fax (9)42-73 30 36
Sra Ana Rivas

Categories ★★ and ★★★ **Rooms** 34 and 16 with telephone, bath, WC and satellite TV; elevator. **Price** Single 5,550-6,600Pts - 6,000-7,200Pts, double 7,150-8,200Pts - 8,000-9,100Pts. **Meals** Breakfast 575Pts, served 9:00-11:00. **Restaurant** Service 13:00-16:00, 21:00-23:00; menu 3,000Pts, also à la carte. Specialties: regional cooking.**Credit cards** All major. **Pets** Dogs not allowed. **Facilities** Swimming pool, tennis, parking. **Nearby** Puerto de Pandetrave, Monastery of Santo Toribio de Liébana - Church of Santa Maria de Lebeña - Santa Maria de Piasca - Torre del Infantado (Potes) - Torre de Mogrovejo - Convento of San Raimundo. **Open** Feb 15 - Jan 1.

Between Oviedo and Santander is a region dominated not only by the towering Picos de Europa with their wild landscape of gorges and mountain passes but also by lovely green valleys and rivers brimming with fish. The Hotel del Oso, which has been run by the same family over several generations, is undoubtedly the hotel the most professionally operated, offering guests the finest accommodation in the Liebana Valley, along with a swimming pool. It is a truly attractive place in the mountains where two old houses face each other across the river, one with rooms slightly larger than the other, explaining the one-star difference in rating. The only ones to be avoided are those overlooking the parking lot. Here you find stunning flowers everywhere, and the restaurant offers a menu with numerous regional specialties. This a family hotel where outdoor tourism is very much the tradition.

How to get there *(Map 4): 140km west of Santander (to Gijón) at half-way road to Potes, Camaleño and Coscaya.*

El Rebeco

39588 Fuente Dé (Cantabria)
Tel. (9)42-73 66 01/02 - Fax (9)42-73 66 00
M. Ottomar Casado Polantinos

Category ★★ **Rooms** 30 with telephone, bath, WC and satellite TV. **Price** Single 5,500Pts, double 7,500Pts, 4 pers. 10,900Pts. **Meals** Breakfast 500Pts, served 8:30-10:00. **Restaurants** Service 12:30-15:00, 20:00-23:00; menu 1,600Pts. Specialties: regional cooking. **Credit cards** All major. **Pets** Dogs not allowed. **Facilities** Parking. **Nearby** Monastery of Santo Toribio de Liébana - Church of Santa Maria de Lebeña - Santa Maria de Piasca - Torre del Infantado (Potes) - Torre de Mogrovejo - Convento of San Raimundo - Naturel Park of Covadonga. **Open** All year.

You leave the Cantabrian coast, the sea and the heat to travel inland on N621 for some seventy kilometers and reach a height of over 1,500 meters. The vegetation changes rapidly along this magnificent highway leading to the towering Picos de Europa. The Hotel Rebeco is in the center of a kind of amphitheater surrounded by mountains rising to 2,600 meters and resembling a lunar landscape. It is a small chalet built of stone and wood with warm and simple decoration based on bright colors, mostly reds, livening up the dark heavy wood of the furniture. You shouldn't miss the view of the Picos and better still, ask for a room with a small terrace. The restaurant offers local specialties plus a year-long panoramic vista. There is a lift and you will have an excellent opportunity for hiking and visiting the wild animal preserve.

How to get there *(Map 4): 140km west of Santander to Gijón) at half-way road to Potes, Camaleño and Fuente Dé.*

La Casona de Treviño

Treviño 39587 Camaleño (Cantabria)
Tel. (9)42-73 30 26
Mme Maria Ester Velez

Rooms 4 (1 with bath and WC, 3 with communal bath). **Price** 4,200Pts, 5,700Pts (with bath). **Meals** Breakfast 400Pts, served 8:00-10:00; half board 7,000Pts (per pers.). **Evening meals** Menu 1,200Pts. **Credit cards** Not accepted. **Pets** Dogs not allowed. **Facilities** Parking. **Nearby** Monastery of Santo Toribio de Liébana - Church of Santa Maria de Lebeña - Santa Maria de Piasca - Torre del Infantado (Potes) - Torre de Mogrovejo - Convento of San Raimundo - Naturel Park of Covadonga. **Open** All year.

The back country behind the coast is a particularly pretty mountainous region, crisscrossed by valleys where environmental tourism has increasingly developed. When you leave the road from Camaleño, you travel through two kilometers of extraordinary countryside where flowered plains follow pine forests at the foot of the majestic Picos de Europa. It is here in these delightful surroundings that you will find the Casona de Treviño at the end of a long rose-lined alley, an 18th-century farm house that has been very well preserved. The parquet floors are particularly interesting with a patina that grows ever more attractive. There is the same rustic authenticity in the four furnished rooms with their large, solid-wood beds and luxurious eiderdowns. In the morning, you can open the windows for a splendid view of the mountain or the valley. Here is a simple hotel in which only one room has a private bath, but the whole place offers a genuine change of scene.

How to get there *(Map 5): 140km west of Santander to Gijón) at half-board road to Potes, Camaleño and Treviño.*

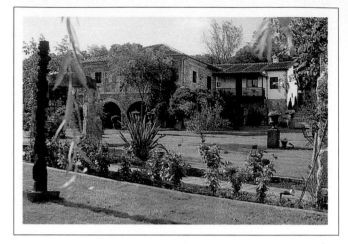

Hotel San Roman de Escalante

39795 Escalante (Cantabria)
Carretera de Escalante a Castillo, km 2
Tel. (9)4-267 77 45 - Fax (9)4-267 76 43 - Sr Melis

Category ★★★★ **Rooms** 10 with air-conditioning, telephone, bath, WC, TV and minibar. **Price** Double 13,000-25,000Pts. **Meals** Breakfast 1250Pts, served 8:00-10:30; half board + 5,200Pts, full board + 8,250Pts (per pers.). **Restaurant** Service 13:00-16:00, 21:00-23:00; menu 3,000Pts, also à la carte. Specialties: Almejas en salsa verde con setas - Mero con manteca de cacao i vanilla con verduritas - Filetto de pato en costra de sesamo i crujiente de Ibèrico - helado de vinagre de Modena. **Credit cards** All major. **Pets** Dogs allowed. **Facilities** Parking. **Nearby** In Santoña: Church of Santa Maria and Monastery of Montehano - Noja - Romanesque church of Bareyo - Beaches of Isla and Ajo. **Open** Jan 18 - Dec 18.

Escalante is a few kilometers away from the important fishing port of Santoña whose fortress has defended the deep bay cutting into the land since the 17th-century. The hotel owes its name to the hermitage dating from Roman times and on the property. The house is a former noble residence whose fine walls rise out of a garden shaded by trees, and in which sculptures by contemporary artists are on display. Here one actually lives surrounded by works of art, both old and modern, as the hotel also has an art gallery and boutique selling antiques. The former stables have been converted into a very good gastronomic restaurant which contributes to the reputation. Comfort is excellent in the rooms which are large with their little lounge areas. This is a very good address from which to discover – in luxury – the Cantabrian coastland.

How to get there *(Map 4 and 5): 42km east of Santander*

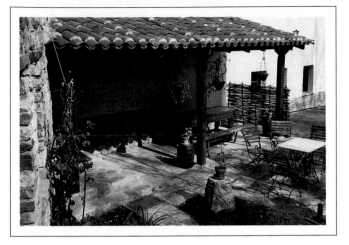

La Tahona de Besnes

33578 Alles (Cantabria)
Tel. (9)8-541 57 49 - Fax (9)8-541 57 49

Rooms 25 with telephone, bath, WC and TV. **Price** Single 5,280-6,880Pts, double 6,600-8,600Pts, 4 pers. 11,000-15,000Pts. **Meals** Breakfast 750Pts, served 8:30-10.30; half board + 2,600Pts, full board 4,200Pts. **Restaurant** Service 13:00-16:00, 20:00-23:00; menu 1,850Pts. Specialties: regional cooking. **Credit card**s Visa, Eurocard, MasterCard. **Pets** Dogs not allowed. **Facilities** Parking. **Nearby** Covadonga National Park - The Cares Route (C632) between Cangas de Onis and Panes - Walks in the Cares Gorges. **Open** All year.

Between Oviedo and Santander stretches the mountain chain of the 'Picos de Europa' (the Peaks of Europe), that offers magnificent attractions to all nature lovers: trails, gorges and rivers filled with salmon and trout. This site has favored rural tourism such as one finds it at Allès. Access to the little village is through of a forest with many winding little streams. Several former farm buildings shelter the rooms, and the decor is very rustic, very sober and very authentic-but one finds all the comforts of a traditional hotel, although you should note that all bathrooms only have small hip-baths. All is calm and one rediscovers the scents of the countryside-and with the cock's crow for alarm clock ! A young and enthusiastic team runs the house and they suggest all kinds of activities: bike rental, canoe outings through the gorges of the Cares and the Deva, 4x4 excursions, horse riding-and more. If you add the sea, some thirty kilometers away, to the program one has everything for a very good holiday.

How to get there *(Map 4): 89km west of Santander to Panes and Alles. Then, take road to Cangas de Onis for 10,5km.*

Hotel Hosteria de Quijas

39590 Quijas (Cantabria)
Carret. N 634
Tel. (9)42-82 08 33 - Fax (9)42-83 80 50
Sr Castañeda

Category ★★★ **Rooms** 14 and 5 suites with telephone, bath, jacuzzi, WC, satellite TV and minibar. **Price** Single 6,800Pts, double 8,500Pts, suite 17,000Pts. **Meals** Breakfast 700Pts, served 7:00-11:00. **Restaurant** Service 13:30-15:30, 20:30-23:00; à la carte. Specialties: Ensalada templada de mollejas de pato y habitas - Calabacines rellenos de bacalaò tres salsas. **Credit cards** All major. **Pets** Dogs not allowed. **Facilities** Swimming pool, parking. **Nearby** Santander - Altamira Caves; Pedreña golf course (18-Hole). **Open** Jan 5 - Dec 21.

A longing for peace and quiet? Then go and hide in the Hotel Hosteria de Quijas. This former 18th-century palace is set in a magnificent garden with its centuries-old trees and superb magnolias. The bedrooms are refined and furnished with pieces from the 17th and 18th centuries. Choose the ones facing the garden, quieter than those that face the street. Small lounges are scattered through the hotel. Uncovered stonework, caisson ceilings and the 'Thonet-style' all contribute to its charm. The dining room is welcoming with its wooden beams and pillars. A variety of trips can be planned starting from this site.

How to get there *(Map 4): 25km southeast of Santander to Torrelavega, towards Oviedo, Puente San Miguel and Quijas.(N634).*

Hotel Real

39005 Santander (Cantabria)
El Sardinero - Paseo Pérez Galdós, 28
Tel. (9)42-27 25 50 - Fax (9)42-27 45 73
Sr Lezius

Category ★★★★★ **Rooms** 123 with air-conditioning, telephone, bath, WC, satellite TV and minibar; elevator. **Price** Single 15,850-29,800Pts, double 19,800-37,200Pts, suite 40,000-130,000Pts. **Meals** Breakfast 1,500Pts, served 7:00-11:00; half board + 4900Pts, full board + 6720Pts (per Pers.). **Restaurant** Service 13:30-15:30, 21:00-23:30; menu 3,400Pts, also à la carte. Specialties: regional and international cooking. **Credit cards** All major. **Pets** Dogs not allowed. **Facilities** Parking. **Nearby** Santander - Altamira Caves; Pedreña golf course (18-Hole). **Open** All year.

This hotel, a racecourse and casino were built in Santander when the royal family used to have its summer quarters in this town, and one sought to give the town those facilities to satisfy all the requirement of such visitors. No details were spared and the hotel was given a privileged site overlooking the Bay of Santander and the Magdalena Beach. Since then it has of course been transformed and renovated, but it has retained all the magnificence and luxury of an old and rather dated hotel 'de luxe'. All the bedrooms open onto terraces or balconies, which are often flowered. The atmosphere here is one of calm and the furniture is classical Empire style. One 'plus' is the dining room with its veranda and stone arcades, and carefully selected furnishings. Next door are cosy lounges. All this to constitute a luxurious staging post in Cantabria.

How to get there *(Map 4): 3.5km northeast of Santander (El Sardinero).*

Parador Gil Blas

39330 Santillana del Mar (Cantabria)
Plaza Ramón Pelayo, 11
Tel. (9)42-81 80 00 – Fax (9)42-81 83 91
Sr Garralda Iribarren

Category ★★★ **Rooms** 56 with telephone, bath, WC, TV and minibar; elevator. **Price** Double 15,000-17,500Pts. **Meals** Breakfast 1,300Pts, served 8:00-11:00 **Restaurant** Service 13:00-16:00, 20:30-22:30; menu 3,500Pts, also à la carte. Specialties: Cocido - Merluza - Lubina - Salmón - Ternera al queso. **Credit cards** All major. **Pets** Dogs not allowed. **Facilities** Sauna, garage, parking. **Nearby** Colegiata de Santillana del Mar - Altamira Caves - Comillas - Picos de Europa - Beaches of Cobreces and Suances. **Open** All year.

Situated on the village square, the hotel occupies the very old and imposing home of the Barreda-Bracho family. The interior architecture is typical of the region: simple wooden columns give structure to most rooms, while the floors are shingled or of polished large parquet chips. On each floor there is a large lounge by the corridor leading to the rooms, which are very attractive: beds with columns in the Spanish style and everywhere a very beautiful choice of furniture, various objects and pictures. However, a special mention must be made of room 222 with its panoramic terrace over the village roofs and countryside. You will thus appreciate the calm in this region, while the caves of Altamira attract a large number of visitors.

How to get there *(Map 4): 31km southwest of Santander via N634, then C6316.*

Hotel Altamira

39330 Santillana del Mar (Cantabria)
Calle Canton, 1
Tel. (9)42-81 80 25 - Fax (9)42-84 01 36 - Sr Oceja Bujan

Category ★★★ **Rooms** 32 with telephone, shower, WC and satellite TV. **Price** Single 6,850-9,170Pts, double 7,800-11,950Pts, triple 10,075-15,265Pts, 4 pers. 12,350-18,580Pts. **Meals** Breakfast included, served 8:00-11:00; half board 7,350-25,380Pts, full board 8,440-29,740Pts (per pers.) **Restaurant** With air-conditioning, service 13:15-16:00, 20:00-22:45; menu 1,650Pts, also à la carte. Specialties: Cocido montañes - Ensalada cantabra de salmon y almejas - Solomillo al vino tinto de rioja. **Credit cards** All major. **Pets** Dogs not allowed. **Nearby** Colegiata de Santillana del Mar - Altamira Caves - Comillas - Picos de Europa - Beaches of Cobreces and Suances. **Open** All year.

The Hotel Altamira now occupies one of the aristocratic houses of Santillana, a medieval town classified as a historic monument, that has conserved a beautiful collection of residences and palaces. Many still wear the shields and arms of the knights and hidalgos who lived in them. This palace of the Valdevesco, rebuilt at the start of the 19th century, is a simple hotel but in goodtaste. The decor is sober and rustic in the lounges and two restaurants, with one of them serving only regional specialties. Beside the staircases and on the half-landings, one finds small corners for reading, TV rooms and other amenities. The bedrooms offer good comfort but those on the upper floor are smaller and only have showers. To be noted: a delightful terrace and a nice place to enjoy a drink.

How to get there (Map 4): 31km southwest of Santander via N634, then C6316.

Hotel Los Infantes

39330 Santillana del Mar (Cantabria)
Avenida le Dorat, 1
Tel. (9)42-81 81 00 – Fax (9)42-84 01 03
Sr G. Mesones

Category ★★★ **Rooms** 30 with telephone, bath and WC. **Price** Single 4,500-10,500Pts, double 6,500-14,700Pts. **Meals** Breakfast 650Pts, served 8:00-11:00; half board 5,900-10,000Pts, full board 7,200-11,300Pts (per pers.) **Restaurant** Service 13:00-16:00, 20:00-23:00; menu 2,000Pts, also à la carte. Specialties: Cocido montañes - Quesada en lechefritas - Solomillo al queso. **Credit cards** All major. **Pets** Dogs allowed (except in restaurant). **Nearby** Colegiata de Santillana del Mar - Altamira Caves - Comillas - Picos de Europa - Beaches of Cobreces and Suances. **Open** All year.

The Hotel Los Infantes now occupies the ancient house of the Calderon and its facade still bears their shield and arms. Right from the entrance one notices the intimate atmosphere that reigns in the hotel, where everything has been designed so that the traveller should feel a little bit at home. On the ground floor one finds a welcoming reception area and dining room with an open fireplace. Upstairs there is a beautiful lounge. One finds the same spirit in the bedrooms, but our favorites are those on the main front facade, which are more spacious, and two of them also have small lounges. Good regional cuisine, a cordial welcome and a discotheque are found here, but the latter does not annoy those staying.

How to get there *(Map 4): 31km southwest of Santander via N634, then C6316.*

Hotel Don Pablo

39710 Solares (Cantabria)
General Mola, 6
Tel. (9)42-52 21 20 – Fax (9)42-52 20 00
Sr Oceja Mazas

Category ★★ **Rooms** 27 with air-conditioning, telephone, bath, WC and Satellite TV. **Price** Single 8,000Pts, double 10,000Pts. **Meals** Breakfast 500Pts, served 8:00-11:00; half board + 2,000Pts, full board + 3500Pts. **Restaurant** Service 13:00-16:00, 20:00-24:00; menu 1500Pts. Specialties: regional cooking. **Credit cards** All major. **Pets** Dogs not allowed in restaurant. **Facilities** Garage, parking. **Nearby** Santander - Palacio de Acevedo in Hoznayo - Palacio de L'Eseldo in Pàmanes - Casa de Cantolla and Palacio de Rañada in Liérganes - Puento Viergos Caves. **Open** All year.

In the back-country behind the Cantabrian coast, Solares is a thermal spa known for its mineral waters, but the village and hotel are only really interesting because they are some twenty kilometers away from all the bustle of Santander. The building is an aristocratic house from the 16th century, and has retained its superb coat of arms and beautiful chapel. All the rest has been converted in the traditional, even standard manner: a rustic atmosphere with stylish furniture, beams and terra cotta tiled flooring. Comfort is fully assured with one or two extra services such as an internal video channel and satellite TV. There's only a few rooms but no less than three restaurants, so one can understand that the hotel hosts a lot of receptions. An agreeable staging post rather than a place to stay long.

How to get there (Map 4): 16km east of Santander.

Es Castell

Mallorca
Binibona 07314 Caimari
Tel. (9)71-87 51 54 - Fax (9)71-87 51 54
Sra Mìa Amer

Rooms 7 with bath. **Price** Single 18,000Pts, double 24,000Pts. **Meals** Breakfast included; half board 21,500Pts (1 pers.), 31,000Pts (2 pers.). **Restaurant** By reservation, only for residents. **Credit cards** Visa, Eurocard, MasterCard. **Pets** Dogs not allowed. **Facilities** Swimming pool. **Nearby** Campanet caves - Ruins of Alarò castel - Palma: Cathedral, Majorque museum, Château de Bellve, Pollensa golf course. **Open** All year.

The finca Es Castell has been in the same family since the 11th century. It was recently renovated and its exterior has preserved its original appearance and you readily understand the owners' unwillingness to alter the magnificent stone work so much in harmony with the subtle nuances of its surroundings. The property's 750 hectares are covered with olive trees and pines. Rooms for guests are in the main house which has a large living room with a fireplace and sofas which create a truly friendly atmosphere. The dining room in Mediterranean style is more intimate and its fine food is made from products of the farm itself. The rooms are simple and decorated in Majorcan style with terra cotta floors, lime-treated walls and colorful fabrics. A charming hotel in a bucolic setting.

How to get there *(Map 10): 50km northeast of Palma via N713 to Inca, Caimari and Binibona.*

Scott's

Mallorca
07350 Binissalem
Plaza Iglesia, 12
Tel. (9)71-87 01 00 - Fax (9)71-87 02 67 - Dr George Scott

Rooms 14 with air-conditioning, telephone, bath, WC. **Price** Single 14,500Pts, double 23,000Pts. **Meals** Breakfast included. **No Restaurant** See p. 244. **Credit cards** All major. **Pets** Dogs not allowed. **Facilities** Swimming pool. **Nearby** Palma: Cathedral, Majorque museum, Château de Bellve, Pollensa golf course. **Open** All year.

Luxurious, elegant and refined is Scott's, a terribly British oasis in the center of Majorca. The owner is, naturally, English and carefully maintains the hotel's coziness. The rooms with their antique furniture and floral percales offer incomparable sleeping accommodation which can be modified to suit the guest's requirements. A number of lounges, a library and a terrace with pleasant vegetation allow you to get away from it all with a minimum of effort. Breakfasts are a treat with a large choice of fruit juice plus pastries, yogurt and eggs along with local cold cuts. For an additional 1,000 pesetas, you can enjoy a typical English breakfast under the patio's lemon tree. Children are admitted over the age of 12.

How to get there *(Map 10): 18km northeast of Palma, Consell/Binissalem exit.*

Son Espases

Mallorca – 07012 Ciutat
Camino Son Espaces, 7
Tel. (9)71-75 06 14 – Fax (9)71-75 06 14
Sr Felio de Cabrera

Rooms 3 with shared bath and 1 suite with private bath. **Price** Single 6,000Pts, double 12,000Pts, suite 14,000-16,000Pts. **Meals** Breakfast included. **No Restaurant** (See p.244). **Credit cards** Not accepted. **Pets** Dogs not allowed. **Facilities** Swimming pool. **Nearby** Palma: Cathedral, Majorque museum, Château de Bellver. **Open** All year.

This superb property very close to Palma has an absolutely magnificent 18th-century house. It is, however, the vast garden overflowing with tropical vegetation that catches your eye. The ground floor is a series of rooms surrounding the courtyard. Large paintings adorn the walls and the lounges have remarkable antique furniture. Rooms for the guests are upstairs, and of them, the suite is the most comfortable as the others share one bathroom. The suite is very large with a fine view of both the courtyard and the garden. You also have access to a swimming pool surrounded by pleasant greenery.

How to get there *(Map 10): take the exit going north out of Palma.*

La Residencia

Mallorca 07179 Deiá (Mallorca)
Finca Son Canals
Tel. (9)71-63 90 11 - Fax (9)71-63 93 70 - Sra Cariuu

Category ★★★★ Rooms 63 with air-conditioning, telephone, bath, WC. **Price** Double 35,000Pts, suite 56,600Pts. **Meals** Breakfast included, served 8:00-11:30. **Restaurant** «El olivo»: Service 12:30-15:00, 20:00-23:00; à la carte 4,400-7,150Pts. **Credit cards** All major. **Pets** Dogs not allowed. **Facilities** Swimming pool, tennis, private beach, parking. **Nearby** Palma - Northroad (Miramar, San Marroig, Lluc Alcari, Cala) - Monastery Real Cartuja de Valdemossa; Son Vida golf course (18-Hole). **Open** All year.

A real love affair is possible with La Residencia hotel. Fifteen kilometers from Majorca and far from the tourist traps, lies a hidden village full of charm. Residencia is 16th-century manor house converted into a hotel; today one of the most delightful in the whole of Spain. One discovers hectares of woodlands, terraces with flowers sprouting out of the old stonework, flowered balconies and a succession of patios around the hotel. With its swimming pool facing the mountains, La Residencia is a genuine oasis. The owner is a great collector of pictures which cover all the walls. The bedrooms are vast and well furnished, all with great refinement. La Residencia is without doubt one of our favorite hotels for reconciling you and the Balearics, all too often stripped of all charm by the affluence of tourists.

How to get there *(Map 10): 27km north of Palma, towards Valldemosa.*

Hotel Costa d'Or

Mallorca
Llucalri 07179 Deià (Mallorca)
Tel. (9)71-63 90 25 - Fax (9)71-63 93 47

Rooms 42 with air-conditioning, telephone, bath or shower, WC, TV and safe. **Price** Single 5,100Pts, double 9100-12800Pts (with terrace and view on the see). **Meals** Breakfast included, served 8:00-11:30; half board 5,450-7,300Pts (per pers.). **Restaurant** Service 12:30-15:00, 20:00-23:00; menu and also à la carte. **Credit cards** Visa, Eurocard, MasterCard. **Pets** Dogs not allowed. **Facilities** Swimming pool, tennis, minigolf, parking. **Nearby** Northroad (Miramar, San Marroig, Lluc Alcari, Cala) - Monastery Real Cartuja de Valdemossa - Son Vida golf course (18-Hole) - Palma - Bendinat golf course (9-Hole). **Open** May - Oct 27.

You leave Palma on a winding mountain road and pass through a majestic countryside with pine forests and cliffs that fall away to the sea. The Costa d'Or has a magnificent location overlooking a small bay. The older buildings have been renovated and the result is a comfortable and thoroughly modern hotel. A number of the rooms have terraces overlooking the sea which were those we preferred. The decoration is, unfortunately, reminiscent of the 70s. The hotel offers a swimming pool and tennis courts, a good panoramic restaurant plus a setting that makes it well worth a detour to enjoy it.

How to get there *(Map 10): 28km north of Palma, towards Valldemosa or Sòller.*

Sa Plana

Mallorca
07192 Estellencs (Mallorca)
Eusebi Pascual
Tel. (9)71–61 86 66 / 61 85 86

Rooms 4 doubles and 1 for 4 pers. with bath. **Price** Double 9,100Pts. **Meals** Breakfast included, served 8:00-11:30. **Evening meals** Service 12:30-15:00, 20:00-23:00; menu. **Credit Cards** Not accepted. **Pets** Dogs not allowed. **Facilities** Parking. **Nearby** Monastery Real Cartuja de Valldemossa - Palma - Son Vida golf course (18-Hole) - Bendinat golf course (9-Hole). **Open** All year.

Estellenes is one of the typical Majorcan mountain villages that is not far from the sea. This charming guest house is located on the edge of the village and its calm, family-like atmosphere is ideal for spending a relaxing vacation. You soon find a favorite spot, either in the living room or in the garden. The soberly-decorated rooms enjoy old furniture and are most comfortable. After a day of swimming, bicycle riding or fishing, the guests gather around a large table in the garden for dinner. Meals here offer produce direct from the vegetable garden, and you will thoroughly enjoy Sa Plana's simplicity, friendliness and fine natural surrounding, all allowing you to simply take it easy.

How to get there (Map 10): 20km north of Palma.

Sa Posada d'Aumallia

Mallorca
07200 Felanitx
Camino Son Prohens
Tel. (9)71-58 26 57 - Fax (9)71-72 12 21 - Familia Marti Gomilla

Rooms 14 with air-conditioning, bath, WC, TV, minibar. **Price** Single 17,120Pts, double 23,340Pts. **Meals** Breakfast included; half board + 3,210Pts (per pers.). **Restaurant** Service 12:30-15:00, 20:00-23:00. Specialties: Mallorquines with products from the property. **Credit cards** Amex, Visa, Eurocard, MasterCard. **Pets** Dogs not allowed. **Facilities** Swimming pool, tennis. **Nearby** Palma: Cathedral, Majorque museum, Château de Bellver. **Open** All year.

In a lovely country setting and far from seaside tourist madness, the Posada d'Aumilia offers lodging at once refined and romantic. Two wings have been added to this old farm house but the spirit of the original architecture has been scrupulously respected. The dining room, the bar and the living room, all on the ground floor, are vast and you find furniture from the 30s peacefully coexisting with imposing pieces in solid wood, clearly in Spanish style. The rooms are in much the same spirit with beds of dark wood with twisted columns, chests of drawers and chairs in 19th-century style. Some of them are at garden level, but the rooms on the third floor are bigger, more imaginative and enjoy a terrace looking out on the olive trees. The others, in the wings of the building, are rather more ordinary, but there's always the swimming pool and tennis courts.

How to get there *(Map 10): 60km east of Palma. In the center of Felanitz, go towards Prohens.*

Es Rafal Podent

Mallorca
07500 Manacor
Carretera Calas de Mallorca, km 6
Tel. (9)71-18 31 30 - Fax (9)71-18 31 30 - Sr Juan Parera

Rooms 5 (2-5 pers.) with kitchenette, lounge, telephone, bath or shower, WC, TV.
Price 8,900-14,500Pts, 13,000-16,500Pts (per pers., by day). **Meals** Breakfast
900Pts. **Restaurant** Service 12:30-15:00, 20:00-23:00.; menu and also à la carte.
Credit cards Not accepted. **Pets** Dogs not allowed. **Facilities** Swimming pool. **Nearby**
Palma: Cathedral, Majorque museum, Château de Bellver. **Open** All year.

This 15th-century farm house lies peacefully in the shade of some
olive trees with its smaller buildings built around a large square
tower. Each of them has an independent entrance as well as a
different decor although all have impressive interior stone walls,
ceilings with exposed beams, antique furniture and a private terrace.
The most attractive of them is on the third floor overlooking the
olive grove. The garden is very pleasant with trees and a superb
swimming pool. If you choose, you can make arrangements to have
meals prepared or take advantage of the fine produce grown on the
farm and do your own cooking. This is an excellent place for a
family vacation.

How to get there *(Map 10): 60km east of Palma to Manacor, then towards Calas*
de Mallorca for 7km.

Palacio Ca Sa Galesa

Mallorca – 07021 Palma de Mallorca
Carrer de Miramar, 8
Tel. (9)71-71 54 00 – Fax (9)71-72 15 79 – Sr Crespi
E-mail: reserves@fehm.es

Category ★★★★★ **Rooms and suites** 12 with air-conditioning, telephone, bath, WC, satellite TV, safe, minibar; elevator. **Price** Double 27,500Pts, suite 31,000-36,000Pts. **Meals** Breakfast 2,200Pts served 8:30-11:00. **No Restaurant** (see p.244). **Credit cards** Amex, Visa, Eurocard, MasterCard. **Pets** Dogs not allowed. **Facilities** Swimming pool, sauna, parking (1,500Pts). **Nearby** Palma: Cathedral, Majorque museum, Château de Bellver. **Open** All year.

Here, the cathedral is a close neighbor and that is one of the reasons we found this intimate and refined palace irresistible, plainly one of the best hotels in Palma. Once through the entrance way, you discover a stone staircase leading to different salons that take up the entire second floor. These are beautifully decorated with inspiration from a number of sources and they include impressive Spanish furniture, a mahogany dining room set that is very English in style as well as the owner's highly personal touch, an exact replica of the dining room in Monet's house in Giverny. This is a splendid setting for tea and a slice of nut cake some quiet afternoon. Relaxation is the order of the day as well on the small patio with a refreshing fountain. The rooms, each bearing the name of a composer, have received particular attention from the owner and are elegant and comfortable. The service and facilities are absolutely perfect as you have a roof garden with an excellent view of the cathedral and the Old Town, while in the basement there is a Roman-style swimming pool plus a fitness center with a sauna. This is quite simply a marvelous place to stay.

How to get there *(Map 10): near the cathedral.*

Hotel San Lorenzo

Mallorca – 07012 Palma de Mallorca
C./ San Lorenzo, 14
Tel. (9)71–72 82 00 – Fax (9)71–71 19 01 – Sr Schmid
E-mail: sanlorenzo@fehm.es – Web: http://www.fehm.es/pmi/sanlorenzo

Category ★★★★ **Rooms** 6 with air-conditioning, telephone, bath, WC, satellite TV, minibar. **Price** Single 14,000-29,000Pts, double 16,000-31,000Pts. **Meals** Breakfast 1,000-1,400Pts, served 8:30-11:00. **No restaurant** See p.244.**Credit cards** All major. **Pets** Dogs allowed on request. **Facilities** Swimming pool. **Nearby** In Palma: Cathedral, Majorque museum, château de Bellver. **Open** All year.

We immediately fell in love with the San Lorenzo, much as we did with the preceding hotel and the one that follows. The three of them truly are the most charming in Palma. You push open the ornate iron gate on this street in the Old Town and discover a paradise of good taste and refinement. On the ground floor is the bar, not unlike a Paris bistro with a zinc counter, bar stools and naval maps, a perfect place for breakfast. One floor up is a terrace with a swimming pool whose design is inspired by the lay-out of the Palma of historical times. Beyond it are the rooms, comfortable, elegant, spacious and bright with attractive regional ceramics in the bath rooms. Two of the rooms have large terraces overlooking the roofs of the city. Whatever your budget, you are sure to be well housed in Palma.

How to get there *(Map 10): in the old town.*

1998

Hotel Born

Mallorca
07012 Palma de Mallorca
C/. Sant Jaume, 3
Tel. (9)71-71 29 42 – Fax (9)71-71 29 42 / 71-71 86 18
E-mail: hborn@bitel.es

Category ★★ **Rooms** 26 and 3 suites with telephone, bath, WC and TV. **Price** Single 6,550-8,000Pts, double 9,000-13,000Pts, suite 15,500Pts. **Meals** Breakfast included. **No restaurant** (See p. 244). **Credit cards** Visa, Eurocard, MasterCard. **Pets** Dogs not allowed. **Nearby** In Palma: Cathedral, Majorque museum, château de Bellver. **Open** All year.

The Hotel Born, located in the historical center of the city, is, for its category, one of our favorite hotels in Palma. Formerly a 16th-century residence having belonged to the Marquis Ferandell, it has conserved its grandiose architecture. Its spectacular entrance way opens onto a patio with three tall palm trees and impressive marble columns holding up large stone arches. A wide staircase leads to a lounge which serves the five most attractive rooms, some of which still have original frescoes on their ceilings. The decor is subtle with antique furniture and soft colors. It is advisable to take a room giving on the patio as those on the street are not all that far from the houses facing them. You should not miss the pleasure of having your breakfast on the marvelously cool patio. A delightful hotel in the very heart of the city.

How to get there *(Map 10): in the center of town near the Plazza Rei Joan Carlesi.*

Arabella Golf Hotel

Mallorca
Son Vida 07013 Palma de Mallorca
Carrer de la Vinagrella
Tel. (9)71-79 99 99 - Fax (9)71-79 99 97

Category ★★★★★ **Rooms** 59 and 24 suites with air-conditioning, telephone, bath, WC, satellite TV, safe, minibar; elevator. **Price** 17,450-60,500Pts. **Meals** Breakfast inclued, served 8:00-11:00. **Restaurant** Le plat d'Or (dinner), à la carte 3,500-5,000Pts. **Credit cards** All major. **Pets** Dogs not allowed. **Facilities** Covered swimming pool, tennis, Arabelle beauty & Holistic, Sauna, 18-Hole golf, parking and garage. **Nearby** Palma: Cathedral, Majorque museum, Château de Bellver. **Open** All year.

The Arabella, six kilometers from Palma, overlooks the city. It is one of many hotels built near the Son Vida golf course. Surrounded by luxurious tropical vegetation, the new buildings maintain a distinctly Spanish style. The immense reception area has a marble floor, leather sofas and a multi-lingual staff as befits an international luxury hotel. The rooms are of different sizes, all providing the same sense of comfort. The hotel's proximity to the golf course explains the presence here of numerous golfers but there are other facilities that allow you to combine sports with the usual tourist pleasures.

How to get there *(Map 10): near the cathedral.*

Son Brondo

Mallorca
07012 Palma a Valdemosa
C/. Sant Jaume, 3
Tel. (9)71-61 61 90 - Fax (9)71-61 61 90 - Sra Possello

Rooms 3 with telephone, bath, WC, TV, minibar. **Price** Suite 22,500Pts. **Meals** Breakfast included; half board + 3,000Pts. **Evening meals** Specialties mallorquines. **Credit cards** Visa, Eurocard, MasterCard. **Pets** Dogs not allowed. **Facilities** Swimming pool, sauna, solarium. **Nearby** Palma: Cathedral, Majorque museum, Château de Bellver. **Open** All year.

Nicely located between the sea and the mountain, this is among the most beautiful settings on the entire island with the green of the pine trees harmonizing perfectly with the yellow of the hills. The road leads upward through the countryside and you soon find yourself at this noble and rustic house. The courtyard is surrounded by large earthenware jars, each overflowing with flowers. A staircase goes off it leading to vast lounge. The rooms for guests are on the fourth floor, well-furnished with regional furniture and Majorcan fabrics, offering all the comfort of a hotel. The garden is only a few meters away with its swimming pool and solarium; even the sea is not far. A few kilometers from the famous charter house, Son Brando enjoys surroundings that are ideal for casual country strolls.

How to get there *(Map 10): 14km from Palma.*

Finca Ses Rotetes

Mallorca - 07509 Porto Cristo
Carretera Porto Colom, km 13,900
Tel. (9)71-18 32 56 - Fax (9)71-18 32 56
Sr José-F. Moragues Villalonga

Rooms 2, 1 apartment (2 pers.), 1 house with 3 rooms (6 pers.), bath, WC, TV. **Price**
14,000-37,500Pts (per day). **Meals** Breakfast 900Pts. **No restaurant** (see p.244)
Credit cards Not allowed. **Pets** Dogs not allowed. **Facilities** Swimming pool. **Nearby**
Palma: Cathedral, Majorque museum, Château de Bellver. **Open** All year.

Ses Rotetes is a typical Majorcan finca built of pink limestone with
green shutters on its two levels and surrounded by olive groves.
The rooms on the third floor are rather small, but there are two
apartments, decorated with regional fabrics which are more pleasant
and private. The garden is set up for serving breakfast and meals
throughout the day. There is a swimming pool and solarium at a
lower level. A fine hotel offering at once the peace and quiet of its
inland location while being close to beaches.

How to get there *(Map 10): 60km east of Palma towards Manacor, then Porto
Cristo.*

Ca'n Coll

Mallorca - 07100 Sòller
Cami de Ca'n Coll, 1
Tel. (9)71-63 32 44 - Fax (9)71-63 19 05
Sra Emma Rodrìguez

Rooms 5 and 3 suites with air-conditioning, bath, WC, satellite TV (in suite). **Price** Single 17,120Pts, double 24,240Pts, suite 37,450Pts. **Meals** Breakfast included; half board + 3,745Pts. **Evening meals** For dinner; menu 3,500Pts. Specialties: Mallorquines. **Credit cards** Visa, Eurocard, MasterCard. **Pets** Dogs not allowed. **Facilities** Swimming pool, bicycle rentals, parking. **Nearby** Beaches in Puerto de Sòller - Palma: Cathedral, Majorque museum, Château de Bellver. **Open** All year.

Ca'n Coll is one of the best hotels on this island with a splendid location, impeccable service plus the ever-so-friendly welcome you receive here. A large red leather sofa stands in the center of a vast lounge giving onto the garden and has attractive modern furniture as well as fine paintings. The same things are found in the well-kept rooms, while the suites are absolutely sumptuous, one of which, the exception to the rule, is furnished with authentic antiques and has a terrace overlooking the valley. Summertime is a time to stretch out beside the pool, stroll among the orange and lemon trees and dine under the garden's palm trees. A real find if you choose "rural tourism."

How to get there *(Map 10): 30km north of Palma*

1998

Finca Ca N'ai

Mallorca
07100 Sòller
Camì Son Puça, 48
Tel. (9)71-63 24 94 – Fax (9)71-63 18 99
Sr Domingo Morell–Marti

Rooms 8 with air-conditioning, telephone, bath or shower, minibar. **Price** Double 15,400-28,500Pts. **Meals** Breakfast included; half board + 3,500Pts (per pers.). **Restaurant** Closed Monday; menu 3,500Pts, also à la carte. **Credit cards** All major. **Pets** Dogs not allowed. **Facilities** Swimming pool, parking. **Nearby** Beaches in Puerto de Sòller - Palma: Cathedral, Majorque museum, Château de Bellver. **Open** Feb - Nov 15.

The reputation of Ca N'Ai has long been established among Majorcans who have recognized it as a truly gastronomic restaurant. Visitors cannot help but fall in love with this authentic finca surrounded by colorful and fragrant orange trees. The house is truly exquisite with delightful and refined rooms, especially the one with a mezzanine and terrace overlooking the countryside. The garden has been skillfully designed to let you take full advantage of the magnificent panorama whether beside the fountain, under the palm trees or from poolside. The restaurant here uses only the finest produce grown on the property. Fourteen generations have followed one another here as evidenced by the documents and family portraits that cover the walls of the house. An excellent hotel.

How to get there *(Map 10): 30km north of Palma.*

Ca S'Hereu

Mallorca
07550 Son Servera
Rue Elisa Servera
Tel. (9)71-59 15 41 – Fax (9)71-59 14 16 – Sr Ventura Rubì

House with 6 rooms, telephone, bath, WC, TV. **Price** 20,000-36,000Pts (per pers./day). **No restaurant** (see p. 244.) **Credit cards** Not accepted. **Pets** Dogs allowed. **Nearby** Palma: Cathedral, Majorque museum, Château de Bellver, Son Servera (9-Hole). **Open** All year.

This vast residence in stone with a turret was one of the twelve houses that belonged to the island's nobility in the 16th century. It now belongs to one of the oldest families on Majorca. It is in the northeastern part of the island on open country and very close to the sea. On the ground floor is a large stone kitchen, a long dining room covered by a brick arch plus a vast lounge with attractive wrought-iron furnishings. Upstairs are rooms decorated in regional style with engravings depicting the conquest of the island along with religious paintings. There is a pleasant garden and you can swim only a few kilometers away.

How to get there *(Map 10): 70km east of Palma towards Manacor, then Porto Cristo and Son Cervera.*

La Ventana

07800 Ibiza
Dalt Vila – Sa Carossa, 13
Tel. (9)71–39 08 57 – Fax (9)71–39 01 45
Sr Monseby

Rooms 13 and 2 suites with air-conditioning, telephone, shower, satellite TV, minibar.
Price Double 13,000-22,000Pts, suite 25,000-44,000Pts. **Meals** Breakfast included.
Restaurant By reservation (tel.: (9)71-30 35 37). **Credit cards** Visa, Eurocard,
MasterCard. **Pets** Dogs not allowed. **Nearby** Dalt Vila and the Cathedral of Ibiza -
Jesus-church - Beach of Talamanca - Roca Lisa golf course (9-Hole). **Open** All year.

This small hotel is a real treasure. It is located at the edge of the
city's fortifications and in one of the houses surrounding the
cathedral. Coming here is much like visiting a private home as you
find family furniture and personal items in the reception area and the
bar. Although slightly monastic, the rooms are truly adorable in their
simplicity with blue walls, white bed linen and muslin mosquito
netting: some look out on the trees of the square (noisy in summer
but, don't forget, the nightly *fiesta* is a tradition in Ibiza), the others
face the courtyard. The only one with air-conditioning are the
suites. They have beautifully arranged terraces with a view of the old
city.

How to get there *(Map 9): in the Old Town - "Dalt Vila."*

La Torre del Canónigo

07800 Ibiza - Calle Mayor, 8
Tel. (9)71-30 38 84
Sr Viader

Apartments 4 and 5 studios with telephone, bath or shower, satellite TV. **Price** Studio 35,000-85,000Pts (2 pers./week), apartment 50,000-175,000Pts (4 pers./week). **No restaurant** (see p. 244). **Credit cards** Allowed. **Pets** Dogs not allowed. **Nearby** Dalt Vila and the Cathedral of Ibiza - Jesus-church - Beach of Talamanca - Roca Lisa golf course (9-Hole). **Open** All year.

The Torre del Canònigo was built in the 16th century in pure Catalan Gothic style as a lookout to stand watch over the port, the chateau and the entire city. Splendidly renovated, its 980 square meters offer apartments on two floors. They are of different sizes and can, if required, be combined. They are all very pleasant and well organized, using attractive traditional materials with nicely embroidered benches and headboards. On the ground floor are the large lounges and the bar where you can have your breakfast. The atmosphere is much like that of a summer house. In addition, Apartment 6 has a small private swimming pool. The service is attentive and efficient. This is an ideal hotel for an extended stay provided you avoid the months of July and August - unless, of course, you are a dyed-in-the-wool Ibiza fancier.

How to get there *(Map 9): in the Old Town.*

El Corsario

07800 Ibiza
Poniente 5 Dalt Vila
Tel. (9)71-30 12 48 – Fax (9)71-39 19 53
E-mail: elcorsario@ctv

Rooms 14 with air-conditioning, telephone and shower. **Price** Single 10,000-18,000Pts, double 12,000-20,000Pts, suite 25,000-30,000Pts. **Meals** Breakfast included. **Restaurant** By reservation. **Credit cards** Visa, Eurocard, MasterCard. **Pets** Dogs not allowed. **Nearby** Dalt Vila and the cathedral of Ibiza - Beach of Talamanca; Roca Llisa golf course (9-Hole) **Open** All year.

An agreeable small hotel hidden in the old town, El Corsario is one of the oldest hotels on Ibiza, and the simplicity of this old house is one of its major charms. The hotel is very well kept and the service friendly; breakfast may be taken on the terrace. This abounds with pots of flowers, and from it you have one of the best views of Ibiza. One can dine at the hotel but a reservation is needed; prices are very modest compared to others on this island.

How to get there *(Map 9): by boat from Barcelona and Valencia: contact the Cia. Transmediterránea company (Tel. (9)71-72 67 40); in the old town (Dalt Vila).*

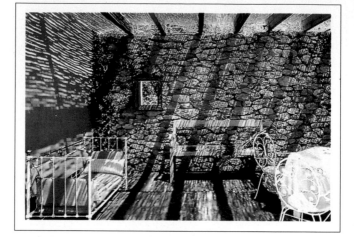

Les Terrasses

07800 Ibiza
Carret. de Santa Eulalia, km 1
Tel. (9)71-33 26 43 – Fax (9)71-33 11 61
Sra Pialoux

Rooms 9 with heating or air-conditioning, telephone, bath and WC. **Price** Single 13,000-15,000Pts, double 16,500-19,500Pts, suite 22,000-26,000Pts. **Meals** Breakfast included. **Restaurant** Open Tue and Fri evening, (everyday for residents) Menu 2,500-3,500Pts, also à la carte. Specialty: Fish. **Credit cards** Visa, Eurocard, MasterCard. **Pets** Dogs allowed. **Facilities** 2 Swimming pools, tennis, parking. **Nearby** Dalt Vila and the cathedral of Ibiza - Beach of Talamanca; Roca Llisa golf course (9-Hole). **Open** All year.

Les Terrasses has nothing to with a hotel–one comes here as a friend! A confidential location, only a large indigo blue stone at 1km on the road from Santa Eulalia indicates the entrance. Françoise, your host, is French and has converted this old house of the Ibizan countryside with a lot of talent. The washed ocres and indigos, the white chalked walls set off with blue door and window frames–all give the house a truly authentic character. There is the same charm indoors where the antique furniture, carefully selected at the local 'flea markets', is mingled with the family pieces. The bedrooms have this same simplicity and good taste. The cuisine is good: light and fresh at lunch-time, but more prepared dishes at dinner. One can be deliciously idle by the swimming pool or on the beautiful shaded terrace, where a delightful time may be had despite its location on a touristy island. This is a very agreeable place to stay.

How to get there *(Map 9): on the road towards Santa Eulalia, a blue stone on the right indicates the way.*

Hotel Pikes

07800 Ibiza
San Antonio de Portmany
Tel. (9)71-34 22 22 – Fax (9)71-34 23 12
Sr A. Pikes

Category ★★★★★ **Rooms** 24 with air-conditioning, telephone, bath, WC, TV and minibar. **Price** Single 15,300-20,000Pts, double 18,000-25,000Pts, suite 30,000-55,000Pts, duplex 60,000-90,000Pts. **Meals** Breakfast included, served 8.30-12.00. **Restaurant** Service 13:00-15:30, 20:30-24:00; carte. Specialties: international and regional cooking. **Credit cards** All major. **Pets** Dogs allowed. **Facilities** Swimming pool. **Nearby** Dalt Vila and the cathedral of Ibiza - Beach of Talamanca; Roca Llisa golf course (9-Hole). **Open** Mar 1 - Jan 31.

To uncover a hotel hidden away between gardens and pine woods on Ibiza is something of a miracle! This is, however, the case with the Hotel Pikes, a residence that is 600 years old. With only twenty rooms all differently decorated, but each in the typical style of the island, the Hotel Pikes offers all the advantages of a hotel 'de luxe' along with the informal ambiance of a friend's home. Not very far from the nightlife, you can rest and recover here during the afternoon beside the swimming pool after a heavy night out! With a bit of luck, you may also spot Julio (Iglesias) or possibly Grace (Jones). All things said, this is a tiny paradise.

How to get there *(Map 9): by boat from Barcelona and Valencia: contact the Cia. Transmediterránea company (Tel. (9)71-72 67 40).*

Hotel Hacienda-Na Xamena

07080 Ibiza
Apartado 423 – San Miguel
Tél. (9)71-33 45 00 – Fax (9)71-33 45 14

Category ★★★★★ **Rooms** 53 and 10 suites with air-conditioning, telephone, bath, WC, satellite TV, minibar, safe; elevator. **Price** Single 19,700-29,700Pts, double 25,000-39,600Pts, Junior suite 33,000-42,300Pts. **Meals** Breakfast 2,300Pts, served 8:00-13:00; half board +8,600Pts and full board +15,100Pts. **Restaurant** Service 13:30-16:00, 20:30/21:00-23:00, also à la carte. **Credit cards** Allowed. **Pets** Dogs allowed in room only. **Facilities** 3 swimming pool (1 with air-conditioning), hammam, sauna, tennis, montain bikes, hairdresser, parking. **Nearby** Dalt Vila and the Cathedral of Ibiza - Jesus-church - Beach of Talamanca - Roca Lisa golf course (9-Hole). **Open** May 1 - Oct 30.

The Hacienda is one of Ibiza's top hotels. It is splendidly located and its architect drew all his inspiration from the surrounding countryside. Its buildings look down 180 meters on a delightful inlet with gleaming rocks. The truly courageous go there to swim. The lounges look out on a large patio, and its luxurious vegetation assures a pleasant temperature even on the hottest days. The rooms are lovely and truly comfortable, and there are bathtubs offering hydro-massage in most of them. All enjoy the impressive and exceptional view for which the hotel is famous. The swimming pools are superb, one of which is even air-conditioned, and you can tour the countryside on foot or bicycle, or simply enjoy the peace and quiet, an often rare commodity in Ibiza. There are several fine restaurants. Renting a car will allow you to take even greater advantage of this attractive island.

How to get there *(Map 9): from the airport, go towards Ibiza. At the first traffic circle, take the road to Sta Eulalia-San Juan for 7km, then towards San Miguel in the direction of the port for 4km. The hotel is marked with an arrow on the left side of the road.*

Ca's Pla

07800 Ibiza
San Miguel de Balanzat - P.O.Box N° 777
Tel. (9)71-33 45 87 - Fax (9)71-33 46 04
Sr N. Sanchez de Fenaroli

Rooms 14 with telephone, bath, WC and satellite TV. **Price** Double 16,000-22,000Pts, suite 18,000-32,000Pts. **Meals** Breakfast 900-1200Pts. **Restaurant** Reservation for dinner; lunch at the swimming pool. Specialties: Fish, barbecue, paella. **Credit cards** Visa, Eurocard, MasterCard. **Pets** Dogs not allowed. **Facilities** Swimming pool, tennis (800Pts), parking. **Nearby** Dalt Vila and the cathedral of Ibiza - Beach of Talamanca; Roca Llisa golf course (9-Hole). **Open** Apr 1 - Nov 30.

In the northwest of the island and some twenty kilometers from Ibiza and close to the port of San Miguel, the owners of this large villa have opened 14 rooms for their guests. You are here in a holiday home, received as friends, which means that you will be living in a very personalized and very warm atmosphere: lots of objects, souvenirs, books, bouquets of dried flowers and so on. All the public rooms open wide onto the garden alive with plants and flowers, while the shady terrace offers many small and restful corners, and hammocks and armchairs allow one to be comfortably idle. The rooms have all been decorated with a care for decor, comfort and your well-being. You are asked not to just drop by on the off-chance, but to book well in advance so that "the bees can get to work" to better receive you.

How to get there *(Map 9): To the northwest of Ibiza, at 3km of San Miguel take the road for the port. At 14km take the roadon your right.*

Parador Raimundo de Borgoña

05001 Avila
Marqués de Canales de Chozas, 16
Tel. (9)20-21 13 40 – Fax (9)20-22 61 66
Sr della Torre Alcala

Category ★★★ Rooms 62 with air-conditioning, telephone, bath, WC, satellite TV and minibar. **Price** Double 13,500-17,500Pts. **Meals** Breakfast 1,300Pts, served 8:00-11:00. **Restaurant** Service 13:00-16:00, 20:30-23:00; menu 3,700Pts, also à la carte. Specialties: Judias del barco - Cochinillo asado. **Credit cards** All major. **Pets** Dogs not allowed. **Facilities** Parking. **Nearby** In Avila: Cathedral, Murallas (walls), Basilica de San Vicente, Monastery of Santo Tòmas - Cebreros. **Open** All year.

This Parador bears the name of the man who reconquered, repeopled and reconstructed Avila, also giving it the fantastic walls, which like an immense crown encircle the ancient 'Town of the Knights'. The hotel was built on the ruins of the Benavides palace and still conserves some of the original structure: one of its facades, backing onto the walls, forms one side of the square, which you enter via one of the nine town gates, La Puerta del Carmen. This ideal location is the main 'plus' of the hotel, apart from which the decor is all rather standardized. This said however, there are no complaints about the rooms and all are comfortable and well-equiped. One should certainly try for a room overlooking the square. Construction work is planned at the parador, so be sure to check about this.

How to get there (Map 12): 97km southeast of Salamanca via N501: or 111km northwest of Madrid via A6, exit Villacastín, then N110.

Hostería de Bracamonte

05001 Avila
C./ Bracamonte, 6
Tel. (9)20-25 12 80 / 21 28 66 - Sr Costa

Category ★★★ **Rooms** 18 and 6 suites with telephone, bath, WC and TV. **Price** Single 6,000Pts, double 8,000-10,000Pts, suite 15,000-17,000Pts. **Meals** Breakfast 500Pts, served 8:00-10:30; full board + 4,590Pts (per pers.). **Restaurant** Service 12:30-16:00, 20:00-24:00; menu 2,500-3,500Pts, also à la carte. Specialties: regional cooking. **Credit cards** Eurocard, MasterCard, Visa. **Pets** Small dogs allowed (except in the restaurant). **Nearby** In Avila: Cathedral, Murallas (walls), Basilica de San Vicente, Monastery of Santo Tòmas - Cebreros. **Open** All year.

In the heart of Avila and two paces from the Plaza de la Victoria, a pretty little hotel has opened in which particular care has been given to the decor. The entry hall attracts with its plain stonework, discreet lighting, the magnificent tapestries on the walls and the bright tiles of the floor. Around are spread the different restaurant rooms, which one enters under some pretty vaulting. The bar is decorated with photos of personalities of Spanish life who have honored it with their presence, and it is a very lively spot. A stone staircase leads to the rooms furnished in an elegant Castillian style; one suite deserves special mention for its slightly mansarded ceiling, which is very delightful. In a town not famous for night-life, you will find a very attractive ambiance both in the restaurant and bar, before dropping peacefully off to sleep sheltered by such beautiful walls.

How to get there *(Map 12): 97km southeast of Salamanca via N501: or 111km northwest of Madrid via A6, exit Villacastín, then N110.*

Parador de Gredos

05132 Novarredonda (Avila)
Carretera Barraco, km 43 – Bejar
Tel. (9)20-34 80 48 – Fax (9)20-34 82 05
Sr Miguel Angel Chica

Category ★★★ **Rooms** 77 with telephone, bath, WC, satellite TV and minibar. **Price** Double 13,500-15,000Pts. **Meals** Breakfast 1,300Pts (buffet), served 8:00-10:30. **Restaurant** Service 13:30-15:30, 20:30-23:00; menu 3,200Pts, also à la carte. Specialties: Castilian and international cooking. **Credit cards** All major. **Pets** Dogs not allowed. **Facilities** Tennis, riding, parking (1,500Pts). **Nearby** Sierra de Gredos - Puerto del Pico (1,352 m/4,435 ft) - Cuevas del Valle - Monbeltràn - Avila. **Open** All year.

Not far from Madrid rises the large hill called the 'Sierra de Gredos', and in 1926 King Alfonso XIII ordered that the first parador in Spain should be built on it. Hereabouts the winter is particularly severe, which is why the architecture relies on massive stonework, so attractive and giving a real impression of grandeur, notably to the columns and terraces. Inside, and as if to counter the cold, the lase of wood has been generous: it is everywhere and very attractive as well. The rooms are vast as in every parador, and furnished in the Castillian style. From the hotel one can enjoy all the pleasures of both hunting and fishing, while Avila is only 60 kilometers away and absolutely deserves a visit, as it is one of the most mythical and most attractive towns of Spain.

How to get there *(Map 12): 116km west of Madrid via A6, on the road linking Avila to Talavera de la Reina.*

Landa Palace

09000 Burgos
km 236 Carret. Madrid Irun
Tel. (9)47-20 63 43 - Fax (9)47-26 46 76 - Sr Revuelta

Category ★★★★★ **Rooms** 37 and 5 suites with air-conditioning, telephone, bath, WC, satellite TV, safe and minibar. **Price** Single 18,400Pts, double 21,000-30,000Pts, suite 28,000-35,000Pts. **Meals** Breakfast 1,600Pts, served 8:00-11:00. **Restaurant** Service 13:00-16:00, 21:00-23:30; menu 5,800Pts, also à la carte. **Credit cards** Visa, Eurocard, MasterCard. **Pets** Dogs not allowed. **Facilities** Swimming pool, garage (1,200Pts). **Nearby** In Burgos: Cathedral - Monasterio de las Huelgas Reales (Royal Convent) - Cartuja de Miraflores (Gothic charterhouse) - Monasterio de San Salvador at Oña - Church Santa Maria la Real de Sasomòn. **Open** All year.

The owner of a restaurant in Madrid, Mr Landa bought an ancient 14th-century military tower some thirty years ago. He had it taken down and rebuilt stone by stone some twenty kilometers from its original site. Two wings were added and the hotel opened its doors in 1964. The Landa Palace is very beautiful, very luxurious, very refined, and shelters some charming collections as well: a collection of carriages in the courtyard, of watch movements on the ground floor, of pressing irons, tools, and weighing scales–among others. The service and fittings of the rooms are perfect, but if you really prefer the truly 'grande luxe', go for the royal suite. For more silence, opt for those rooms overlooking the countryside and swimming pool. The pool is 'Hollywoodian' and covered with a gothic vaulting roof.

How to get there *(Map 4): 3km south of Burgos via N1.*

Mesón del Cid

09003 Burgos
Plaza Santa Maria, 8
Tel. (9)47-20 59 71 - Fax (9)47-26 94 60
Sr Lopez Alzaga

Rooms 28 with bath or shower, WC and TV. **Price** Single 8,000Pts, double 14,500Pts, suite 19,500Pts. **Meals** Breakfast 900Pts, served 7:00-11:30. **Restaurant** Service 13:00-16:00, 20:00-24:00; menus 3,000-4,500Pts. Specialties: Alubias rojas - Cordero Lechal asado - Postre del abuelo. **Credit cards** All major. **Pets** Dogs allowed. **Facilities** Garage (1,000Pts). **Nearby** In Burgos: Cathedral - Monasterio de las Huelgas Reales (Royal Convent) - Cartuja de Miraflores (Gothic charterhouse) - Monasterio de San Salvador at Oña - Church Santa Maria la Real de Sasomòn. **Open** All year.

This imposing building is just in front of the superb cathedral of Burgos, on a small tiled square decorated with a pretty stone fountain, and has been the property of the same family for several generations. They first opened a well-known restaurant in a 15th-century house, the former printing shop of a disciple of Gutenberg. Decorated in the style of the period, a typically Castillian cuisine is served. In the newer hotel they have kept the most representative elements (woodwork and tiled floors) of its past. In fact, the rooms are more functional than elegant, and lack originality. Some of them overlook the cathedral while others look over the town roofs. The location is ideal for discovering the charms of Burgos, best known among other things for speaking the purest form of Castillian.

How to get there *(Map 4): facing the cathedral.*

Hotel Arlanza

09346 Covarrubias (Burgos)
Plaza Mayor, 11
Tel. (9)47-40 64 41 - Fax (9)47-40 63 59 - Sr and Sra Briones
E-mail: arlanza@ctv.es - Web: http://www.ctv.es/users/arlanza

Category ★★★ **Rooms** 38 and 2 suites with telephone, bath or shower, and WC; elevator. **Price** Single 5,200-5,500Pts, double 9,000-9,300Pts. **Meals** Breakfast 650Pts, served 8:00-10.30. **Restaurant** Service 13:00-15:45, 20:30-22:45; closed Sun night, menus 2,700Pts; also à la carte. Specialties: Sopa serrana - Cordero. **Credit cards** All major. **Pets** Dogs not allowed in the restaurant. **Nearby** Collegiata de Covarrubias - Church Santa Maria in Quintanillas de la Viñas - Monastery Santo Domingo de Silos - Lerma - Burgos. **Open** Mar 1 - Dec 1

Simple and without pretentions, this hotel deserves its selection thanks to its superb siting: it dominates the square of Covarrubias, a charming Castillian village. The hotel is installed in a former noble's home and has been restored in a rustic style, and the interior refurbished with a desire for sobriety. The rooms would merit a rather brighter decor, and this is why we prefer those looking out from the facade as they are larger, and enjoy the view of the square. No sophisticated cuisine is served but good house dishes based on the produce of the area.

How to get there *(Map 4): 39km south of Burgos via N234, to Cuevas de San Clemente, then small road to Covarrubias.*

Hotel Tres Coronas de Silos

09610 Santo Domingo de Silos (Burgos)
Plaza Mayor, 6
Tel. (9)47–39 00 47 – Fax (9)47–39 00 65
Sr Martín

Category ★★★ Rooms 16 with telephone, bath, WC, TV. **Price** Single 6,500-6,700Pts, double 9,700-10,200Pts. **Meals** Breakfast 950Pts, served 8:30-11:00; half board 9,200Pts (per pers.). **Restaurant** Service 13:30-15:30, 20:30-23:30; carte 3,500-4,000Pts. Specialties: Morcillos - Jamón - Picadillo - Menestra de verduras naturales. **Credit cards** Amex, Visa, Eurocard, MasterCard. **Pets** Dogs allowed. **Nearby** Monastery Santo Domingo de Silos - Collegiata de Covarrubias - Salas de los Infantes - Caves of the Yecla. **Open** All year.

Santo Domingo de Silos is a very beautiful and very authentic Castillian village renowned for its convent dating from the year 1000 (note the very fine cloisters where one can hear the Gregorian chant every day). Opposite the main square and the church, a large 18th-century house restored by the local craftsmen has become this intimate family hotel. A charming dining room with a large wood-burning stove allows one to sample the house's regional cuisine. At the top of an attractive wooden staircase, the delightful and snug rooms match the Castillian style of the whole residence. The welcome is friendly and relaxed. If you cannot find the hotel ask for the Casa Grande (Big house), as it is known by the village people.

How to get there *(Map 4): 58km south of Burgos via N234 to Hacinas, then take the small road to Santo Domingo.*

Hospederia del Monasterio de Valvanera

26322 Anguiano (La Rioja)
Tel. (9)41-37 70 44 - Fax (9)41-37 70 44
Fraï Martín

Category ★★ **Rooms** 28 with shower, WC. **Price** Single 3,850Pts, double 5,550Pts. **Meals** Breakfast 600Pts, served 9:00-10:30; half board + 2,000Pts, full board + 3,000Pts (per pers.). **Restaurant** Service 13:30-15:00, 20:30-21:30; menu 1,500Pts. Specialties: regional cooking. **Credit cards** Not accepted. **Pets** Dogs not allowed. **Facilities** Parking. **Nearby** San Millàn de la Cogolla - Santo Domingo de la Calzada. **Open** Jan 8 - Dec 21.

At the peak of a very green mountain an immense red-stone monastery looks out each evening on a real postcard sunset. The hotel occupies the rear part of the monastery to which one has access via the gallery-cloister. The architecture has remained sumptuous, as it always was. The rooms are modest but very clean. If you want to fill your lungs with good clean air in an exceptional environment of beauty and peace, the Hospederia del Monasterio de Valvanera is well worth a detour (by a very difficult road as well). However, if you are looking for comfortable and cosseted rooms it is better to drive on, for an air of great sobriety reigns here: do not forget you are in a monastery after all.

How to get there (Map 5): 48km southwest of Logroño via N120 to Nájera, then C113.

Parador Marco Fabio

26500 Calahorra (La Rioja)
Era Alta - Quintiliano
Tel. (9)41-13 03 58 - Fax (9)41-13 51 39

Category ★★★ **Rooms** 62 with telephone, bath, WC, satellite TV and minibar. **Price** Double 13,500-15,000Pts. **Meals** Breakfast 1,300Pts, served 8:00-10:30. **Restaurant** Service 13:00-15:30, 20:30-23:00; menu 3,500Pts, also à la carte. Specialties: Cordero. **Credit cards** All major. **Pets** Dogs not allowed. **Facilities** Parking. **Nearby** Arnedo. **Open** All year.

This is a rather classical parador whose facade has an austere aspect, but which is surrounded by a flowery terrace at the back of the building. As in all paradors, the rooms are particularly large and great use has been made of wood, which gives them a warmer character. The furniture is classical and the floor-tiles polished. Even if you are just passing through, do not leave without visiting the town cathedral known as the 'Cathedral of the Sacristy'.

How to get there (*Map 5*): *100km southwest of Pamplona via A15, then A68 towards Logroño, exit Calahorra.*

Hotel Los Agustinos

26200 Haro (La Rioja)
Calle San Agustin, 2
Tel. (9)41-31 13 08 – Fax (9)41-30 31 48
Sr de Miguel Luengo

Category ★★★★ **Rooms** 62 with air-conditioning, telephone, bath, WC, satellite TV and minibar; elevator. **Price** Single 7,600-10,200Pts, double 9,800-12,800Pts, suite 24,200Pts. **Meals** Breakfast 1,100Pts, served 7:30-10:30; half board + 2,800 Pts, full board + 5,700Pts (per pers.). **Restaurant** Service 13:30-15:30, 20:30-23:00; closed Sun and Aug; menu 2,800Pts, also à la carte. Specialties: Patatas a la riojana - cordero. **Credit cards** All major. **Pets** Dogs allowed (except in restaurant). **Nearby** Villages of Briones, San Vicente de la Sonsierra and de Casalareina - Balcòn de Rioja. **Open** All year.

A 14th-century convent, and then a military hospital, prison, bus station and now a hotel, this is a real pleasure for us because the restoration here has been made with taste. Our greatest delight was in the terrace formed around the cloister, which is also the setting for a patio, where the former torture chamber of the prison once stood! The cloister arcades aligned the prisoners' cells and on the stonework one can still read their scribblings, which are sometimes very amusing. The church has become the lounge. As for the rooms, they are very classical. The restaurant cellars offer a particularly wide choice of regional wines. An excellent halting place for a trip through this area of renowned wines.

How to get there *(Map 5): 90km south of Bilbao via A68.*

Motel de Pradorrey

24700 Astorga (León)
Tel. (9)87-61 57 29 - Fax (9)87-61 92 20
Sr Sanchez

Category ★★★ **Rooms** 64 with telephone, bath, WC, satellite TV and minibar. **Price** Single 7,500-8,600Pts, double 10,500-11,800Pts, suite 11,500-12,900Pts. **Meals** Breakfast 850Pts, served 8:00-12:00. **Restaurant** With air-conditioning, service 13:00-16:00, 21:00-24:00; menu 2,000Pts. Specialties: Cames rojas - Embutidos. **Credit cards** All major. **Pets** Dogs allowed (except in restaurant). **Facilities** Parking. **Nearby** In Astorga: the cathedral - Monastery Santa Maria de Carrizo - La Bañeza - Church of Luyego - Castrillo de los Polvazares. **Open** All year.

At an altitude of 950 meters, the Motel de Pradorrey is housed in a medieval edifice that still bears on its facade, as well as inside, some vestiges of the constructions of the Templers' Order. The beauty of its stones and the wrought ironwork are remarkable but the interior is less attractive. Why sacrifice to comfort the charm one might have expected from admiring the hotel's outside ? This being said, the hotel is in a part of León that is a region still preserved from tourism, and where one can drive through some of the most typical villages of Spain, such as Castrillo de Los Polvazares. Three kilometers away, one can also visit the famous cathedral of Astorga. Please note, the hotel's restaurant has a good reputation.

How to get there *(Map 3): 52km west of León via N120, then N6 towards La Coruña.*

Parador Hostal San Marcos

24001 León
Plaza San Marcos, 7
Tel. (9)87-23 73 00 – Fax (9)87-23 34 58
Sr Alvarez Montoto

Category ★★★★★ **Rooms** 256 with telephone, bath, WC, satellite TV; elevator.
Price Double 19,000-21,500Pts. **Meals** Breakfast 1,400Pts, served 7:45-11:30.
Restaurant With air-conditioning, service 13:30-15:30, 21:00-23:30; menu 3,800Pts.
Specialties: Trout "Hostal" - Cecina. **Credit cards** All major. **Pets** Dogs not allowed.
Nearby In Leòn: Cathedral, Monastery San Marcos, Basilica San Isidoro - Monastery
San Miguel de Escalada - Castle of Valencia of Don Juan - Caves of the Robla. **Open**
All year.

No, this is not a museum entrance but it really is the hotel San Marcos! A historical monument, the former Santiaguista convent is the pride of the province of León. Its facade is a beautiful example of the 'plateresque' style, so called because of its resemblance to silver plate work. Inside, the massive and grandiose architecture of the cloister that surrounds the garden, is in contrast to the grace of the arches of the upper gallery, where tables are set out. A very beautiful lounge occupies the former chapter house with its astonishing 'mudejar' ceiling. There is unmatched comfort in all rooms, but naturally one prefers those of the main building as the annex has much less charm. An impeccable service and great friendliness are still the qualities of this classy hotel.

How to get there *(Map 3): in the town center.*

Hotel Castillo de Monzòn

34410 Monzòn de Campos (Palencia)
Tel. (9)79-80 80 75 - Fax (9)79-80 83 03

Category ★★★ Rooms 9 and 1 suite with telephone, bath, WC and TV. **Price** Single 8,000Pts, double 8,000-13,000Pts, suite 28,600Pts. **Meals** Breakfast 850Pts, served 8:00-11:00; full board + 4,760Pts (per pers.). **Restaurant** Service 13:30-15:30, 20:30-23:30; carte. Specialties: Meat, regional cooking. **Credit cards** Amex, Visa, Eurocard, MasterCard. **Pets** Dogs not allowed. **Facilities** Parking. **Nearby** In Monzòn: the church - Cathedral of Palencia - Ribas de Campos - Amusco - Piña de Campos - Tamara. **Open** All year.

The town of Monzòn is a former royal residence and it has converted its historic castle into a hotel. The arrival at this fortress on its small hill is impressive enough, with a very imposing building and its high tower and window-less walls. The interior however is welcoming and even if the architecture has been restored, the most attractive elements, such as a Roman arch and some beautiful ceilings, have been preserved. Comfort is also here in the rooms with their canopied beds and heavy drapes, to remind you that you are staying in a 'chateau'. In a rustic atmosphere, a fine restaurant offers good braised meats and an excellent menu of regional specialties. The hotel is isolated but in fact only eleven kilometers from Palencia, which has conserved a magnificent Gothic cathedral from its past and is well worth a visit. This is a most pleasant staging post.

How to get there *(Map 4): 11km north of Palencia.*

Hosterìa El Convento

34492 Santa Maria de Mave (Palencia)
Tel. (9)79-12 36 11
Familia Moral

Category ★★ **Rooms** 25 with bath. **Price** Single 5,000Pts, double 7,000Pts, suite 9,000-12,000Pts. **Meals** Breakfast 600Pts, served 8:00-12:00; half board + 5,000Pts, full board + 6,500Pts (per pers.). **Restaurant** Service 13:30-15:30, 20:30-22:30; menu 1,500Pts; also à la carte. Specialties: Sopa castillana - cordero. **Credit cards** All major. **Pets** Dogs not allowed. **Facilities** Parking. **Nearby** Hunting and fishing - Aguilar de Campoò - Monastery de Santa Maria La Real. **Open** All year.

Between Santander and Palencia in a region rich in Roman ruins, this very beautiful medieval priory shelters a hotel run in the family style, and where the charming daughters of the house look after the reception. Attached to the building, a pretty church is still in use. Understandably the rooms respect the spirit of the house and have a rather monk-like aspect. Their furniture is restricted to the essential, their walls bare and the entry doors small, but the bathrooms contribute a more contemporary touch. A little more sophisticated, the suites have canopied beds. The main room of the restaurant, with its beams, stone walls and tiled floors, is cheered by pretty lighting and intimate tabling. It is with a great pleasure that you relax in the garden, and as your eyes wander out over the rocky canyon of the Horadada and the surrounding limestone formations. Peace and well-being are to be found here.

How to get there (Map 4): 116km south of Santander, towards Palencia via N611.

Hotel Rector

37008 Salamanca
Paseo Rector Esperabé, 10
Tel. (9)23-21 84 82 - Fax (9)23-21 40 08
Sr Ferrán

Category ★★★★ **Rooms** 14 with air-conditioning, telephone, bath, WC, satellite TV, safe and minibar; elevator. **Price** Single 10,5000-12,500Pts, double 16,000Pts, suite 20,000-22,000Pts. **Meals** Breakfast 1,000Pts, served 8:00-11:00. **Restaurant** See p.245. **Credit cards** All major. **Pets** Dogs not allowed. **Facilities** Garage (850Pts). **Nearby** Castillo de Buen Amor - Peñaranda de Bracamonte - Ciudad Rodrigo - Candelario - La Alberca. **Open** All year.

The hotel is in a beautiful house of golden stone from the Villamayor region, like most of the other buildings in the town of Salamanca. Famous for its university, this is one of the most attractive towns in Spain. With a great wealth of monuments, it retains admirable remains from both the Renaissance and baroque periods, among them the Plaza Mayor, to name only one of them. The hotel has been fully renovated but with great refinement. The reception lounges on the ground floor have been made very light and airy. The furniture and chairs in mahogany and covered with salmon-pink fabrics, and assorted drapes give the decor an air of gentleness. Blue has been chosen for the rooms, which are very comfortable indeed, with their attractive bathrooms all in white marble. The hotel's small capacity ensures a very attentive service, along with a very friendly welcome. This is a very good staging post in a town that really deserves a visit.

How to get there (*Map 11*): *205km northwest of Madrid via A63, towards Avila; at 98km from Avila, via N501.*

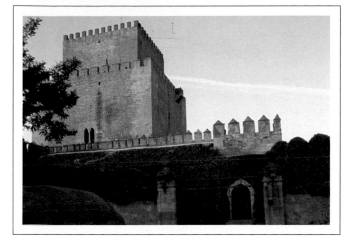

Parador Enrique II de Trastamara

37500 Ciudad Rodrigo (Salamanca)
Plaza del Castillo, 1
Tel. (9)23-46 01 50 - Fax (9)23-46 04 04
Sr Aliste Lopez

Category ★★★ **Rooms** 27 with air-conditioning, telephone, bath, WC, satellite TV and minibar. **Price** Double 13,500-15,000Pts. **Meals** Breakfast 1,200Pts, served 8:00-10:30. **Restaurant** Service 13:00-16:00, 20:30-23:00; menu 3,200Pts, also à la carte. Specialties: regional cooking. **Credit cards** All major. **Pets** Dogs not allowed. **Facilities** Parking. **Nearby** In Ciudad Rodrigo: the cathedral - Ruins of Urueña in Fuenteguinaldo - Villages: Peña de Francia and La Alberca. **Open** All year.

Ciudad Rodrigo is a fortified 12th-century town built on the orders of Fernando II. The chateau-alcazar that shelters the parador is in the center of the town on the banks of the River Agueda. As with many of these chateaux, their austere and rather severe side is relieved by beautiful flower gardens. The best rooms are those which, like the lounge and dining room, have a view of the river and town. Classified a historical monument, Ciudad Rodrigo well merits a visit.

How to get there (Map 11): 88km from Salamanca via N620, towards Portugal.

Hotel Infante Isabel

40001 Segovia
Plaza Mayor Isabel la Catolica, 1
Tel. (9)21-44 31 05 – Fax (9)21-43 32 401
Sr E. Canada Cardo

Category ★★★ **Rooms** 29 with air-conditioning, telephone, bath, WC, satellite TV, safe and minibar; elevator. **Price** Single 9,000Pts, double 9,100-11,400Pts. **Meals** Breakfast 875Pts, served 8:30-11:00. **Restaurant** See p. 245-246. **Credit cards** All major. **Pets** Dogs not allowed. **Facilities** Garage (1,000Pts). **Nearby** In Segovia: Roman aqueduct, the cathedral, churches of San Martìn, San Millàn and San Estebàn (tower), Alcàzar, Monastery de El Parral - Turégano - Pedraza de la Sierra - Castle Castilnovo - Sepùlveda - Royal Palace of La Granja - Palacio de Riofrio. **Open** All year.

A royal city, Segovia is one of the most attractive towns in Spain, and one comes here to visit its architectural treasures and also sample the gastronomic specialties (trout and above all its sucking pig roasted over a wood fire), which have made its reputation. The hotel is admirably situated opposite the cathedral, and it is a charming little hotel full of elegance and refinement. Everything is in good taste: modern comforts, classical decor and impeccable service. Breakfast is delicious and the welcome most attentive. The rooms are enchanting, bright and quiet, and most have a view of the cathedral. This is a very attractive address.

How to get there (Map 13): 87km northwest of Madrid.

El Hotel de la Villa

40172 Pedraza della Sierra (Segovia)
Calle Calzada, 5
Tel. (9)21-50 86 51 - Fax : (9)21-50 86 53
Sr Martín

Category ★★★ **Rooms** 22 and 2 suites with air-conditioning, telephone, bath, WC, satellite TV and minibar; elevator. **Price** Double 13,100Pts, suite 17,300Pts. **Meals** Breakfast 800Pts, served 7:30-11:00. **Restaurant** Service 13:00-16:00, 20:30-23:00; menus 3700Pts; also à la carte. **Credit cards** All major. **Pets** Dogs not allowed. **Nearby** Pedraza - hiking and riding in Sierra of Guadarramaand in the Naturel Park of Hyedo de Tejera Negra. **Open** All year.

Located in the north of the triangle formed by Segovia, Madrid and Burgos, Pedraza is a city well worth a detour where you will find a medieval village with well-preserved 15th-century architecture which includes the castle of the Velasco nobles where the French king François I was imprisoned. The Hotel de la Villa, located in one of the impressive houses in this attractive ochre-colored village, is at once refined, traditional and modern, something you recognize immediately in the lounges on the ground floor. The dining room is a pure delight where you can see meals prepared on an impressive stove dating back to the Arab invasion. The rooms are spacious and elegant, each one different and each superb. It is difficult to choose among them as all have identical comfort, exceptional decoration and beautifully appointed bathrooms. This is a hotel which, while quite expensive, lives up to its well-deserved reputation.

How to get there *(Map 13): 36km Northeast of Segovia via N110 until Matabuena (towards Soria) then on left to pedraza.*

La Posada de Don Mariano

40172 Pedraza della Sierra (Segovia)
Tel. (9)21-50 98 86 – Fax (9)21-50 98 87 – Sr Mariano

Category ★★ **Rooms** 18 with telephone, bath, WC and TV. **Price** Single 10,000Pts, double 12,000Pts, suite 16,000Pts. **Meals** Breakfast 950Pts, served 8:00-11:00. **Restaurant** Closed Monday, Jan 15 - 25 and June 15 - 25. Service 13:15-15:30, 20:00-22:00; menu 2,950Pts. Specialties: regional cooking. **Credit cards** All major. **Pets** Dogs not allowed. **Facilities** Parking. **Nearby** Segovia - Castle Castilnovo - Sepùlveda. **Open** All year.

Behind a discreet facade, La Posada de Don Mariano reveals a real jewel decorated throughout by the director of the Spanish version of 'House & Garden'. Pedraza is a small medieval village straight off a postcard, situated on a huge rock and surrounded by walls. Preserved admirably, you can admire aristocratic homes with their shields and arms, along with the Plaza Mayor and its porched houses. The owner of La Posada has created an original style based on the typical elements: Castilian ceramics, furniture from Andalusia and Extremadura, mixed with creations such as fabrics from Canovas found on the beds, curtains and wall hangings. The tones vary with the rooms. White, and with a superb canopied bed, number 101 is a magnificent marital chamber. Along the corridors and in the patio, a host of green plants create a charming atmosphere, which is never precious or affected. In the restaurant the white-covered tables promise romantic 'tête-à-têtes' by candlelight. This is a true hotel of charm in a village that has attracted and inspired many an artist.

How to get there *(Map 13): 36km northeast of Segovia via N110 towards Soria until Matabuena, then Pedraza.*

Molino de Río Viejo

40170 Collado Hermoso (Segovia)
Carretera N–110, km 172
Tel. (9)2–40 30 63 – Fax (9)2–40 30 51 – M. Antonio Armero

Rooms 6 with bath and WC. **Price** Double 9,000Pts. **Meals** Breakfast 800Pts, served 7:00-11:00. **Restaurant** (weekend only). Service 13:00-15:30, 20:30-22:30; à la carte 3,000-4,000Pts. **Credit cards** Visa, Eurocard, MasterCard. **Pets** Dogs not allowed. **Facilities** Riding (for 3 houres - 1week: 8,000-30,000Pts), parking. **Nearby** Pedraza - hiking and riding in Sierra of Guadarramaand in the Naturel Park of Hyedo de Tejera Negra. **Open** All year.

When asked to describe El Molino in terms of its being a restaurant or a hotel, its owner prefers to leave it to you, saying that it will, over time, become something very much like your own home. Standing in the middle of the imposing Sierra de Guadarrama, this old mill, already enjoying a long and often colorful past, has been resuscitated and is now a warm and friendly hotel. Relics of its past are on display in the large dining room, among them old farm tools and wheat sheaves, side by side with elegant wicker furniture. The low ceilings create a cozy atmosphere which permeates the entire house, especially the rooms located under the roof. Of these, your best choice would be those at the rear. The food is flawless and all the more pleasant on summer weekends when you can eat under the poplars and oaks that line the river. This, however, is by no means all of the Molino's attractions. If you enjoy riding horses, there are unforgettable trails in the region, where you will be accompanied by the Molino's owners who have been riding them for twenty years. Antonio Amero's slogan is simple: "Get to know Spain on horseback!"

How to get there *(Map 13): 36km northeast of Segovia via N110 towards Soria until Matabuena, then Pedraza.*

Posada de Sigueruelo

Sigueruelo (Segovia)
Calle Badén, 40
Tel. (9)21-50 81 25 - Fax (9)21-50 81 25
Sra Concepcíon Alarcos Rodriguez

Open All year. **Rooms** 6 with shower and WC. **Price** Double 9,700Pts. **Meals** Breakfast 800Pts, served 7:30-11:00; half board: 12,000Pts (per pers.). **Evening meals** Menus 1,200Pts (lunch), 1,500Pts (dinner). **Credit cards** Visa, Eurocard, MasterCard. **Pets** Small dogs allowed. **Facilities** Parking. **Nearby** Pedraza - hiking and riding in Sierra of Guadarramaand in the Naturel Park of Hyedo de Tejera Negra. **Open** All year.

In the heart of a wild and sunny landscape sits the tiny village of Sigueruelo between the Sierra de Guadarrama and Ayll overlooking the square. In addition, the hotel has a shady terrace where you can have lunch or a quiet drink and enjoy the life of the ing that include hiking and horseback riding in the neighboring natural parks as well as canoeing with experienced guides on the Río Duratquare. In addition, the hotel has a shady terrace where you can have lunch or a quiet drink and enjoy the life of the lection of its surroundings, both rural and rustic. In it you see beams, stone walls, regional furniture and works of naïve art while enjoying the comfort of its rooms which are not altogether spacious. Among them, the best are upstairs, ideally the ones with a view. After putting in a strenuous day, you are sure to appreciate the traditional cooking as well as the friendly family atmosphere that always is part of your stay here.

How to get there *(Map 13): 50km Northeast of Segovia via N110 (towards Soria) to Sigueruelo.*

Hotel Mesón Leonor

42005 Soria
Paseo del Mirón
Tel. (9)75-22 02 50 - Fax (9)75-22 99 53
Sr Heras Varea

Category ★★★ **Rooms** 32 with air conditioning, telephone, bath or shower, WC, TV, safe and minibar. **Price** Single 5,875-6,250Pts, double 8,500-9,500Pts, "Special" 9,400-9,900Pts, suite 11,000-12,000Pts. **Meals** Breakfast 575Pts, served 8:00-11:00; half board + 2,525 Pts, full board + 3,875Pts (per pers.). **Restaurant** Service 13:00-16:00, 21:00-23:00; menu 1,950Pts, also à la carte. Specialties: Meat. **Credit cards** All major. **Pets** Dogs allowed in the rooms. **Facilities** Garage (1,200Pts). **Nearby** In Soria: cathedral San Pedro, churches of Santo Domingo and of San Juan de Duero - Vinuesa - Agreda - Sierra de Urbiòn: road of Laguna Negra de Urbìon to Laguna egra de Neila. **Open** All year.

Soria is one of those towns from "Lands of Castille" about which Antonio Machado has spoken so well. The large house sheltering the hotel is austere, while the interior is in Castilian style. The rooms however are more welcoming and comfortable; some of them, with mezzanines, are more spacious and will cost you a few extra pesetas. This is a very pleasant halt for those planning to walk in the beautiful Sierra de Urbiòn.

How to get there (Map 14): 106km south of Logroño via N3.

Parador Rey Fernando II de León

49600 Benavente (Zamora)
Paseo de Ramon y Cajal
Tel. (9)88-63 03 00 - Fax (9)88-63 03 03
Sr Don Pedro Hernande Muñoz

Category ★★★★ **Rooms** 30 with air-conditioning, telephone, bath, WC, satellite TV and minibar. **Price** Double 15,000-16,500Pts. **Meals** Breakfast 1,300Pts, served 8:00-11:00. **Restaurant** Service 13:00-16:00, 20:30-23:00; menu 3,500Pts, also à la carte. Specialties: regional cooking. **Credit cards** All major. **Pets** Dogs not allowed. **Facilities** Garage (1,000Pts). **Nearby** Villalpando - Monastery of Moreruela - Church ofe Santa María de Tera. **Open** All year.

Built in the 12th-century, this chateau was the residence of King Fernando II who installed his court here in 1176. But after so many centuries it was practically destroyed during some battle between the French and English. Only the imposing Torre del Caraco remains today. To install the parador, it was thus necessary to build one wing for the rooms and a second for the dining room and reception. The lounge has been placed in the tower, whose main decorative element is the magnificent 'mudejar' ceiling in wood marquetry. In the TV room it was a good idea to make a mosaic from all the ceramic pieces found on the site. Apart from the comfort, one can also appreciate the terraces with their splendid panorama of the countryside.

How to get there (Map 3): 69km south of León via N630.

Parador Condes de Alba de Aliste

49001 Zamora
Plaza Viriato, 5
Tel. (9)80–51 44 97 – Fax (9)80–53 00 63
Sra Pelegrín

Category ★★★★ **Rooms** 47 with telephone, bath, WC, satellite TV and minibar; elevator. **Price** Double 15,000-18,500Pts. **Meals** Breakfast 1,300Pts, served 8:00-10:30. **Restaurant** Service 13:00-16:00, 20:30-23:00; menu 3,500Pts, also à la carte. Specialties: Castilian cooking. **Credit cards** All major. **Pets** Dogs allowed. **Facilities** Swimming pool, garage (600Pts). **Nearby** In Zamora: the cathedral, Museo Catedralicio (Flamencos tapestries) - Church at Arcenillas - Church at San Pedro de la Nave - Colegiata de Toro. **Open** All year.

This 15th-century palace is right in the heart of Zamora on the edge of the old quarter. Largely destroyed during the revolt of the 'Comuneros' in the 16th century, it was then restored by the Counts of Alba and of Aliste, and became a hospital in the 18th century. The magnificent Renaissance cloister still survives today, along with a double gallery, the balcony, and the grand monumental staircase at the foot of which one can admire a superb coat of arms. Lounges and dining room succeed each other to the garden with its swimming pool. The rooms are very well furnished but the suite, facing the square, deserves a special mention for its comfort and reasonable price. The personnel are friendly and the lady director charming, and they do everything to ensure that your stay is one of the happiest times of your journey.

How to get there *(Map 11): 62km north of Salamanca via N630.*

Hostería Real de Zamora

49000 Zamora
Cuesta de Pizarro, 7
Tel. (9)80-53 45 45 – Fax (9)80-53 45 22
Sr Ramón

Category ★★★★ **Rooms** 18 with telephone, bath or shower, WC, TV and minibar. **Price** Single 7,260Pts, double 9,475Pts. **Meals** Breakfast included; half board 13,400Pts, full board 16,000Pts (per 2 pers. 3 days min.). **Restaurant** "Pizarro" service 14:00-16:00, 21:00-23:30; menu 1,975Pts, also à la carte. Specialties: Basque and Castille cooking. **Credit cards** All major. **Pets** Dogs allowed. **Facilities** Parking. **Nearby** In Zamora: the cathedral, Museo Catedralicio (Flamencos tapestries) - Church at Arcenillas - Church at San Pedro de la Nave - Colegiata de Toro. **Open** All year

The hotel occupies a former palace of the Inquisition, itself built on an earlier Jewish building that legend links with the famous discoverer of Peru, Pizarro. A beautiful stone staircase leads to the rooms arranged around a pretty patio. Some of them, the largest, have a view of the River Ebro: the only nuisance is the noise from the street, but other rooms look onto the patio. All are attractive and fresh with their tiled floors and light walls. The bathrooms are without reproach and some astonishing ancient Jewish baths have been conserved; while the water comes from natural rock sources. Via a small staircase one reaches the garden and a terrace up against the medieval walls of the town, where you can look out over the river. During Holy Week a series of classical music recitals is given in the patio or the beautiful restaurant room.

How to get there (Map 11): 62km north of Salamanca via N630.

132

Parador de la Mancha

02000 Albacete
Al Sureste
Tel. (9)67-50 93 43 – Fax (9)67-22 60 92
Sr Cornero Fandiño

Category ★★★ **Rooms** 69 with air-conditioning, telephone, bath, WC, TV and minibar. **Price** Double 13,500-15,000Pts. **Meals** Breakfast 1,300Pts, served 8:00-10:30. **Restaurant** Service 13:00-16:00, 20:30-23:00; menu 3,500Pts, also à la carte. Specialties: Bacalão a la manchega - Pimientos rellenos - Pierna de cabrito al romero. **Credit cards** All major. **Pets** Dogs not allowed. **Facilities** Swimming pool, tennis, parking. **Nearby** In Albacete: Archeological Museum (Roman ivory dolls), Feria (September) - Alcaraz. **Open** All year.

A good staging post towards the coast if coming from Madrid, the Parador is also a starting point for discovering the vast plain of La Mancha, the setting for Don Quixote's adventures. The Parador de la Mancha will meet your needs as it is a comfortable hotel in country style, built around a large patio with its fountain. One feels good in the large fresh rooms, each with its own small terrace. The swimming pool is always welcome in summer, while one will also appreciate the hotel's cuisine full off the specialties of La Mancha, famous, among other things, for its cheese.

How to get there *(Map 21): 183km southwest of Valencia via N430, and 5km from Albacete.*

133

Parador de Almagro

13270 Almagro (Ciudad Real)
Ronda de San Francisco
Tel. (9)26-86 01 00 – Fax (9)26-86-01 50
Sr Muñoz Romera

Category ★★★★ **Rooms** 55 with air-conditioning, telephone, bath, WC, satellite TV and minibar. **Price** Double 15,000-17,500Pts. **Meals** Breakfast 1,300Pts, served 8:00-10:30. **Restaurant** Service 13:30-16:00, 21:00-23:00; menu 3,700Pts, also à la carte. Specialties: Pisto manchego - Mojete - Migas. **Credit cards** All major. **Pets** Dogs not allowed. **Facilities** Swimming pool, tennis, parking. **Nearby** In Almagro: Plaza Mayor - Bolaños de Calatrava - Church of Moral de Calatrava - Calzada de Calatrava - National Park of Lagunas de Ruidera. **Open** All year.

The parador is built on the ancient convent of San Francisco (1506). Almagro rises out of the vast La Mancha plain and is a key staging post on the route of Cervantès. It is the town of lace and the center of the Order of Calatrava. It is also interesting for its Plaza Mayor, which is a real jewel with its extensive uninterrupted glazed windows, and the Corral de Comedias, the only surviving theater of the Siglo de Oro. The parador has no less than sixteen patios with galleries, where the flowers and fountains combine to create a magic atmosphere. Terra-cottas and faiences are often used in decorating the pretty rooms and the magnificent cellar next to the bar. The hotel is right in the heart of town, and has private parking, while the service is very good.

How to get there *(Map 19): 22km east of Ciudad Real via C415.*

Parador Marqués de Villena

16213 Alarcón (Cuenca)
Avenida Amigos del Castillo
Tel. (9)69-33 03 15 – Fax (9)69-33 03 03
Sra Aurora Lozana

Category ★★★★ **Rooms** 13 with telephone, bath, WC, satellite TV and minibar; elevator. **Price** Double 18,500-19,000Pts. **Meals** Breakfast 1,300Pts, served 8:15-11:00. **Restaurant** Service 13:15-16:00, 21:00-23:00; menu 3,700Pts, also à la carte. Specialties: Bacalão a la Manchega. **Credit cards** All major. **Pets** Dogs not allowed. **Facilities** Parking. **Nearby** Motilla del Palancar - Valverde - Minglanilla - Puebla del Salvador - Yémeda. **Open** All year.

The parador is in the chateau of the little fortified town of Alarcón, and it seems to be the most beautiful and best conserved in the province of Cuenca. Set on the edge of the town on a huge rock almost entirely surrounded by the River Jucar, it enjoys a perfect tranquility. The rooms are pleasantly decorated and the bathrooms comfortable. Go for those in the tower, for even if they are rather sombre; their tiny windows, or sometimes loopholes, give them an added attraction. A special mention goes to Room 105, from which you can walk onto the circular pathway with its unmatched view over the surrounding country. Breakfast is perfect, particularly generous and excellent, and served in the imposing restaurant hall.

How to get there *(Map 20): 85km south of Cuenca via N320 to Motilla del Palencar, then N3 towards Madrid.*

Posada de San José

16001 Cuenca
Calle Julián Romero, 4
Tel. (9)69-21 13 00 – Fax (9)69-23 03 65
Sra Morter and Sr Cortinas

Category ★★ **Rooms** 30 (21 with bath, 9 with basin). **Price** Single 2,500-2,800Pts (with basin), 4,000-4,600Pts (with bath), double 4,000-4,600Pts (with basin), 7,000-8,900Pts (with bath), triple 5,400-6,200Pts (with basin), 10,800-12,000Pts (with bath), 4 pers. 12,800-14,200Pts (with bath). **Meals** Breakfast 500Pts, served 8:00-11:00. **Bar-Restaurant** Service 17:30-22:30; closed Mon; à la carte. Specialties: Tapas, morteruedo, trucha escabechada. **Credit cards** All major. **Pets** Dogs allowed in the rooms. **Nearby** In Cuenca: the cathedral, las Casas Colgadas (Hanging Houses), Museo de Arte Abstractado (Museum of Spanish Abstract Art) - La Ciudad Encantada (Enchanted City) - Las Torcas - Hoz del Huecar (views). **Open** All year.

The posada occupies the former residence of the painter Martinez del Mazo, which is now a hotel full of charm with a magnificent view over the cliffs and vegetable gardens. Cuenca has been celebrated since the 14th century for its houses suspended above the Júcar gorges and, more recently, for its modern art museum. You will like this hotel for its simplicity and the comfortable rooms (apart from Number 9 with its 'lavabo'), and all are imbued with that same atmosphere of a well run house. The furniture and floor-tiles are well-polished, the curtains stitched by the seamstresses of Cuenca, cotton napkins and towels, and so on. Those rooms with bathrooms also have a beautiful view, while Rooms 15, 21, 32 and 33 also have terraces. A pretty garden and a friendly welcome are good reasons for choosing this posada, which also offers very reasonable prices.

How to get there *(Map 14): 63km southeast of Madrid.*

Hotel Cueva del Fraile

16001 Cuenca
Hoz del Huecar
Tel. (9)69-21 15 71 - Fax (9)69-25 60 47 - Sr de la Torre

Rooms 63 with telephone, bath, WC and TV. **Price** Single 5,900-8,500Pts, double 7,500-13,900Pts. **Meals** Breakfast 795Pts, served 8:00-11:00; half board + 2,770Pts, full board + 4,033Pts (per pers.). **Restaurant** Service 13:00-16:00, 20:00-23:00; menu 1,975Pts, also à la carte. Specialties: regional and national cooking. **Credit cards** All major. **Pets** Dogs not allowed. **Facilities** Swimming pool, tennis (350Pts), parking. **Nearby** In Cuenca: the cathedral, las Casas Colgadas (Hanging Houses), Museo de Arte Abstractado (Museum of Spanish Abstract Art) - La Ciudad Encantada (Enchanted City) - Las Torcas. **Open** Mar 1 - Jan 7.

It is seven kilometers from Cuenca, in the midst of mountainous outcrops, that the 'Cueva del Fraile' is to be found. Before being converted some ten years ago into a welcoming and quiet hotel, this 15th-century building was first a convent and then a farm. The rooms are nothing extraordinary, their Castilian furnishings and lighting are not very welcoming. The most attractive are those reached via the covered gallery and overlooking the pretty interior courtyard. One will appreciate the dining room with its large open fireplace, or the bar with its mezzanine, for their rustic atmosphere. A friendly welcome and quality regional cuisine add to the charm of this peaceful establishment without any pretentions.

How to get there *(Map 14): 170km southeast of Madrid to Cuenca, then the road to Palomera for 6km, then to the left on the road to Buenache for 1.2km.*

Parador de Sigüenza

19003 Sigüenza (Guadalajara)
Tel. (9)49-39 00 01 - Fax (9)49-39 13 64
Sr José Menguiano

Category ★★★ **Rooms** 77 with air-conditioning, telephone, bath, WC, satellite TV and minibar; elevator. **Price** Double 13,500-15,000Pts. **Meals** Breakfast 1,300Pts, served 8:15-11:00. **Restaurant** Service 13:15-16:00, 20:30-22:30; menu 3,700Pts, also à la carte. Specialties: regional cooking. **Credit cards** All major. **Pets** Dogs not allowed. **Facilities** Parking. **Nearby** In Sigüenza: the cathedral (Tomb of Don Martìn Vàsquez de Arca in the Chapel of the Doncel, the sacristy, Chapel of Santa Librada) - Village of Medinaceli. **Open** All year.

At the summit of the fortified town of Sigüenza, which rises in terraces on the side of the hill, stands the imposing Moorish fortress which became a Bishop's Palace, and now a parador. The restoration and reconstruction work has been careful to respect the proportions of this enormous four-sided building of 7,000 m2. To soften the austerity of the site, courtyards and gardens have been laid out, while two immense rooms shelter the lounge and dining room with their sober Castilian furniture. The rooms, whether giving onto the courtyard or valley, are all comfortable while some have terraces with long reclining chairs. From the large tiled courtyard one has a magnificent view over the pink roofs of Sigüenza, and one can trace out the maze of tiny streets. In the marvellous cathedral do not miss the funeral monument of Doncel, from the 15th century, and one of the most beautiful sculptures in the history of Spanish art.

How to get there *(Map 14): 130km northeast of Madrid; at 70km from Guadalajara via N11 to Alcolea del Pinar, then C204 towards Sigüenza.*

Parador de Oropesa

45460 Oropesa (Toledo)
Plaza del Palacio, 1
Tel. (9)25-43 00 00 - Fax (9)25-43 07 77

Category ★★★★ **Rooms** 48 with air-conditioning, telephone, bath, WC, satellite TV and minibar; elevator. **Price** Double 15,000Pts. **Meals** Breakfast 1,300Pts, served 8:00-10:30. **Restaurant** Service 13:00-16:00, 20:00-23:00; menu 3,570Pts, also à la carte. Specialties: Cordero del campo - Perdiz de tiro a la toledana. **Credit cards** All major. **Pets** Dogs not allowed. **Facilities** Parking. **Nearby** "Ceramic road" from Talavera de la Reina, via Puente de Arzobispo, Valdeverdeja - Lake of Azutàn - Lagartera. **Open** All year.

The magnificent feudal 'château' of Oropesa was the first historic building to be converted into a parador in 1930. This is a superb gothic-mudejar building, square in plan, and flanked with towers and keeps that look out over the valley of the Campo Arañuelo, with the plain of Gredos in the far distance. It shares the site with a renaissance palace that one can visit. In the interior the large forms and original floors have been preserved, which give a lot of charm and character to the well-furnished reception rooms. The rooms have all the comforts of a grand hotel and terraces, some of which look over the valley. At the foot of the historic building is a magnificent swimming pool, bordered by lawns, which also offers a superb panorama. A very beautiful address that should not be missed.

How to get there (Map 12): *70km southwest of Madrid via N401; close to the Puerta de Bisagra.*

139

Hostal del Cardenal

45004 Toledo
Paseo de Recaredo, 24
Tel. (9)25-22 49 00 – Fax (9)25-22 29 91
Sr Gonzalez Luis Golzalbo

Category ★★★ Rooms 27 with air-conditioning, telephone, bath, WC, satellite TV and minibar (suite). **Price** Single 5,475-7,300Pts, double 8,850-11,800Pts, suite 12,038-16,050Pts. **Meals** Breakfast 850Pts, served 7:15-11:00. **Restaurant** Service 13:15-16:00, 20:30-23:00; closed Dec 24; menu 2,650Pts, also à la carte. Specialties: Cochinillo y cordero asado - Sopa de ajo - Perdiz estofado a la toledana. **Credit cards** All major. **Pets** Dogs allowed. **Nearby** In Toledo: Cathedral, Church of Santo Tomé ("El Entierro del Conte de Orgaz" by Greco), El Trànsito Synagogue, Museum of Santa Cruz - Aranjuez - "Don Quixote country": (N301,south of Aranjuez): Consuegra, Corral de Almaguer, Quintanar de la Orden, El Toboso, Mota del Cuervo Belmonte, Tomelloso, Argamasillo de Alba. **Open** All year.

In Toledo there are many reasons for staying at the Hostal del Cardenal: Its location, in the heart of the imperial city, facing the Puerta de Bisagra, one of the jewels of Toledo. Its site in a Toledan palace of the 18th century, former summer residence of Cardinal Lorenzana, archbishop of the city. The calm of its Moorish gardens where only the birdsong and fountains are to be heard. Its comfort and good cuisine, its summer dinners in the garden. And for a last evening stroll around the circular pathway of the 11th-century bastion of walls.

How to get there *(Map 13): 70km south of Madrid via N401; near to the Porte de Bisagra.*

Hotel Residencia La Almazara

45080 Toledo
Carret de Cuerva
Tel. (9)25-22 38 66 - Fax (9)25-25 05 62
Sr Villamor

Category ★★ **Rooms** 21 with telephone, bath and WC. **Price** Single 3,500Pts, double 5,500-6,200Pts. **Meals** Breakfast 450Pts, served 8:00-11:00. **Restaurant** See p. 246. **Credit cards** All major. **Pets** Dogs not allowed. **Facilities** Parking. **Nearby** In Toledo: Cathedral, Church of Santo Tomé (El Entierro del Conte de Orgaz od Greco), El Trànsito Synagogue, Museum of Santa Cruz - Aranjuez - "Don Quixote country": (N301, south of Aranjuez): Consuegra, Corral de Almaguer, Quintanar de la Orden, El Toboso, Mota del Cuervo Belmonte, Tomelloso, Argamasilla de Alba. **Open** Mar 6 - Dec 11.

Protected by 500 hectares of olive trees, oaks and junipers, this hotel was the former vacation home of Cardinal Quiroza in the 16th century. It is the oldest hotel in the city and it featured in the El Greco painting, 'General view of Toledo'. The rooms are simple but very attractive with their brand new bathrooms. Rooms 1 to 9 also have terraces with a breathtaking view. The countryside around and the softness of the light make this place a real haven that one is always happy to return to after a tiring visit to Toledo or its surroundings.

How to get there *(Map 13): 73.5km south of Madrid to Toledo via N401; then 3.5km on the road to Arges, near to the restaurant Monterrey-Aire de Cigarrales*

Parador Conde de Orgaz

45001 Toledo
Cerro del Emperador
Tel. (9)25-22 18 50 - Fax (9)25-22 51 66
Sr Molina Aranda

Category ★★★★ **Rooms** 76 with air-conditioning, telephone, bath, WC, TV and minibar; elevator. **Price** Double 18,500Pts. **Meals** Breakfast 1,300Pts, served 8:00-10:30. **Restaurant** Service 13:00-16:00, 20:30-23:00; menu 3,700Pts, also à la carte. Specialties: Duelos y quebrantos - Perdiz a la toledana - Ponche toledano. **Credit cards** All major. **Pets** Dogs not allowed. **Facilities** Swimming pool. **Nearby** In Toledo: Cathedral, Church of Santo Tomé ("El Entierro del Conte de Orgaz" Greco), El Trànsito Synagogue, Museum of Santa Cruz - Aranjuez - "Don Quixote country": (N301,south of Aranjuez): Consuegra, Corral de Almaguer, Quintanar de la Orden, El Toboso, Mota del Cuervo Belmonte, Tomelloso, Argamasilla de Alba. **Open** All year.

The parador, which takes its name from the famous painting by El Greco, 'The burial of the Count of Orgaz', is on the 'Emperor's Hill', in the privileged quarter of Cigarrales. This quarter dominates Toledo and offers an unmatched view between the Alcántara and San Martin bridges. This remarkable site has conditioned the layout of the buildings. With its completely Toledan character, the hotel is very comfortable and air-conditioned, and also has a swimming pool, both major 'pluses' when visiting Toledo in summer.

How to get there *(Map 13): 70km south of Madrid via N401; facing the city on the other side of the River Tagus (Tajo).*

Hotel Domenico

45002 Toledo
Cerro del Emperador
Tel. (9)25-25 00 40 - Fax (9)25-25 28 77
Sr R. Vidales Sànchez–Infantes

Category ★★★★ **Rooms** 48 and 2 suites with air-conditioning, telephone, bath, WC, satellite TV, safe and minibar; elevator. **Price** Single 9,800-10,200Pts, double 14,150-14,850Pts, 3 pers. 16,400-17,200Pts, suite 22,550-23,650Pts. **Meals** Breakfast 1,100Pts, served 8:00-10:30; half board + 4,100Pts, full board + 6,000Pts (per pers., 2 days min.). **Restaurant** Service 13:00-16:00, 20:30-23:00, menu 3,000Pts, also à la carte. Specialties: regional cooking. **Credit cards** All major. **Pets** Dogs not allowed. **Facilities** Swimming pool, parking. **Nearby** In Toledo: Cathedral, Church of Santo Tomé ("El Entierro del Conte de Orgaz" Greco), El Trànsito Synagogue, Museum of Santa Cruz - Aranjuez - "Don Quixote country": (N301, south of Aranjuez): Consuegra, Corral de Almaguer, Quintanar de la Orden, El Toboso, Mota del Cuervo Belmonte, Tomelloso, Argamasilla de Alba. **Open** All year.

The Hotel Domenico is not in the town center but on the high ground close by, which allows you to admire this ancient city as El Greco painted it. The architecture of the hotel has all the rigor of the arid mineral countryside surrounding it. The interior is very ordinary, the decor modern but without style, but all the rooms have terraces offering magnificent views over the countryside and, even better, over the old town. The lounge and bar are very lively areas, while the swimming pool with its shady corner terraces is much appreciated. The site, services and quality of facilities all quickly make you forget the banality of the decor.

How to get there *(Map 13): 70km south of Madrid via N401; facing the town on the other bank of the Tagus.*

Hotel Husa Palace - Ritz

08010 Barcelona
Gran Via de les Corts Catalanes, 668
Tel. (9)3-318 52 00 - Fax (9)3-318 01 48
Web: http://www.ritzbcn.com

Category ★★★★★ **Rooms** 149 and 12 suites with air-conditioning, telephone, bath, WC, satellite TV, safe and minibar; elevator. **Price** Single 24,000Pts, double 35,000-36,000Pts, suite 43-160,000Pts. **Meals** Breakfast 2,300Pts, served 7:00-11:00. **Restaurant** Service 13:30-16:00, 20:30-23:00; à la carte 5,500Pts. Specialties: Pollo con langostinas - Escudella i carn d'olla. **Credit cards** All major. **Pets** Dogs not allowed. **Facilities** Parking. **Nearby** Sitges (beach) - Monastery of San Cugat del Valle - Montserrat - Vich; Prat golf course (9-and 18-Hole), San Cugat golf course (18-Hole). **Open** All year.

Since its opening in 1919, time has not tarnished its image, as one would expect from 'The Ritz'. The building and its interior are very splendid: from the entrance, the grand double staircase, the main hallway and all the attention you are given do not deceive, you are in a real palace. The rooms are more impersonal even if all are very comfortable. The hotel restaurant offers international cuisine but also a good variety of Catalan dishes. The terrace of the small interior garden is also a pleasant spot for having a drink, while a visit to the bar in the basement is obligatory.

How to get there (Map 8): on the 'Diagonal'; close to the Plaza de Catalunya.

Hotel Claris

08007 Barcelona
Pau Claris, 150
Tel. (9)3 487 62 62 – Fax (9)3 215 79 70 – Sr P. Bouisset

Category ★★★★★ **Rooms** 120 and 18 junior suites, 18 duplex, 2 suites with air-conditioning, telephone, bath, WC, satellite TV, minibar, safe; elevator. **Price** Single 19,800Pts (weekend)-23,000Pts, double 22,000Pts (weekend)-34,100Pts, suite 42,000-90,000Pts. **Meals** Breakfast 2,400Pts. Served 7:00-11:00. **Restaurant** «Beluga». Service 20:30-1:00; closed Sunday evening. «Le Barbacoa», at the swimming pool, open evening. **Credits cards** All major. **Pets** Dogs allowed (except in restaurant). **Facilities** Swimming pool, sauna, garage. **Nearby** Sitges (beach) - Monastery of San Cugat del Valle - Montserrat - Vich; Prat golf course (9- and 18-hole), San Cugat golf course (18-hole). **Open** All year.

The Claris is near the Barrio Gotic and a short distance from the celebrated buildings designed by Antonio Gaudi (1852-1926). It was built in the 19th century and has retained its Neo-Gothic facade while adding a metallic gray extension which nicely weds the two styles. This architecture is a prelude to the interior decoration which skillfully plays on the contrasts of its building materials and the refinement of its furnishings. You find large concrete pillars, an extensive use of marble plus exotic wood superbly put to use in the hotel's modern chairs and 1930-style light fixtures. In addition, there are mosaics from the Roman era. The same luxury is present in the resolutely modern rooms although some have very attractive antiques. Art and culture are everywhere and the hotel houses a small museum with a fine collection of Egyptology. This is one of the most beautiful hotels in the Catalan capital.

How to get there *(Map 8): on the Diagonal.*

Hotel Condes de Barcelona

08008 Barcelona
Paseo de Gracia, 75
Tel. (9)3-488 22 00 - Fax (9)3-488 06 14
Web: www.gulliver.es/publicit/condes/ben

Category ★★★★ **Rooms** 183 with air-conditioning, telephone, bath, WC, satellite TV, video and minibar; elevator. **Price** Double 15,500-25,000Pts (1 pers.), 16,500-27,000Pts - suite "Gaudi" 20,000-63400Pts, suite "Barcelona" 40,000-60,000Pts. **Meals** Breakfast 1,700Pts, served 7:00-11:00. **Restaurant** Service 13:00-22:30; menu 3,700Pts, also à la carte. Specialties: Catalan and international cooking. **Credit cards** All major. **Pets** Dogs not allowed. **Facility** Swimming pool, garage (2,000Pts). **Nearby** Sitges (beach) - Monastery of San Cugat del Valle - Montserrat - Vich; Prat golf course (9-and 18-Hole), San Cugat golf course (18-hole). **Open** All year.

A few meters away from the famous house of Gaudi, "La Pedrera", there stood another 'Art Nouveau' house, "La Casa Batllo," which is now one of the best hotels in Barcelona. The interior architecture is very pure, with modern black furniture, halogen lighting, and a very refined setting for a select clientele patronizing the lounges and bar. Whatever the layout of the rooms, they are comfortable: those on the courtyard look out onto a beautiful terrace and gardens; the rooms on the street are well insulated from the noise; and in the older building all those on the upper floor have been renovated. We recommend the Gaudi or Barcelona suites. Very fashionable and a little bit sophisticated, yet no way pretentious.

How to get there *(Map 8): on the 'Diagonal'; Plaza de Catalunya, then Paseo de Gracia.*

St-Moritz Hotel

08007 Barcelona
Diputacìon, 262/264
Tel. (9)3 412 15 00 – Fax (9)3 412 12 36

Category ★★★★ **Rooms** 80 and 12 suites with air-conditioning, telephone, bath, WC, satellite TV, minibar, safe; elevator - Wheelchair access. **Price** Single 16,900-21,400Pts, double 19,900-26,800Pts. **Meals** Breakfast 1,950-2,100Pts, served 7:00-11:00. **Restaurant** Service 13:30-16:00, 20:30-23:00, menu 2,500Pts; also à la carte. **Credits cards** All major. **Pets** Dogs allowed (except in restaurant). **Facilities** Garage. **Nearby** Sitges (beach) - Monastery of San Cugat del Valle - Montserrat - Vich; Prat golf course (9- and 18-hole), San Cugat golf course (18-hole). **Open** All year.

The St. Moritz is located on the periphery of the Barrio Gotic which came into existence as a result of 19th-century urban planning. Today, as numerous offices occupy its renovated buildings, it stands to reason that an efficient and luxurious hotel should be among them. This is an impressive building dating from 1883 and classed as "historical landmark" by the Ministry of Tourism. For this reason its architecture has been preserved and includes an immense entry in gray marble leading to a huge staircase with a glass roof assuring very pleasant light. The decor is sober and elegantly modern and this equally applies to the rooms which in addition to standard comfort and elegant bathrooms, offer a mini-gymnasium equipped with a bicycle-exerciser. On the second floor is the St. Gallen, the hotel's restaurant which enjoys the esteem of the residents and businessmen of Barcelona. On the roof is a terrace where you can have lunch.

How to get there *(Map 8): on the Diagonal.*

Hotel Duques de Bergara

08002 Barcelona
Calle Bergara, 11
Tel. (9)3-301 51 51 - Fax (9)3-317 34 42
Sra M. Jané

Category ★★★★ Rooms 151 with air-conditioning, telephone, bath, WC, satellite TV and minibar; elevator. **Price** Single 16,900Pts, double 20,900Pts. **Meals** Breakfast 1,500Pts, served 7:00-10:30. **Restaurant** Service 13:00-16:00, 20:30-23:00; menu 1,800Pts. Specialties: international cooking. **Credit cards** All major. **Pets** Dogs not allowed. **Nearby** Sitges (beach) - Monastery of San Cugat del Valle - Montserrat - Vich; Prat golf course (9-and 18-Hole), San Cugat golf course (18-Hole). **Open** All year.

This is a private house built in 1903 and converted into a hotel a few years ago. The entrance is beautiful enough to take your breath away: its 'caisson' ceiling of incredible height opens onto a glass roof that fills the hotel with the sort of light that photographers dream about. Marble covers all the staircase right up to the magnificent doors. Alas, like almost all older hotels trying to keep abreast of the demands of the modern visitor, nothing in the bedrooms recalls the past of such an attractive building. This being said, even if they are modern, it does not make them any less pleasant. The bathrooms are specially functional. The dining room, although sadly neglected, is still a comfortable staging post that deserves noting.

How to get there (Map 8): on the 'Diagonal'.

148

Astoria Hotel

08036 Barcelona
Calle Paris, 203
Tel. (9)3-209 83 11 - Fax (9)3-202 30 08

Category ★★★ **Rooms** 114 with air-conditioning, telephone, bath or shower, WC, satellite TV, safe and minibar; elevator. **Price** Single 12,700Pts, double 15,100Pts. **Meals** Breakfast 1,250Pts, served 7:00-11.00. **Restaurant** See pp. 247-250. **Credit cards** All major. **Pets** Dogs allowed. **Facilities** Parking. **Nearby** Sitges (beach) - Monastery of San Cugat del Valle - Montserrat - Vich; Prat golf course (9 and 18-Hole), San Cugat golf course (18-Hole). **Open** All year.

This beautiful hotel with its Art-Deco facade, even though only built in the 1950's, is in the residential quarter of Barcelona, the Estoril. A very solemn hallway, marble columns and large mirrors all set the tone. The rooms are double-glazed and decorated simply, but offer all the comforts. In the bathrooms some elements have been covered with marble. There is no restaurant but a bar with pleasant lamps has a snug atmosphere, along with an attractive rest lounge. The general ambiance is discreet and elegant.

How to get there (Map 8): on the 'Diagonal'.

Hotel Gran Vía

08007 Barcelona
Gran Vía, 642
Tel. (9)3-318 19 00 – Fax (9)3-318 99 97
Sr Garcia

Category ★★★ **Rooms** 53 with air-conditioning, telephone, bath, WC, TV, minibar.
Price Single 9,000Pts, double 12,000Pts. **Meals** Breakfast 600Pts, served 7:00-11:00.
Restaurant See pp.247-250. **Credit cards** All major. **Pets** Dogs not allowed. **Facilities**
Parking (2,300Pts). **Nearby** Sitges (beach) - Monastery of San Cugat del Valle -
Montserrat - Vich; Prat golf course (9 and 18-Hole), San Cugat golf course (18-Hole).
Open All year.

In the heart of Barcelona, the Hotel Gran Vía has been here since
1936. It was first of all a beautiful private hotel of which a large
part of the furniture and original pictures still remain. Without being
luxurious, the Gran Vía still has that charm of all cozy establishments
and one is rapidly won over by the snug atmosphere. After an
attractive hall, the arcaded gallery and the colonnade of the first floor,
one is a little disappointed by the lack of character of the rooms.
Though comfortable, they lack the glory of the public rooms with
their rococo style. The very beautiful dining room is now only used
for breakfast, served in summer on the sunny terrace behind the
building. The quieter rooms are also on this side. All in all the
welcome is warm.

How to get there *(Map 8): close to the Paza de Catalunya.*

Hotel Méridien Barcelone

08002 Barcelona
Ramblas, 111
Tel. (9)3-318 62 00 - Fax (9)3-301 77 76

Category ★★★★ **Rooms** 201 and 7 suites with air-conditioning, telephone, bath, WC, satellite TV, video and minibar; elevator - Wheelchair access. **Price** Single 26,000Pts, double 30,000Pts, suite 73,000Pts. **Meals** Breakfast 2,250Pts. **Restaurant** Service 13:00-15:30, 20:00-23:30; menu, also à la carte. Specialties: Mediterranean cooking. **Credit cards** All major. **Pets** Dogs not allowed. **Facilities** Garage. **Nearby** Sitges (beach) - Monastery of San Cugat del Valle - Montserrat - Vich; Prat golf course (9 and 18-Hole), San Cugat golf course (18-Hole). **Open** All year.

Here again the 'Ramblas' has been chosen to modernize an old hotel. The services are those of a grand hotel intended for a clientele of wealthy tourists or businessmen. One must however recognize the special effort that has been made in matters of decor. The lounges are luxurious. The rooms with their immense beds are furnished in the style of the 1930's, with an abundance of fabrics in soft colors that create an elegant and subtle atmosphere. If you would like to reserve a suite, then ask for 918. This is a hotel to stay to see the lights of the town, while also profiting from its voluptuous comfort. The interesting rates for weekends should be noted.

How to get there *(Map 8): on the Ramblas.*

Hotel Colón

08002 Barcelona
Avenida de la Catedral, 7
Tel. (9)3-301 14 04 – Fax (9)3-317 29 15
Sr Gretz Badia

Category ★★★★ **Rooms** 147 with air-conditioning, telephone, bath, WC, satellite TV and minibar; elevator. **Price** Single 15,500-18,400Pts, double 23,000Pts, executive 36,500Pts, suite 41,500Pts. **Meals** Breakfast 1,700Pts (buffet), served 7:00-11:00; half board + 4,800Pts, full board + 6,480Pts. **Restaurant** Service 13:00-15:00, 20:00-22:30; menu 3,500Pts, also à la carte. Specialties: Catalan and international cooking. **Credit cards** All major. **Pets** Dogs allowed. **Nearby** Sitges (beach) - Monastery of San Cugat del Valle - Montserrat - Vich; Prat golf course (9 and 18-Hole), San Cugat golf course (18-Hole). **Open** All year.

The Hotel Colón has an unequaled site: in the heart of the gothic quarter and facing the 13th-century cathedral. This is an institution for foreign tourists, and even if some fittings and equipment are now rather dated, it still remains a very agreeable hotel to live in. The ambiance is cosy, as with any good old hotel, making the lounges and bar a nice place to visit in the evenings. The rooms vary but one goes first for those on the top floor with their superb terraces. With the 'Ramblas' a few paces away, this is the ideal spot in Barcelona!

How to get there (Map 8): *facing the cathedral.*

Hotel Regencia Colón

08002 Barcelona
Avenida de la Catedral, 7
Tel. (9)3-318 98 58 - Fax (9)3-317 28 22
Sr Gretz Badia

Category ★★★ **Rooms** 55 with air-conditioning, telephone, bath or shower, WC, TV, safe and minibar; elevator. **Price** Single 8,600-11,600Pts, double 14,500Pts, triple 17,500Pts. **Meals** Breakfast 1,100Pts (buffet), served 7:00-11:00. **Restaurant** See pp 247-250. **Credit cards** All major. **Pets** Dogs allowed. **Facilities** Parking (2,500Pts). **Nearby** Sitges (beach) - Monastery of San Cugat del Valle - Montserrat - Vich; Prat golf course (9 and 18-Hole), San Cugat golf course (18-Hole). **Open** All year.

Situated just next to its 'big brother', the Regencia Colón is very much less expensive but offers the same convenient site, along with comfortable and well equiped rooms. Nothing is very original but with its vast and rather solemn entry hall this is a well-meaning hotel, which is very relaxing after a long walk through the small lanes of the gothic quarter or along the 'Ramblas'.

How to get there *(Map 8): facing the cathedral.*

Hotel Metropol

08002 Barcelona
Carreer Ample, 31
Tel. (9)3 310 51 00 – Fax (9)3 319 12 76
Sra Gema Mal

Category ★★★ **Rooms** 68 with air-conditioning, telephone, bath or shower, WC, satellite TV, minibar; elevator. **Price** Single 8,900Pts, double 11,900Pts. **Meals** Breakfast 1,000Pts, served 7:30-10:30. **No restaurant** (see pp. 247-250). **Credit cards** All major. **Pets** Dogs not allowed. **Nearby** Cimenterie became the Taller de arqutectura de Ricardo Bofill and Walden 7 in Sant Just Desvern - Sitges (beach) - Monastery of San Cugat del Valle -Montserrat - Vich - Prat golf course (9 and 18-Hole golf), San Cugat golf course (18-Hole). **Open** All year.

Among the small hotels in the Barrio Gotic, the Metropol is one of the best, nicely located between the Plaza Real and the port. The lobby, once the patio, is all in pink, a tradition in Spanish houses. The rooms are not large but very pleasant and enjoy good light because of their bay windows. Rooms on the second floor have balconies and we prefer the ones giving on the street. The decor is modernistic, dating from the Olympic Games held in Barcelona, and is marked by sober and elegant contemporary furniture and marble bathrooms. The hotel has no restaurant but you can enjoy Catalan specialties in the small bars and restaurants in the surrounding streets.

How to get there (Map 8): In the Old Town.

Hotel Jardí

08001 Barcelona
Pl. Sant Josep Oriol, 1
Tel. (9)3 301 59 00 - Fax (9)3 318 36 64

Rooms 39 with telephone, bath or shower, WC (10 with TV). **Price** Single 4,000Pts, double 6,500-7,700Pts, triple 7,200-9,200Pts. **Meals** Breakfast 750Pts. Served 8:30-11:30. **No restaurant** (see pp. 247-251). **Credit cards** All major. **Pets** Dogs not allowed. **Nearby** Cimenterie became the Taller de arqutectura de Ricardo Bofill and Walden 7 in Sant Just Desvern - Sitges (beach) - Monastery of San Cugat del Valle - Montserrat - Vich - Prat golf course (9- and 18-Hole golf), San Cugat golf course (18-Hole). **Open** All year.

The Jardì is included in this guide only because of its location on one of the prettiest squares in the neighborhood, one that is about as typical and popular as you ask for. It is in a small 19th-century building with a yellow exterior, simple and without much charm. The rooms are sober and undistinguished but very well kept up. Some of them offer a view on the Plaza del Pi but our favorites are those overlooking the Plaza Sant Josep Oriol.

How to get there (Map 8): in the Old Town near the Ramblas.

Hotel San Sebastián Playa

08870 Sitges (Barcelona)
Port Alegre, 53
Tel. (9)3-894 86 76 – Fax (9)3-894 04 30
Sr José Llaurado

Rooms 51 with air-conditioning, telephone, bath, WC, satellite TV, video, safe and minibar; elevator. **Price** Single 11,000-14,250Pts, double 14,500-20,000Pts, suite 21,260-25,500Pts (view on the see: + 3,500Pts). **Meals** Breakfast included, served 7:00-12:00; half board + 2,100Pts. **Restaurant** "La Concha" Service 13:30-16:00, 20:30-23:00; à la carte 3,200-6,500Pts. Specialties: Catalan and international cooking. **Credit cards** All major. **Pets** Dogs not allowed. **Facilities** Swimming pool, garage, parking. **Nearby** Monastery of Santes Creus - Monastery Santa Marìa Poblet - Barcelona - Costa Dorada; Terramar golf course (18-Hole). **Open** All year.

The Hotel San Sebastiàn Playa is relatively new and built in a neo-classical style recalling the architecture of the palaces of the early years of the century. Its site in the seaside resort of Sitges is incomparable at only a hundred meters from the historic center and facing the sea, and it promises its clientele in the front rooms some exceptional morning wakenings. Prices vary with room location. In the reception rooms the decor is modern and uses beautiful and elegant materials. One finds the same sobriety in the rooms, which gives them a rather cold atmosphere, but all are very comfortable. The beach is right close by but the hotel has its own attractive and well sheltered swimming pool. A very good address in this tourist town, very animated in summer, which allows you to alternate calm and distractions.

How to get there (Map 8): 39km south of Barcelona via C246, corniche road along the sea.

Hotel Romántic

08870 Sitges (Barcelona)
Sant Isidre, 33
Tel. (9)3-894 83 75 – Fax (9)3-894 81 67
Sr Vendrell i Sobrer

Rooms 55 with telephone, bath or shower, WC. **Price** Single 6,600-9,000Pts, double 9,400-12,000Pts, triple + 2,800-3,650Pts. **Meals** Breakfast included, served 7:00-11:00. **Restaurant** See pp. 251. **Credit cards** All major. **Pets** Dogs not allowed. **Nearby** Barcelona - Costa Dorada ; Terramar golf course (18-Hole). **Open** Oct 15 - Mar 31.

This is a charming hotel in a beautiful house in the town of Sitges, some forty kilometers away from the Catalan capital, and very much the fashionable beach. All the hip citizens of Barcelona are to be found here, and the ambiance in summer is exceptional, especially in the evenings at aperitif- and tapas-time, when all the parties start–only to finish in the wee hours of the morning! The rooms are indeed well kept but rather basic and only fitted with showers. On the other hand, the atmosphere is very lively. Painters staying at the hotel have left their frescoes on the walls, while from 6pm onwards one can have a drink, with classical music, at the bar. The shaded garden has many small corners for reading or unwinding in full peace and quiet. The welcome is very friendly and the atmosphere very informal, but the hotel is better suited for bachelors than for family groups.

How to get there (*Map 8*): *29km south of Barcelona via the C246, the corniche along the sea coast.*

1998

Termes La Garriga

08530 La Garriga (Barcelona)
Banys, 23
Tel. (9)3 871 70 86 – Fax (9)3 871 78 87
Sr Monnet – Sr Vola

Category ★★★★ Rooms 22 with air-conditioning, telephone, bath, WC, satellite TV, minibar, safe; elevator. **Price** Single 9,900-15,400Pts, double 16-24,000Pts, suite 30,960-47,160Pts. **Meals** Breakfast 1,500Pts; served 8:00-11:00; half board + 5,100Pts. **Restaurant** Service 13:30-16:00, 20:30-23:00; menus and also à la carte. **Credit cards** All major. **Pets** Dogs not allowed. **Facilities** Swimming pool, sauna, Health Center, bikes, parking and garage (800Pts). **Nearby** Barcelona - Costa Daurada; Tarramr golf course (18-Hole). **Open** All year.

If the idea of getting back in shape should suddenly appeal to you, the Termes La Garriga would be an excellent choice as it neatly combines all that is necessary for doing just that with a setting and ambiance reminiscent of the glorious days of Biarritz and Baden Baden. Nothing here even smacks of a clinical atmosphere; this a place where executives can get plenty of exercise both indoors and out for a few days while the ladies can get themselves ready for the summer. The rooms are elegant and each is decorated differently. The garden has a swimming pool for those not interested in the hotel's fitness programs. A few kilometers from Barcelona, this is a useful place to know as it offers a base from which to visit the Catalan region and also take advantage of the arts of relaxation which La Garriga so skillfully practices.

How to get there *(Map 8): 35km north of Barcelona via A7 or N152. Take the La Garriga exit. The hotel is well indicated in the city center.*

Fonda Europa

08400 Granollers (Barcelona)
Anselm Clavé, 1
Tel. (9)3 870 03 12 - Fax (9)3 870 79 01
Sr Font

Category ★★★ **Rooms** 7 with air-conditioning, telephone, bath, WC, satellite TV, minibar, safe; elevator. **Price** Single 8,000Pts, double 12,000Pts. **Meals** Breakfast included, served 8:00-11:00. **Restaurant** Service 13:30-16:00, 20:30-23:00; à la carte: 3,000-4,000Pts. **Credit cards** All major. **Pets** Dogs allowed. **Facilities** Garage (1,000Pts). **Nearby** Barcelona - Costa Daurada; Tarramr golf course (18-Hole). **Open** All year.

This is one of the old hotels that everyone in the province of Barcelona knows, especially for its restaurant which is both highly popular and very much in keeping with local traditions. The Perellada family has been in this lovely building with its orange façade adorned with eye-catching friezes since 1714. Here, you find rooms very nicely furnished offering refinement and good taste plus particularly efficient service. We especially liked Room 7 with its bathroom reminiscent of old Pompeii. In addition, two days a week, Thursdays and Sundays, are market days here in this small and friendly city.

How to get there *(Map 8): 28km north of Barcelona via A7 or N152. Take the La Garriga exit. The hotel is well indicated in the city center.*

Parador Duques de Cardona

08261 Cardona (Barcelona)
Castillo de Cardona
Tel. (9)3-869 12 75 – Fax (9)3-869 16 36
Sr Soria Alvarez

Category ★★★★ **Rooms** 60 with air-conditioning, telephone, bath, WC, TV, (50 with minibar); elevator. **Price** Double 15,000-17,500Pts. **Meals** Breakfast 1,300Pts, served 8:00-11:00. **Restaurant** Service 13:30-16:00, 20:30-22:30; menu 3,500Pts, also à la carte. Specialties: Catalan cooking. **Credit cards** All major. **Pets** Dogs not allowed. **Facilities** Parking. **Nearby** In Cardona: Church Sant Vicenç - Salt mountain of Salina. **Open** All year.

Raised by the Dukes of Cardona, this fortress was built at the very beginning of the Middle Ages and modified over the course of the centuries, and for a long time served as a military barracks. Despite its rather impressive proportions, the new occupants have learned how to make the place welcoming: ceilings with caissons and numerous copper-colored carpets all help warm the public rooms. The bedrooms are attractive and well furnished. The view, superb in earler times, is now somwhat compromised as Cardona is one of the major mining towns of the north of the country.

How to get there *(Map 8): 97km northwest of Barcelona to Manresa, then C1410.*

Gran Hotel Rey don Jaime

08860 Castelldefels (Barcelona)
Torre Barona - Avenida del Hotel, 22
Tel. (9)3-665 13 00 - Fax (9)3-665 18 01
Sra Nuria Rubios

Category ★★★★ **Rooms** 240 with air-conditioning, telephone, bath, WC, TV and minibar. **Price** Double 14,000-18,000Pts, suite 20,500Pts. **Meals** Breakfast included, served 7:30-10:30; half board and full board, + 4,000Pts. **Restaurant** Service 13:30-15:30, 20:30-22:00; menu 3,900Pts. Specialties: arroz negro. **Credit cards** All major. **Pets** Dogs allowed. **Facilities** Indoor swimming pool, squash, fitness center, garage, parking. **Nearby** Sitges (beach) - Villafranca del Peredes - Barcelona; Vallomanas golf course (18-hole). **Open** All year.

The Gran Hotel Rey don Jaime is right next to the Barona Tower dating from the 12th century, which, with the chateau, dominated the ancient town of Castrum de Fels, today's Castelldefels. Situated on a small hill, it has a pretty view over the 'gran playa' of Barcelona. The hotel is of very good standing and comfort reigns throughout. Recently restructured, itl has been enormously enlarged and the rooms are vast, some with terraces. There is a shady garden with a pretty swimming pool set at the foot of the tower, all adding to the calm of the site. The proximity to Barcelona makes this an ideal staging post on a Costa Brava that is too overpopulated in the summer.

How to get there *(Map 8): 20km south of Barcelona via C246.*

Hotel Llicorella

08880 Cubelles (Barcelona)
Carret. C 246 – Camino de San Antonio, 101
Tel. (9)3-895 00 44 – Fax (9)3-895 24 17 – Sra de Adria

Category ★★★★ Rooms 16 with air-conditioning, telephone, bath, WC, satellite TV, safe and minibar. **Price** Single 10,000Pts, double 13,000-20,000Pts, suite 20,000Pts. **Meals** Breakfast 1,100Pts, served 7:00-11:00; half board 15,370Pts, full board 19,540Pts (per pers., 3 days min.). **Restaurant** Service 13:30-16:00, 20:30-23:00; menu 5,618Pts, also à la carte. Specialties: Pimientos del piquillo rellenos de gambas - Higado de pato sobre cebolla y manzana confitadas - Tocinillo de cielo sobre coulis de frambuesa. **Credit cards** All major. **Pets** Dogs not allowed in the restaurant (+ 530Pts). **Facilities** Parking. **Nearby** Sitges (beach) - Villafranca del Penedes - Barcelona. **Open** All year.

Hardly has one left the many lights of Barcelona than one enters into the heart of Catalonia, where stretches of countryside ever more beautiful than the preceding one follow after each other. In one of these privileged little corners you will find the Hotel Llicorella, a handsome stone residence with a careful recipe of elegance and sobriety. The owner is known to a large number of Catalans as he ran a well-known picture gallery in Barcelona, and has remained in contact with many artists. Still a lover of the arts, he has filled his hotel with many works of recognized artists. All details are aesthetic. The kitchen is run by Renata Dabbert, whose excellent cooking is an original interpretation of traditional Catalan culinary tradition combined with touches of French cuisine. The rooms, are each dedicated to a different painter, and mix a taste for art with refined comfort. There is also a very good restaurant.

How to get there *(Map 8): 54km southwest of Barcelona via A7, exit Villafranca (No. 29), then C244 and C246.*

Hotel San Bernat

08460 Montseny (Barcelona)
Tel. (9)3-847 30 11 - Fax (9)3-847 30 11
Sr Pérez

Category ★★★ **Rooms** 21 with telephone, bath, WC and TV. **Price** Half board 8,560Pts (per pers.). **Meals** Breakfast included, served 8:00-11:00. **Restaurant** Service 13:30-16:00, 20:30-22:00; menu 2,710Pts, also à la carte. Specialties: Catalan cooking. **Credit cards** All major. **Pets** Dogs not allowed. **Facilities** Parking. **Nearby** Sierra of Montseny from San Celoni to Massanet de la Selva, 120 km (Ermitage de Santa Fe, Brull, Tona, Viladrau). **Open** All year.

One gets to the hotel via a small winding and very green-lined lane that climbs up to the high ground of Montseny. The entrance is really attractive: a building covered with ivy, lawns on which the owner's Saint Bernard dogs are playing, and a small pond reflecting the large willow trees. The rooms, small and simple, are pleasant and in good taste, while the bathrooms are ravishing. The quietest rooms face the valley. Do not miss taking your tea on the lawn behind the hotel, to enjoy both the irreplaceable view over the valley and neighboring mountains, and the calm of the spot. The pretty little church is where Saint Bernard halted in earlier days. The San Bernat is the ideal place for a relaxing country stay if no very special reception is expected.

How to get there (Map 8): 70km northeast of Barcelona; or 8km northwest of Montseny, on the road to Tona.

Parador de Vich

08500 Vich (Barcelona)
Tel. (9)3-888 72 11 - Fax (9)3-888 73 11
Sr Martinez

Category ★★★★ **Rooms** 36 with air-conditioning, telephone, bath, WC, TV and minibar; elevator. **Price** Double 13,500-15,000Pts. **Meals** Breakfast 1,300Pts, served 8:00-10:30. **Restaurant** Service 13:30-16:00, 20:30-22:30; menu 3,500Pts, also à la carte. Specialties: Zarzuela de pescado y mariscos, semi-tomba. **Credit cards** All major. **Pets** Dogs not allowed. **Facilities** Swimming pool, tennis, garage, parking. **Nearby** In Vich; Cathedral and Episcopal museum - Costa Dorada - Costa Brava - Barcelona. **Open** All year.

The architecture and decor of this parador are not its major strengths, and the building put up in 1972 under the Franco regime is massive and hardly welcoming. The interior arrangements are not in the best taste either. But its greatest quality is its site. For apart from its isolated setting 14 kilometers from Vich, which makes it quiet and restful, it also has the advantage of a magnificent panorama over the Pantana de Sau lake and the Guilleries massif. It is imperative to ask for a front room with a balcony. The swimming pool is very delightful, facing the lake and in the midst of a well-kept garden.

How to get there (Map 8): *69km north of Barcelona via N152; 15km from Vich, towards Roda de Ter.*

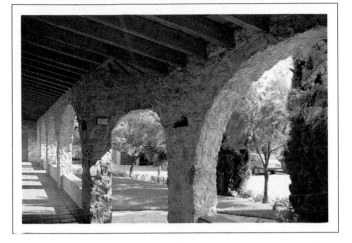

Hotel Mas Pau

17742 Avinyonet de Puigventos
Carretera de Figueres a Olot
Tel. (9)72-54 61 54 - Fax (9)72-54 63 26 - Sr T. Gerez
Web: http://www.6temps.com.maspau

Category ★★★★ **Rooms** 7 with air-conditioning, telephone, bath, WC, satellite TV, safe and minibar. **Price** Double 9,000-13,000Pts, suite 13,000-15,000Pts. **Meals** Breakfast 1,200Pts, served 7:15-10:00. **Restaurant** Service 13:00-16:00, 20:00-23:00; closed Sun night and Mon, in summer, closed Mon lunch; à la carte 4,000-5,500Pts. **Credit cards** All major. **Pets** Dogs not allowed. **Facilities** Swimming pool, parking. **Nearby** In Figueres Museu Dali (Salvador Dali museum) - Cadaqués - Massanet de Cabrenys - Gerona. **Open** Mar 16 - Jan 14.

If you decide to stop at Figueres to visit the famous Salvador Dali museum, a detour via Avinyonet is a must. This is where the 'Mas Pau' is to be found, one of the best known gastronomic addresses in the area. A hotel has recently been added, with charm only equalled by its quality. This ancient farm built in the 16th century is right in the country, surrounded by fields. The rooms have been arranged in a new annexe, in the same spirit as the public rooms in the main building. More modern, they also bear witness to the exquisite taste of the owners. It is beautiful, functional and comfortable, with friendly and stylish personnel.

How to get there *(Map 9): 58km south of Perpignan; 42km from Gerona via A7, exit Figueres, then take the road to Olot.*

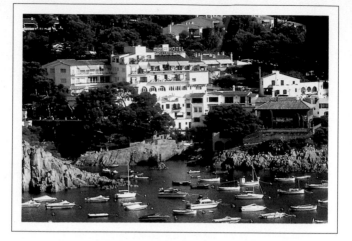

Hotel Aigua Blava

Aigua Blava 17255 Begur (Gerona)
Playa de Fornells
Tel. (9)72-62 20 58 – Fax (9)72-62 21 12

Category ★★★★ Rooms 85 with telephone, bath or shower, WC, TV and minibar.
Price Single 10,000-14,160Pts, double 12,500-17,000Pts, suite 16,900-22,800Pts.
Meals Breakfast 1,500Pts, served 8:00-11:00; half board + 5,000Pts, full board
+ 6,800Pts (per per., 3 days min.). **Restaurant** Service 13:30-16:00, 20:30-23:00;
menu 3,500Pts, also à la carte. Specialties: Spanish and international cooking. **Credit
cards** All major. **Pets** Small dogs allowed. **Facilities** Swimming pool, tennis, volley
ball, garage, parking. **Nearby** Pals - Costa Brava - Barcelona - Gerona - Pals golf
course (18-Hole). **Open** Feb 22 - Nov 8.

At the head of a charming creek where rocks covered with pine
trees surround the limpid sea, the Aigua Blava enjoys a really
beautiful site. It is made up of a group of buildings set around a very
attractive small and flowered park. Go for a room with a terrace
looking over the sea. With their bright moquette and white walls the
rooms are both comfortable and welcoming. As night falls the
swimming pool is floodlit and its glow mixes with the lights of the
villas all around, thus creating a magic atmosphere. Alas, the cuisine
does not live up to the standards of the rest.

How to get there *(Map 9): on the coast north of Barcelona; 46km east of Gerona
via A7, exit No. 6.*

Hotel Jordi's

17255 Begur (Gerona)
Apartado, 47
Tel. (9)72-30 15 70 - Fax (9)72-61 01 12 - Jordi y Maria

Category ★★ **Rooms** 8 with bath. **Price** Double 5,000-7,000Pts. **Meals** Breakfast 600Pts. **Restaurant** Service 13:00-16:00, 20:00-23:00; (in winter, the week ends only); à la carte 3,500Pts. Specialties: Suquet de pescados - Caldereta de langouste - Filete al queso de cabra y bayas de hencero. **Credit cards** Amex, Visa, Eurocard, MasterCard. **Pets** Dogs allowed. **Facilities** Parking. **Nearby** Pals - Costa Brava - Barcelona - Gerona - Pals golf course (18-Hole). **Open** All year .

This is a very good location well away from the surrounding confusion, and personally run by Jordi. The beautiful house is on the high ground that dominates the surrounding country, and is set among cypresses and pine trees that give a welcoming shade and cool. Eight rooms have been arranged on two levels with very great care; they are beautifully simple, their wood furniture married with cooling floor tiles, their bathrooms impeccable. On the ground floor the rooms all have terraces, but those on the upper floor (the house is built on a slope) have smaller windows. In the restaurant hall around the open fireplace, or on the big terrace protected from the sun, you will feel the original atmosphere of this Catalan house. The cuisine is another strong point with delicious specialties varying with arrivals at the market. The welcome is very friendly.

How to get there (Map 9): on the coast north of Barcelona; 46km east of Gerona via A7, exit No. 6.

Chalet del Golf

17463 Bolvir-Puigcerda (Gerona)
Tel. (9)72-88 09 62 - Fax (9)72-88 09 66
Sr Lucarini

Category ★★★ **Rooms** 16 with telephone, bath, WC, TV; elevator. **Price** Single 8,000-10,000Pts, double 12,000-14,000Pts. **Meals** Breakfast 1,250Pts, served from 8:30; half board + 3,750Pts, full board + 6,000Pts. **Restaurant** Service 13:30-16:00, 20:30-22:30; menu 3,300Pts, also à la carte. **Credit cards** All major. **Pets** Dogs allowed in the rooms. **Facilities** Swimming pool, tennis, squash, parking. **Nearby** Cerdanya Valley - Andorra (a duty free principality) - Bellver de Cerdaña (fishing in the rio Segre) - Skiing (La Molina and Maranges) - Llivia; Cerdaña golf course (18-Hole). **Open** All year except fifteen days before Christmas.

Naturally there is a beautiful golf course while the house that serves as hotel and restaurant is no less charming. Woodlands nearby make timber easily available, and great use of it has been made in decorating the hotel, giving it a very warm atmosphere. All the rooms look out over the golf course, and they are simple, but that doesn't matter much—they are mainly used by sports lovers, who spend most of their days outside. In contrast, the management has fitted out a snug restaurant and lounges that make one think of Great Britain.

How to get there *(Map 8): 172km north of Barcelona via N152, then at Puigcerdá via C1313.*

Hotel Torre del Remei

17463 Bolvir de Cerdanya (Gerona)
Cami Reial
Tel. (9)72-14 01 82 - Fax (9)72-14 04 49 - Sr Boix

Category ★★★★★ **Rooms** 4 and 7 suites with air-conditioning, telephone, bath with jacuzzi, WC, satellite TV and safe; elevator. **Price** Double 26,000-31,000Pts, suite 40,000-60,000Pts. **Meals** Breakfast 2,800Pts, served 8:00-12:00. **Restaurant** Service 13:00-16:00, 21:00-23:00; à la carte 6,000Pts. Specialties: Terrina de escalivada y salsa de mostaza - Cola de buey guisada a las siete horas - Medallones de venado marinado con salsa de trufa. **Credit cards** All major. **Pets** Dogs allowed (except in restaurant). **Facilities** Swimming pool, parking. **Nearby** Cerdanya Valley - Andorra (a duty free principality) - Bellver de Cerdaña (fishing in the rio Segre) - Skiing (La Molina and Maranges) - Llivia; Cerdaña golf course (18-Hole). **Open** All year.

Only fifteen minutes from the border at Bourg–Madame in a superb country of vast prairies and mountains in the real heart of Catalonia, the Hotel Torre del Remei has been installed in a beautiful aristocratic residence dating from the begining of the century. Despite renovation the building has lost nothing of its original character, while the decor is remarkable, allying luxury, charm and comfort. Here are polished floors, crystal lamps and caisson ceilings, alongside contemporary art and furniture with studied lines. One has to salute the restaurant and the personnel, stylish yet efficient, and attentive to your slightest request. Thanks to its exceptional situation, the Torre del Remei, open summer and winter, attracts both sports lovers (close to a golf course and to ski resorts) and lovers of nature and good food.

How to get there *(Map 8): 172km north of Barcelona via N152, then 2km from Puigcerdá via C1313.*

1998

Playa Sol

17488 Cadaqués (Gerona)
Playa Pianc, 3
Tel. (9)72-25 81 00/25 81 40 - Fax (9)72-25 80 54

Category ★★★ **Rooms** 45 and 5 suites with air-conditioning, telephone, bath, WC, TV; elevator. **Price** Double 9,900-16,900Pts. **Meals** Breakfast 1,100Pts, served 8:00-11:30. **No Restaurant** in hotel (See pp. 251-252). **Credit cards** All major. **Pets** Dogs allowed. **Facilities** Swimming pool, tennis, parking (1300Pts). **Nearby** In Cadaqués: museum Perrot Moore and Church - Port-Lligat - Costa Brava. **Open** Feb 11 - Jan 6.

You travel a magnificent road overlooking the sea with wind-blown vegetation on either side and finally arrive at Cadaqués. Along with Port Lligat, Cadaqués had its illustrious ambassador in the person of Salvador Dalí who made this small fishing port world famous. This fact may explain why it has retained a certain authenticity with its small white houses lining the bay and its brightly-colored old fishing boats. The hotel was built quite recently but fits into its surroundings very nicely and its location is exceptional as it faces the port and the small beach. The rooms offer more comfort than charm but most have a balcony looking out on the sea. This surely explains why it is usually full to capacity in the summertime. For this reason you are advised to reserve well in advance.

How to get there *(Map 9): 69km north of Gerona.*

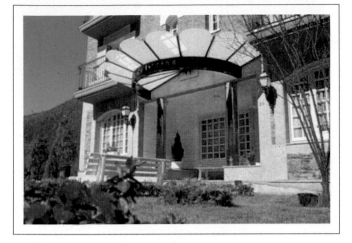

Hotel Edelweiss

17867 Camprodón (Gerona)
Carret. de Sant Joan, 28
Tel. (9)72-74 09 13 – Fax (9)72-74 07 04
Sr Rous

Category ★★★ **Rooms** 21 with telephone, bath, WC and TV; elevator. **Price** Double 9,950Pts. **Meals** Breakfast 700-1,300Pts, served 8:00-10:30. **No Restaurant** in hotel. **Credit cards** All major. **Pets** Dogs allowed. **Facilities** Parking. **Nearby** In Camprodón: Church of San Pedro - Beget (San Cristófol Church and the bell tower) - Llanars (San Esteve Church) - Molló (Santa Cecilia Church) - Ripoll (Santa Marìa Church) - Setcases; Camprodón golf course (18-Hole). **Open** All year except Christmas.

The facade is welcoming and one step inside you immediately notice the refinement of this place. The owner claims he decorated his hotel just as if it was his own home. The pieces of furniture are only copies but not one fault can be found with them. The bathrooms are harmonious. In the dining room, only breakfasts are served—but what breakfast! A sideboard recalls those of our grandmothers, with their large pots of home-made jams, onto which bright labels have been stuck to make them more chic. A warm welcome and plenty of attention mean you will certainly want to keep the hotel's card close at hand.

How to get there *(Map 8): 133km north of Barcelona via N152 to Ripoll, then C151.*

La Mère Michelle

17121 Corça (Gerona)
Calle Mayor, 11
Tel. (9)72-63 05 35 - Fax (9)72-63 05 35
Sra Michelle Amram

Rooms 3 with bath and WC. **Price** Double 9,000Pts. **Meals** Breakfast 1,200Pts, served 8:00-13:00. **Restaurant** Service 12:30-16:30, 20:30-23:30; menu 2,500-3,000Pts. Specialties: French cooking. **Credit cards** Not accepted. **Pets** Small dogs allowed. **Nearby** Gerona - Figueres (Salvador Dali Museum); 10 golf courses. **Open** July, Aug, Sept and all weekends and holidays out of season. Except in Feb.

Close to Gerona everybody knows the small restaurant La Mère Michelle, opened by a French woman living in Spain. The small village of Corça is very well sited for holidays, just a few kilometers away from the regional capital of Gerona, at about twenty kilometers from the beaches and surrounded by golf courses. All the conviviality of a family home has been retained: beams and old furniture give a lot of warmth to the decor. It is the same in the restaurant, very small, where one has to rush to reserve if you wish to try the good French specialties of the house: scents of Mediterranean cuisine but also all the generosity of the cooking of Alsace. Three rooms have recently been opened, prettily decorated and comfortable, but more in the spirit of a boarding house than a traditional hotel (no TV, no direct phone but on the other hand, a small fridge in each room along with tea- and coffee-making facilities and room service). This is a non-typical address for Spain.

How to get there *(Map 9): 30km from Gerona via E15 exit Gerona North, then towards La Bisbal.*

172

Hotel Grévol

17869 Llanars (Gerona)
Carretera de Camprodòn
Tel. (9)72-74 10 13 - Fax (9)72-74 10 87 - Sr Sole

Category ★★★★ **Rooms** 36 with telephone, bath or shower, WC, TV, and minibar; elevator. **Price** Double 15,250-18,700Pts. **Meals** Breakfast 1,375Pts (buffet); half board 11,475-13,200Pts, full board 13,750-15,475Pts (per pers., 3 days min.). **Restaurant** Service 13:00-15:30, 21:00-22:30; closed Mon, 15 days in May and Nov; menu 3,850Pts, also à la carte. Specialties: regional and international cooking. **Credit cards** Amex, Visa, Eurocard, MasterCard. **Pets** Dogs not allowed. **Facilities** Indoor swimming pool, parking. **Nearby** In Llanars: San Esteve Church - Camprodón (Church of San Pedro) - Beget (San Cristófol Church and the bell tower) - Molló (Santa Cecilia Church) - Ripoll (Santa Marìa Church) - Setcases; Camprodón golf course (18-Hole). **Open** All year.

The recently built and very well-equipped Grévol recalls those large Austrian chalet-hotels. The Camprodòn region attracts a family clientele wanting to get some fresh air in the refreshing setting of the Pyrenees, and to do engage in an open-air sport such as golf, skiing or horseback riding. The hotel rooms are charming with panelled walls, furniture in wood and oak in Tyrolian style, which is also found in the main room of the restaurant around an open fireplace. All this creates a very comfortable atmosphere. With a more than complete games room/hall (bowling, table football, billiards, etc.), children will be more than happy. After a day's hiking the family can then swim in the covered pool or unwind in the huge jacuzzi.

How to get there *(Map 8): 129km north of Barcelona via N152 to Ripoll, then C151. At 3km on the road from Camprodòn to Setcases.*

Hotel Santa Marta

17310 Lloret de Mar (Gerona)
Playa de Santa Cristina
Tel. (9)72–36 49 04 – Fax (9)72–36 92 80
Sr Noguera

Category ★★★★ **Rooms** 78 with air-conditioning, telephone, bath, WC, satellite TV and minibar; elevator. **Price** Single 12,000-19,000Pts, double 17,000-34,000Pts, suite 26,5000-46,000Pts. **Meals** Breakfast 1,750Pts, served 8:00-11:00; half board + 7,700Pts, full board + 10,900Pts (per pers.). **Restaurant** Service 13:30-15:30, 20:30-22:30; menu 5,950Pts, also à la carte. Specialties: Rollitos de salmon con cangrejos - Suquet de mero. **Credit cards** All major. **Pets** Dogs allowed in the rooms (+ 800 Pts). **Facilities** Swimming pool, tennis (1,000Pts), beach, parking. **Nearby** Costa Brava - Road from Lloret del Mar to Tossa del Mar; Gerona. **Open** Feb 1 - Dec 15.

This was the most fashionable hotel on the Costa Brava thirty years ago. It is certainly modern, and with an exceptional situation that is unique in the region. It is lost in woodland, with a facade clinging to the rocks and facing the sea. There is also a fully equipped private beach, and all this in such divine peace and quiet. The rooms are very comfortable, the decoration classic (perhaps too much so) and the hospitality is kind and thoughtful !

How to get there *(Map 9): 39km south of Gerona via A7, exit No. 9; 3km from Lloret.*

Cal Borrell

17539 Meranges (Gerona)
Regreso, 3
Tel. (9)72-88 00 33 - Fax (9)72-88 01 44
Sr Forn

Category ★★ **Rooms** 8 with telephone, bath and WC. **Price** Double 8,000-9,000Pts. **Meals** Breakfast 700-800Pts, served 9:00-11:00; half board + 3,500Pts, full board + 6,000Pts. **Restaurant** Service 13:00-17:00, 21:00-23:00; à la carte 3,500-5,500Pts. Specialties: Pork, game. **Credit cards** Visa, Eurocard, MasterCard. **Pets** Dogs not allowed. **Facilities** Parking. **Nearby** Cerdanya Valley - Andorra (a duty free principality) - Bellver de Cerdaña (fishing in the rio Segre) - Skiing (La Molina and Maranges) - Llivia; Cerdaña golf course (18-Hole). **Open** Apr 1 - Dec 31 and the weekends all the year.

Cal Borrell is a former farmhouse refurbished and transformed into a hotel in the heart of a picture-perfect mountain village. The rooms have magnificent wooden ceilings and beams, and all have a view over the valley. Try to get the room called 'The house on the prairie', with its mezzanine and superb panorama. There is a guaranteed warm mountain atmosphere, perfect for relaxing and rest. One also appreciates the good cuisine served in the restaurant as the Cal Borrell is known for its excellent table.

How to get there *(Map 8): 191km north of Barcelona via N152 to Puigcerdá, then C1313 for about 7km; take the small road to the right.*

Hotel Carles Camós Big-Rock

17250 Playa de Aro (Gerona)
Barri de Fanals, 5
Tel. (9)72-81 80 12 - Fax (9)72-81 89 71
Sr Camós

Category ★★★★ Suites 5 with air-conditioning, telephone, bath, WC, TV, and minibar. **Price** Suite 16,000-24,000Pts. **Meals** Breakfast 1,150Pts, served 8:30-11:00. **Restaurant** Service 13:00-15:30, 20:30-22:30; à la carte 3,600-4,800Pts. Specialties: Lomo de merluza con patatitas - Suquet de rape y langostinos - Capriccio de crema con fresitas. **Credit cards** All major. **Pets** Dogs allowed. **Facilities** Swimming pool, parking. **Nearby** Gerona - Costa Brava; Costa Brava golf course (18-Hole). **Open** Feb 1 - Dec 31, closed Mon and Sun night in winter.

Known first for its restaurant, Big-Rock also has a few rooms. Isolated in the country, this is a large and ancient building refurbished with taste in the last century. The owner is an excellent chef and great personality, as he founded the 'Brotherhood of happy Joy', and everything with him is genuine and simply breathes fun. The flowered terraces glory in the sun while the furniture smells sweetly of polished wood. The rooms are in fact all suites, and deserve a special mention for their luxurious amenities. Tasteful pictures decorate the walls, so why be surprised if the King of Spain himself sometimes passes by here ?

How to get there *(Map 9): 37km southeast of Gerona via C250.*

Castell de Peratallada

17113 Peratallada (Girona)
Plaça del Castell, 1
Tel. (9)72-63 40 21 - Fax (9)72-63 40 11 - M. Cesar Sancho

Category ★★★★ **Rooms** 3 and 2 suites with air-conditioning, telephone, bath, WC, safe and minibar. **Price** Double 22,500Pts, suite 27,500Pts. **Meals** Breakfast included, served 9:00-11:00. **Restaurant** Service 13:00-16:00, 20:00-23:30, closed Sun and Mon evening in winter; à la carte 6,000Pts. **Credit cards** All major. **Pets** Dogs not allowed. **Facilities** Gerona - La Costa Brava. **Open** All year.

To the north of Barcelona between Girona and the Mediterranean is a region known as the Ampudán where villages dating from the Middle Ages proudly maintain Catalan traditions. Peratallada, classed as a National Monument, is a genuine treasure of medieval architecture where you will find innumerable examples, among them a vast trench dug in the rock surrounding the city. The city's name - Peratallada is, literally translated, «carved stone.» The hotel, nicely situated in a pedestrians-only zone, is in an 11th-century castle. The ground floor has two long hallways with high vaulted ceilings, a splendid decor for the lounge bar and restaurant. There are few rooms in this luxurious hotel and the furniture, rugs and paintings are absolutely authentic period pieces. It is an ideal place for receptions although the hotel could make an effort to diminish the guests' inconvenience while they are going on. The village is truly historic but at the same time very lively with art galleries, artisans' shops and antiques stores lining a number of its small streets.

How to get there *(Map 9): 120km north of Barcelona via A7 (Barcelona/La Jonquera), take the northern Girona exit; then C-255 towards La Bisbal; 1km after La Bisbal, turn left for Peratallada which is 4km further.*

El Moli

17706 Pont de Molins (Gerona)
Carret. las Escaules
Tel. (9)72-52 92 71 – Fax (9)72-52 91 01 – Sr Llado Grau
E-mail: molipark@speedrom.es

Category ★★ **Rooms** 8 with telephone, bath and WC. **Price** Double 9,500Pts. **Meals** Breakfast 600Pts, served 7:30-10:00. **Restaurant** Service 13:15-15:30, 19:30-22:30; à la carte 2,500-3,800Pts. Specialties: Regional cooking. **Credit cards** All major. **Pets** Dogs allowed in the restaurant. **Facilities** Tennis (800Pts), parking. **Nearby** Figueres (Salvador Dali museum) - Cadaqués - Gerona - Massaner de Cabrenys. **Open** Holy Week - Oct.

Set back from a country road stands a former 18th-century mill, restored and converted into a hotel-restaurant some ten years ago. Here it is clear that someone loves secondhand things: the mill stones now serve as low tables; all the sideboards, cupboards, troughs and beds were bought from local antique dealers. Five meters in front of the hotel terrace flows the River Monje, lined with magnificent trees. The restaurant has a good reputation and attracts a French clientele, as the frontier is only some twenty kilometers away. The rooms are charming, while No. 102 is the largest and overlooks the river. Taking count of the very reasonable prices as well, 'El Moli' certainly merits a detour.

How to get there *(Map 9): 43km north of Gerona via A7, exit No. 2.*

Hostal de la Gavina

17248 S' Agaró (Gerona)
Plaza de la Rosaleda
Tel. (9)72-32 11 00 – Fax (9)72-32 15 73
Sra Requena

Category ★★★★ **Rooms** 74 with air-conditioning, telephone, bath, WC, TV, video, safe and minibar; elevator. **Price** Single 19,800-27,000Pts, double 22,500-39,500Pts, suite 30,500-47,500Pts. **Meals** Breakfast 2,100Pts, served 7:30-11:30; half board + 7,900Pts, + 11,800Pts (per pers.). **Restaurant** Service 13:00-15:30, 20:30-23:30; menu 6,000Pts; à la carte. «Grill Candlelight», open on the evening; à la carte, 4,600-6,650Pts. Specialties: Scampi candlelight. **Credit cards** All major. **Pets** Dogs not allowed. **Facilities** Swimming pool, sauna, paddle-tennis, parking. **Nearby** Gerona - Costa Brava; Costa Brava golf course (18-Hole). **Open** Holy Week - Oct 20.

This is an old house that the owners transformed little by little into a hotel and then a hotel 'de luxe'. It enjoys an enviable situation: all rooms, the flowery terrace and the patio have a superb view over the sea. The rooms are also all different and personalized. If you have the means, go for the royal suite, but you have to pay out in the Louis XV style as well !

How to get there (Map 9): 34km southeast of Gerona via C250.

Balneario Termas Orión

17404 Santa Colomá de Farnés (Gerona)
Tel. (9)72-84 00 65 - Fax (9)72-84 04 66
Sr Campeny

Category ★★ Rooms 66 with telephone, bath or shower, WC (40 with TV); elevator.
Price Single 4,000-6350Pts, double 6,000-10,500Pts, triple 8,300-11,600Pts. **Meals**
Breakfast 600Pts, served 8:30-10:00; full board 7,275-9,600Pts (per per.).
Restaurant With air-conditioning. Service 13:30-15:00, 20:30-22:00; menu 2,100-
2150Pts, also à la carte. Specialties: Catalan cooking. **Credit cards** Visa, Eurocard,
MasterCard. **Pets** Dogs not allowed. **Facilities** Indoor swimming pool, tennis (700Pts),
parking. **Nearby** Thermal station - Gerona. **Open** Feb 15 - Jan 15.

On leaving the village and at the end of an alley of huge trees,
you come upon this gleaming while building with stone
columns. Built in the last century, the hotel has kept all its allure and
atmosphere: everything here has the feel of times past. A
gramophone, a magic lantern, a collection of old spectacles, all seem
to have always been here. There is even a lounge-theater (the former
owner was a great actress). The natural springs have been completely
refurbished in recent times, and only the mosaics of the earlier
swimming pool remain; the former marble baths serve as flower pots.
The rooms are simple and the bathrooms have an unmatched
comfort. Choose the newer rooms or those looking out on the vast
stone terrace on the park. It is all very romantic.

*How to get there (Map 9): 23km southwest of Gerona, and 2km from Santa
Colomá.*

Hotel Mas Torrellas

17246 Santa Cristina de Aró (Gerona)
Carret. Santa Cristina a Playa de Aro, km 1,713
Tel. (9)72-83 75 26 – Fax (9)72-83 75 27
Carrera Family

Category ★ **Rooms** 17 with telephone, bath, WC, TV and minibar. **Price** Double 8,500-11,500Pts. **Meals** Breakfast included, served 8:00-11:00; half board + 2,100Pts, full board + 4,200Pts. **Restaurant** Service 13:00-16:00, 19:30-23:30; menu 2,100Pts, also à la carte. Specialties: Pastel de esparragos - Zarzuela - Capricho de la casa. **Credit cards** All major. **Pets** Dogs not allowed. **Facilities** Swimming pool, tennis, sauna, parking. **Nearby** Gerona - Costa Brava - Costa Brava golf course (18-Hole). **Open** Mar 16 - Oct 14

A real discovery... A few years ago the owners spotted and bought a residence in the midst of ten hectares of land, then restored it and fitted it out as a hotel. It is not luxurious: they have opted for personality and ambiance. The famous Catalan vaultings are everywhere, above all in the former stables now converted into the dining room. A mention for the cellar-bar with its original old beams and wine barrels from all regions of the country! The rooms are neat—the best is choose No. 18, which looks out on the countryside and mountain, and was a round bath. For the moment this hotel has only a one-star rating but, given all the advantages on offer, profit from this quickly before its prices rise to those of a three-star.

How to get there *(Map 9): 31km southeast of Gerona via C250.*

Can Feliciá

17850 Segueró (Gerona)
Tel. (9)72-59 05 23
Sr and Sra Llimona

Rooms 6 and 4 with bath. **Price** 3,000Pts (per pers.). **Meals** Breakfast included, served 7:30-10:00; half board 4,500Pts, full board 6,000Pts. **Evening meals** Service, 19:30-22:30. Carte 2,500-3,000Pts. Specialties: famillial and regional. **Credit cards** Not accepted. **Pets** Dogs not allowed. **Facilities** Parking. **Nearby** Besalú - Santa Pau - Naturel Park de la Garrotya - Gerona. **Open** All year.

Seguero is a spot truly out in the country, yet only ten kilometers from Besalú, a small city known for its numerous and impressive remains of by-gone eras, Roman and Gothic among them. Very recently, Marta opened her property to rural tourism, and Can Feliciá offers several lodgings designed for families; most of them have their own bathrooms. In addition, it is a very friendly place where you can genuinely make yourself at home. The meals all bear the mark of home cooking, and this is an excellent hotel for a weekend or a longer stay.

How to get there *(Map 9): 30km Northwest of Gerona; 10km north of Besalú.*

Mas de Torrent

17123 Torrent (Gerona)
Tel. (9)72-30 32 92 - Fax (9)72-30 32 93
Sr Berengüi

Category ★★★★★ **Rooms** 30 with air-conditioning, telephone, bath, WC, satellite TV, safe and minibar. **Price** Double 27,000-32,000Pts, suite Jardín 29,000-35,000Pts, suite Masia 35,000-40,000Pts. **Meals** Breakfast 2,000Pts; half board + 6,500Pts, full board + 12,000Pts. **Restaurant** Service 13:30-15:00, 20:30-23:30; menus 3,500-6,000Pts, also à la carte. Specialties: regional and international cooking. **Credit cards** All major. **Pets** Dogs allowed in the rooms (2,000Pts). **Facilities** Swimming pool, tennis, squash, bike, parking. **Nearby** Gerona - Costa Brava - Costa Brava golf course (18-Hole), Pals golf course (18-Hole). **Open** All year.

In the heart of Catalonia, nine kilometers from the most fashionable beaches of the Costa Brava (Aigua Blava, Bégur, etc.), a large 18th-century farm building, now completely restored, has been offering its cuisine and suites for some years. The appeal is to a clientele sensitive to comfort and gentle manners. Everything has been arranged in exquisite taste; all the rooms are different and decorated with a lot of finesse. Twenty bungalows have been built for families in a private garden. The restaurant is delightful and one should note a collection of prints in the dining room in honor of Picasso. The ambiance is very calm and relaxed. What more could one want?

How to get there *(Map 9): 36km east of Gerona via A7, exit No. 6, towards Torrent.*

Hotel Caldas

25528 Caldas de Bohi (Lérida)
Tel. (9)73-69 62 30 - Fax (9)73-69 60 30
Sr Moriscot Pidemunt

Category ★ **Rooms** 104 (31 with bath and WC, 73 with WC, 14 with TV). **Price** Single 3,485-4,495Pts, double 3,615-14,435Pts, triple 12,200-18,915Pts, 4 pers. 15,765-24,830Pts. **Meals** Breakfast 595-745Pts, served 8:00-10:30; half board + 2,945Pts, full board + 4,400Pts (per pers.). **Restaurant** Service 14:00-15:30, 21:00-22:00; menu 2,350Pts, also à la carte. Specialties: Truchas de la casa - Carn dolla. **Credit cards** Not accepted. **Pets** Small dogs allowed. **Facilities** Thermal swimming pool, tennis (800Pts), sauna (1,100Pts), garage (500Pts). **Nearby** Bohí Valley from Pont de Suert to Caldes de Bohi (Romanesque churches of Durro, Erill-Aval, Sant Climent de Taùll, Santa Maria) - Excursions in the Aigües Tortes National Park (San Maurici lake) and Vall d'Aran. **Open** June 25 - Sept 30.

The green and winding mountain road ends at a group of hotels at an altitude of 1,500 meters. It was on this site more than sixty years ago that the most important thermal spa in Spain opened. A rare environment and divine peace surround this complex of hotels with its 37 natural springs. A remarkably equiped sporting complex naturally makes this site even more attractive. Our choice has fallen on the very smallest hotel in the complex, which is full of charm. There is a terrace with climbing plants to welcome you both an adorable patio, attractive little corners. The ceilings of all the rooms retain their ancient beams. But make no mistake about it: the whole place is simple, like the people running it, and the prices as well....

How to get there *(Map 7): 145km north of Lérida via N230; 3km after the Suert bridge, take small road to the right.*

Hotel El Castell

25700 La Seu d'Urgell (Lérida)
Carret N 60
Tel. (9)73-35 07 04 - Fax (9)73-35 15 74
Sr Jaume Tápies Travé - Sr Jaume Tápies Ibern

Category ★★★★ **Rooms** 34 and 4 suites with air-conditioning, telephone, bath, WC, satellite TV, safe and minibar. **Price** Single 12,000Pts, double 16,500Pts, junior suite 25,500Pts. **Meals** Breakfast 1,600Pts, served 7:30-10:30. **Restaurant** Service 13:00-15:30, 20:00-22:30; à la carte 5,500-8,000Pts. Specialties: Raviolis de cigalas con mousse de calabacin - Risotto de bogavente con moixernons y trufa. **Credit cards** All major. **Pets** Dogs allowed in the rooms. **Facilities** Swimming pool, parking. **Nearby** In Seu: Santa Marìa Cathedral - Monastery Sant Serni de Tavérnoles in Anserall - Castellciutat - Excursions into the Vall d'Aran - The Cerdanya: Bellver de Cerdanya, Llivia, Puigcerdà - Andorra (Duty Free Principality). **Open** Feb 15 - Jan 15.

It is on the summit of a gently sloping hill, at the foot of which lies the medieval town of Seo d'Urgel, that El Castell is to be found. In this hotel protected by its mountain (the Sierra del Cadí), everything is organized to profit from such a privileged site. A remarkable comfort characterizes the place with the ground floor rooms enjoying a terrace or private garden, while those on the upper floor have just been renovated. In addition, all enjoy a personalized decor. The restaurant is gastronomic. Truly a hotel for those insisting on style, nature and good living.

How to get there *(Map 8): 133km northeast of Lérida via C1313.*

Parador Castillo de la Zuda

43500 Tortosa (Tarragona)
Castillo de la Zuda
Tel. (9)77-44 44 50 – Fax (9)77-44 44 58
Sr Esteban

Category ★★★★ **Rooms** 82 with air-conditioning, telephone, bath, WC, TV and minibar; elevator. **Price** Double 13,500-15,000Pts. **Meals** Breakfast 1,300Pts, served 8:00-10:30. **Restaurant** Service 13:30-14:30, 20:00-22:15; menu 3,500Pts; also à la carte. **Credit cards** All major. **Pets** Dogs not allowed. **Facilities** Swimming pool, parking. **Nearby** In Tortosa: Cathedral - Morella - Hunting and fishing in the Ebro Delta. **Open** All year.

The château of La Zuda takes its name from the well which according to Arab sources was sunk within the walls in the year 944, and which can still be seen today. This ancient Roman town has had a tumultuous history, becoming in turn a Arab fortress, a prison in the 12th century, and then a royal residence before being ceded to the Templars. Inside, the dining room has kept four huge windows and three open fireplaces as witnesses of such a past. The rooms have terraces with a magnificent panorama. But it is from the swimming pool that one has the best view over Tortosa and the fertile valley of the Ebro, all with a backdrop of the mountains of Tortosa and Beceite, a huge hunting reserve.

How to get there *(Map 16): 83km southwest of Tarragona via A7.*

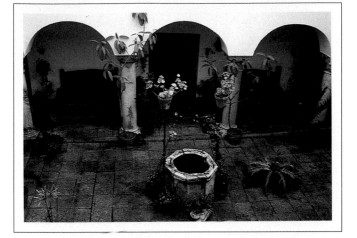

Parador Via de la Plata

06800 Mérida (Badajoz)
Plaza de la Constitución, 3
Tel. (9)24-31 38 00 - Fax (9)24-31 92 08
Sr Victor Teodosio

Category ★★★★ **Rooms** 82 with air-conditioning, telephone, bath, WC, satellite TV and minibar; elevator. **Price** Double 16,500Pts. **Meals** Breakfast 1,300Pts, served 7:30-11:00. **Restaurant** Service 13.00-16:00, 20:30-23:00; menu 3,500Pts, also à la carte. Specialties: Gazpacho extremeno - Pastel del convento. **Credit cards** All major. **Pets** Dogs not allowed. **Facilities** Swimming pool, Fitness center, sauna, garage (500Pts), parking. **Nearby** Roman Mérida: Roman Art Museum, Roman Theater, Roman Amphitheater, Roman bridge - Montijo - Embalse de Proserpina - Medelin. **Open** All year.

Mérida is a major tourist center where one comes to see the numerous Roman, Visigoth and Arab remains, and the parador is installed in an ancient convent, itself built on the ruins of a Roman temple. It has known diverse fortunes, even having been a prison! But have no fear, no traces remain of this former ocupation. Two huge lounges, one in the former chapel, a dining room and some very beautiful rooms have been fitted out around the traditional interior courtyard. There is also a delightful garden decorated with the Roman sculptures brought to light during the building work.

How to get there (Map 17): 68km south of Cáceres via N630.

Hotel Emperatriz

06800 Mérida (Badajoz)
Plaza de España, 19
Tel. (9)24-31 31 11 – Fax (9)24-31 33 05 – Sr Simancas

Category ★★★ **Rooms** 40 with air-conditioning, telephone, bath, WC, and TV. **Price** Single 6,000-9,000Pts, double 10,950-12,500Pts, suite 12,950-14,500Pts. **Meals** Breakfast 700Pts (buffet), served 8:00-11:00; half board + 2,450Pts, full board + 3,570Pts (per pers. 3 days min.). **Restaurant** Service 13:30-16:00, 20:30-23:00; menu 1,750Pts, also à la carte. Specialties: Carne a la brasa - Caldereta de cordero. **Credit cards** Amex, Visa, Eurocard, MasterCard. **Pets** Dogs allowed in the rooms. **Facilities** Garage (500Pts), parking. **Nearby** Roman Mérida: Roman Art Museum, Roman Theater, Roman Amphitheater, Roman bridge - Montijo - Embalse de Proserpina - Medelin. **Open** All year.

Built at the end of the 16th century, this former palace has offered hospitality to numerous crowned heads throughout its history. The interior is arranged around a large covered patio. As the rooms are being fully refurbished, ask for one of the most recent ones, spacious with their pretty bathrooms, while the nicest ones look onto the main square, which is happily animated. Some rooms have small balconies. The Emperatriz is not a 'grand luxe' hotel but rather a comfortable establishment with affordable prices. You will appreciate the Talavera tilework marrying so well with the stone of the walls, and the basement-bar in the former cellars. This is the place to stopover at if you wish to visit the famous Roman ruins of Mérida, or just it you are en route towards Andalusia.

How to get there (Map 17): 68km south of Cáceres via N630.

Parador de Zafra

06300 Zafra (Badajoz)
Plaza Corazon de Maria, 7
Tel. (9)24-55 45 40 – Fax (9)24-55 10 18 – Sr Antonio Atalaya

Rooms 45 with air-conditioning, telephone, bath, WC, satellite TV and minibar.
Price Double 15,000-18,500Pts. **Meals** Breakfast 1,300Pts, served 7:30-11:00; half
board + 4,700Pts, full board + 6,970Pts (per pers., 3 days min.). **Restaurant** Service
13:30-16:00, 20:30-23:00; menu 3,500Pts; also à la carte. **Credit cards** Amex, Visa,
Eurocard, MasterCard. **Pets** Dogs not allowed. **Facilities** Swimming pool, parking.
Nearby In Zafra: Colegiata Ntra. Sra. de la Candeleria, Hospidal de santiago,
convento de Sta Clara, casa palacio de Marqués de Solanda, bodegas Medina -
"Ducado de Feria" road and "Ruta de los Templarios". **Open** All year.

This parador is in the center of a lovely *alcazar* in this charming
little city whose name has not changed since the Moorish
invasion. An imposing turret survives from that period and to it has
been added a building in Andalusian Moorish style with an eye-
catching facade of nicely-blended white and gray. Once past the vast
entrance way, you discover a magnificent patio in white marble. The
lounges are quite luxurious, and a magnificent staircase leads to the
rooms, most of which have balconies overlooking the patio. The
rooms are large with furniture that evokes the charm of the era of the
Spanish *conquistadores*. The ones in the annex are smaller but equally
comfortable. The swimming pool enjoys the shade of the historic
walls surrounding it, a true oasis, especially in the summertime. The
immense dining room is equally cool. Here is a fine hotel, one
bringing to mind the glorious days of the Spanish Empire.

How to get there *(Map 17): 76km south of Badajoz.*

Hotel Huerta Honda

06300 Zafra (Badajoz)
Lopez Asme, 30
Tel. (9)24-55 41 00 – Fax (9)24-55 25 04

Rooms 45 with air-conditioning, telephone, bath, WC, satellite TV and minibar.
Price Single 7,500Pts, double 7,500-13,500Pts. **Meals** Breakfast 800Pts, served
7:30-11:00; half board + 5,000Pts, full board + 6,700Pts (per pers., 3 days min.).
Restaurant Service 12:30-16:00, 20:30-23:30; menu 4,000Pts; also à la carte. **Credit
cards** All major. **Pets** Dogs not allowed. **Facilities** Swimming pool, parking. **Nearby** In
Zafra: Colegiata Ntra. Sra. de la Candeleria, Hospidal de santiago, convento de Sta
Clara, casa palacio de Marqués de Solanda, bodegas Medina - "Ducado de Feria"
road and "Ruta de los Templarios". **Open** All year.

Right next to the Parador, the Hotel Huerta Honda is part of
some 17th-century buildings that have been renovated over
centuries to become a hotel today. Its concept is typical of certain
Spanish hotels: there are three restaurants, two bars and a nightclub
all at your disposal. The interior decoration is nothing if not
surprising; it ranges from blatant bad taste to extreme refinement.
You can find rooms which are at once exquisite and kitsch. On the
other hand, the hotel's restaurant, *La Barbacana,* is magnificent with
its antique furnishings and a kitchen run by the Hotel School of San
Sebastian with truly remarkable results. A good hotel, located nicely
between Madrid and Seville.

How to get there *(Map 17): 76km south of Badajoz.*

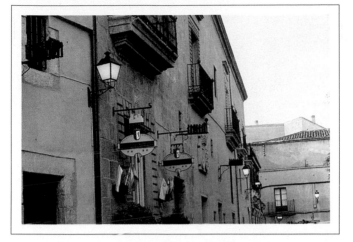

Hotel Meliá Cáceres

10003 Cáceres
Plaza de San Juan, 11
Tel. (9)27-21 58 00 - Fax (9)27-21 40 70

Category ★★★★ **Rooms** 86 with air-conditioning, telephone, bath, WC, satellite TV, safe and minibar; elevator. **Price** Single 15,000Pts, double 19,300Pts, suite 24,500Pts; extra bed + 4,600Pts. **Meals** Breakfast 1,400Pts (buffet), served 7:30-11:00; half board + 4,750Pts, full board + 8,100Pts (per pers.). **Restaurant** "La Indias" Service 13:00-16:00, 20:30-23:00; menu 3,500Pts, also à la carte. **Credit cards** All major. **Pets** Dogs not allowed. **Nearby** In Càceres: Barrio Monumental, Plaza de Santa Maria, Palacio de los Golfines de Abajo; Sanctuario de la Virgen de la Montaña - Arroyo de la Luz. **Open** All year.

A superb town and admirably preserved, the old town ('Barrio Monumental') of Càceres is a real museum of Spanish gothic town architecture. The Melià Càceres is in a former palace of the aristocratic Ovendo family, which distinguished itself in America and had a number of such palaces built. All the original structure has been preserved and one enters by a heavy wooden door opening on to the Plaza de San Juan. A large central patio allows a soft light to enter the hall giving access to the reception rooms. Seating and tables have been arranged around some ancient wells to better exploit the serene atmosphere. The bar has been installed in the former stables, covered with magnificent brick vaulting. The rooms are decorated with taste and we recommend those giving onto the square shaded by its bay trees and palms. Comfort is very good and the breakfasts delicious, while the restaurant is also much appreciated. A very good hotel where one is received by a competent and delightful staff.

How to get there *(Map 17): 300km west of Madrid.*

Hospederia del Real Monasterio

10140 Guadalupe (Cáceres)
Plaza Juan Carlos I
Tel. (9)27-36 70 00 - Fax (9)27-36 71 77
Sr Barerra

Category ★★ **Rooms** 47 with air-conditioning, telephone, bath, WC; elevator. **Price** Single: 5,000Pts, double 7,500Pts, suite 18,000Pts. **Meals** Breakfast 850Pts, served 8:30-10:30; half board 6,900Pts, full board 9,000Pts (per pers. 2 days min.). **Restaurant** Service 13:30-15:30, 21:00-22:30, menu 2,600Pts, also à la carte. Specialties: Migas extremeñas - Cabrito asado - Sopa de tomate. **Credit cards** Visa, Eurocard, MasterCard. **Pets** Dogs not allowed. **Facilities** Parking. **Nearby** Monastery of Guadalupe - Ermitage de Humilladero - Caramero - Logrosán. **Open** Feb 12 - Jan 12.

An impressive and grandiose ensemble, both warrior and monastic, this monastery was an important cultural center, and the Franciscan Community occupying it today has chosen to open a hotel in one part of the monastery. From the hallway one has a very beautiful view on one of the most enchanting corners of the edifice, 'Los Caídos'. Lounges, a dining room and large rooms are spread around the cloister, a small Gothic masterpiece, which is covered with a canopy in summer. Naturally you should visit the monastery with its facade on the town square, and the 'mudejar' cloister and church that has conserved an impressive collection of works of art, including several exceptional pictures by Zurbarán in the sacristy.

How to get there (Map 18): 139km east of Cáceres via N521, then C524 and C401.

Parador Zurbarán

10140 Guadalupe (Cáceres)
Marqués de la Romana, 12
Tel. (9)27-36 70 75 - Fax (9)27-36 70 76
Sr Arias

Category ★★★ **Rooms** 40 with telephone, bath, WC, TV, minibar; elevator. **Price** Double 12,500-13,500Pts. **Meals** Breakfast 1,300Pts, served 8:00-10:30. **Restaurant** Service 13:00-16:00, 20:30-22:30; menu 3,200Pts, also à la carte. Specialties: Cabrito asado - Sopa de arroz cacereña - Bacalao monacal - Caldereta de Cordero. **Credit cards** All major. **Pets** Dogs allowed. **Facilities** Swimming-pool, tennis, garage and parking. **Nearby** Monastery of Guadalupe - Ermitage de Humilladero - Caramero - Logrosán. **Open** All year.

Guadalupe was an important center of pilgrimage and today the grandiose monastery, the Zurbarán and the museum (with a very beautiful collection of lace, among others things), all merit a stop here. The ancient St. John the Baptist hospital from the 18th century now houses the hotel. It certainly does not have the prestige of the monastery but its interior layout has a lot more charm. The lounges and dining room are once again arranged around the patio, whose arcades are invaded by orange trees, and in the summer one lunches in the shade of the gallery. The rooms are very prettily decorated but it is preferable to ask for those in the new building, which have a view over the mountains, village and the incredible monastery situated right in front. On the rear side is the swimming pool in the midst of a very flowery garden, much appreciated in the summer.

How to get there *(Map 18): 139km east of Cáceres via N521, then C524 and C401.*

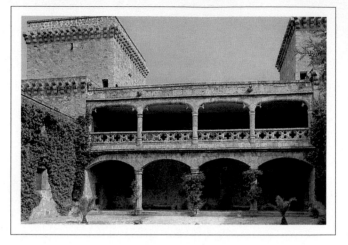

Parador Carlos V

10450 Jarandilla de la Vera (Cáceres)
Tel. (9)27-56 01 17 - Fax (9)27-56 00 88
Sr Fagesa

Category ★★★ **Rooms** 53 with air-conditioning, telephone, bath, WC, satellite TV and minibar. **Price** Double 15,000-17,000Pts. **Meals** Breakfast 1,300Pts, served 8:00-11:00. **Restaurant** Service 13:00-16:30, 20:30-23:00; menu 3,700Pts, also à la carte. Specialties: Cabrito - Calderetas. **Credit cards** All major. **Pets** Dogs not allowed. **Facilities** Swimming pool, tennis, parking. **Nearby** Cuacos de Yuste and Monastery of Yuste - Garganta la Olla - Cathédrale de Plasencia. **Open** All year.

In the north of Extremadura in the wild country of the Vera, this 14th- and 15th-century chateau is to be found. The very well-preserved edifice still has its beautiful surrounding wall, elegant angle towers and a drawbridge. The building is built around a flowered patio, and one facade consists of two arcaded galleries and a stone balcony worked in the oriental style. It is here that Charles V lodged before retiring to the Yuste monastery. The dining room occupies the ground floor while on the upper floor the lounge opens onto a balcony dominating the patio. The furniture is simple but the caisson ceilings, size of the rooms, lamps, medallions and trophees, all contribute to the chateau spirit. The rooms are both perfect and comfortable.

How to get there *(Map 11): 141km northeast of Cáceres via N630 to Plasencia, then C501.*

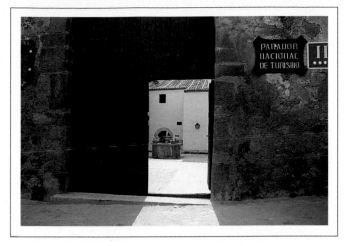

Parador de Trujillo

23003 Trujillo (Cáceres)
Plaza de Santa Clara
Tel. (9)27-32 13 50 - Fax (9)27-32 13 66
Sr Fuentes

Category ★★★★ Rooms 46 with telephone, bath, WC, satellite TV and minibar. **Price** Double 15,000Pts. **Meals** Breakfast 1,300Pts, served 8.00-11:00. **Restaurant** Service 13.30-16:30, 21:00-23:00; menu 3,700Pts, also à la carte. Specialties: Tenca, cordero asado. **Credit cards** All major. **Pets** Dogs not allowed. **Facilities** Swimming pool, tennis, parking. **Nearby** In Trujillo: Plaza Mayor and church of Santa Maria la Mayor - Santa Cruz de la Sierra - Càceres - Guadalupe - National Park of Monfrague. **Open** All year.

Trujillo was the home base of the Conquistadors, as recalled by the equestrian statue of F. Pizarro on the main square, and it is a beautiful town with a host of medieval and Renaissance monuments. The parador is in the ancient convent founded in the 16th century by order of the Immaculate Conception. Built around a courtyard, the cloister is planted with orange trees and has three facades in Renaissance style, with arcatures topped by a gallery with Tuscan small columns. The interior decoration is rather impersonal, particularly in the rooms which, however, lack for no comfort. Some have terraces entirely covered with a trellis, the traditional manner in this region of protecting against the heat. The hotel is air-conditioned and has a swimming pool.

How to get there *(Map 18): 47km east of Cáceres via N521; the parador is located in the lower part of town.*

Posada Finca de Santa Marta

Pago de San Clemente
23003 Herguijuela-Trujillo (Cáceres)
Tel. and Fax(9)27 31 92 03 - Fax (9)1-350 22 17
Sr Helink - Sra Rodriguez-Gimeno

Rooms 12 with bath. **Price** Double 9,000Pts. **Meals** Breakfast included. **Restaurant** Evening meals on request; menu 2,500-3,000Pts. **Credit cards** All major. **Pets** Dogs allowed. **Facilities** Swimming pool, parking. **Nearby** In Trujillo: Plaza Mayor and church of Santa Maria la Mayor - Santa Cruz de la Sierra - Càceres - Guadalupe - National Park of Monfrague. **Open** All year.

On the National V road linking Madrid and Lisbon, Trujillo is a good staging post where one can visit its 'Plaza Mayor', famous for its arcades and renaissance Palace. One can try the regional tomato soup with figs, and its braised pork ('la morada'), while - even better - one can now stay in the countryside at the Finca de Santa Marta, a rare 'cortijò' converted for 'green tourism'. This farm-manor house, known in the region as a 'lagar' - where oil and wine are produced - offers eight beautiful rooms. A long and rigorous restoration has preserved all the authenticity of the buildings: one can still visit the mill, (converted into a vast lounge-dining room), winepress, cellars, stables, sheepfolds and even the little chapel. The rooms have been subjected to all the care of the owner-decorator and have very refined decors: old wood and tiles have been restored to mix in harmony with the regional furniture and the most up-to-date comfort facilities. The garden is delightful, planted with olive, cherry and almond trees, all offering beautiful spring days in white and pink.

How to get there (Map 18): *50km east of Càceres via N521 to Trujillo, then 14km towards Guadalupe via C524 .*

Pazo da Merced

15510 Neda (La Coruña)
Tel. (9)81-38 22 00 - Fax (9)81-38 01 04
Mme Marinela Medina

Category ★★★★ **Rooms** 5 with telephone, bath, WC, satellite TV and minibar.
Price Single 9,600Pts, double 12,000Pts. **Meals** Breakfast 1,200Pts, served 8:00-
11:00. **Restaurant** For residents only, on request (See p. 247). **Credit cards** All major.
Pets Dogs not allowed. **Facilities** Swimming pool, sauna, parking. **Nearby** Les rías.
Open All year.

On the northwest corner of Spain, the highly indented coastline
lets the sea flow inland, forming what the Spanish call rias. Here
on the bank of the Ria de Ferrol, you find the Pazo da Merced, an
L-shaped, 18th-century house to which has been subtly and
harmoniously added new and wholly contemporary architecture. An
attractive glass-covered metal staircase leads up to the rooms. These
are spacious with antique beams and floors and offer a pleasant
combination of Victorian and Biedermeir furniture, while the
bathrooms are distinctly modern. On one side there is a small
French-style garden and on the side facing the sea is a landing dock
which has been made into a terrace where breakfast – and other
meals if you ask for them – is served. A small private beach marks the
end of the hotel's property. The Merced is one of the rare attractive
hotels in this lovely region which has escaped the industrialization
that took place in the 70s and 80s.

How to get there *(Map 1): 60km north of La Coruña, to El Ferrol.*

Parador de Los Reyes Católicos

15705 Santiago de Compostela (La Coruña)
Plaza del Obradoiro, 1
Tel. (9)81–58 22 00 – Fax (9)81–56 30 94 – Sr Morales

Category ★★★★★ **Rooms** 136 with telephone, bath, WC, satellite TV and minibar; elevator. **Price** Single 21,200Pts, double 26,500Pts, suite 35,300Pts. **Meals** Breakfast 1,800Pts, served 7:00-11:00. **Restaurant** Service 13:00-15:30, 21:00-23:30; menu 3,800Pts; also à la carte. Specialties: Merluza con almejas - Caldo gallego - Vieiras a la gallega - Solomillo de ternera gallega al horno - Tarta de santiago - Filloas rellenas de crema. **Credit cards** All major. **Pets** Dogs not allowed. **Facilities** Garage (1,900Pts). **Nearby** In Santiago: Cathedral, Plaza del Obradoiro, Plaza de la Quintana, Barrio antiguo - Church Santa Maria la Real del Sarl - Pazo de Oca (manor and gardens) - Monastery of Santa Maria de Conjo. **Open** All year.

It was in 1499 that the Catholic monarchs Isabel and Fernando established this royal hospital to shelter pilgrims. Situated on the very attractive Plaza del Obratoiro, it remains today a testimony to an epoch when history, religion, art and culture were intimately linked. Today tourists have replaced the 'walkers' on the road to Saint-Jacques, and this parador is one of the best hotels in Spain. The setting is grandiose: the entry and facade in the 'plateresque' style, the four cloistered patios of the 16th- and 17th-centuries, and the former stables now used as the dining room. The rooms are exquisite, in particular Numbers 201, 202 and 204, while the 'Cardinal Suite' and the 'Royal Suite' overlook the square. The service is that of a grand hotel, attentive and discreet.

How to get there *(Map 1): facing the cathedral.*

Casa Grande de Cornide

Cornide (Calo-Teo) 15886 Santiago (La Coruña)
Tel. (9)81-80 55 99 – Fax (9)81-80 57 51
Sra Maria Jesus Castro Rivas

Rooms 7 with telephone, bath, WC, satellite TV and minibar. **Price** Single 10,000-12,000Pts, double 12,000-14,000Pts. **Meals** Breakfast 950Pts, served 8:00-11:00. **No restaurants** See p. 247. **Credit cards** All major. **Pets** Dogs not allowed. **Facilities** Parking. **Nearby** Santiago de Compostela - Church Santa Maria la Real del Sarl - Gardens and manor Pazo de Oca - Monastery of Santa Maria de Conja. **Open** All year.

Only nine kilometers from Santiago, the Casa Grande de Cornide is a hotel of incomparable charm. It enjoys an inland location, you enter through a beautiful old stone entrance where you come upon its different wings, all representative of local architecture, and discover a large garden with magnolias, oak and olive trees along with a palm grove. The owners are connoisseurs of Spanish art and this shows in the way they have restored the house and particularly the library. The rooms here are in the wings, three in the old one, two in the more recent one. Each is furnished differently but all have the same enjoyably subtle atmosphere, the result of a decor of predominantly deep red colors plus furniture in very dark wood. The suite is the most spacious with a glass-covered mezzanine, decorated in a style that tastefully combines Victorian architecture with that commonly found in old-fashioned hay barns. This hotel is a true find, one where you are always warmly received and it's a good place to regain your strength after a pilgrimage to Santiago or before setting out for Portugal.

How to get there (Map 1): *9km south of Santiago, on the Vigo road; at the gas station of Casalonga, turn on left and follow the road during 2km; Casa Grande de Cornide is on right.*

Parador Condes de Villalba

27800 Valeriano Valdesus – Villalba (Lugo)
Tel. (9)82-51 00 11 – Fax (9)82-51 00 90
Sr Vazquez Camara

Category ★★★ **Rooms** 6 with telephone, bath, WC, TV and minibar; elevator. **Price** Double 15,000-17,500Pts. **Meals** Breakfast 1,300Pts, served 8:00-11:00. **Restaurant** Service 13:00-16:00, 21:00-23:00, menu 3,500Pts, also à la carte. Specialties: Pulpo - Filloas - Empanadas - Lacón con grelos. **Credit cards** All major. **Pets** Dogs not allowed. **Facilities** Parking. **Nearby** Lugo (cathedral and fortifications) - Chapel of Baamonde - Monastery of Meira. **Open** All year.

It was really a very long time ago that the Los Andrade tower defended Villalba against its attacking enemies. The recognition due to it was almost forgotten, but the Paradores company saved it 'in extremis' from destruction, while also giving the region a good hotel establishment. The rooms are very large with all the amenities required, while good regional cuisine is served in the dining room on the ground floor. A comfortable staging post on the road to Saint-Jacques de Compostella.

How to get there (Map 2): 36km north of Lugo via N6 to Rábade, then C641.

Parador de Monterrey

32600 Verín (Orense)
Tel. (9)88-41 00 75 - Fax (9)88-41 20 17
Sr Cardo

Category ★★★ **Rooms** 23 with telephone, bath, WC and minibar. **Price** Double 11,500-13,500Pts. **Meals** Breakfast 1,200Pts, served 8:00-10.30. **Restaurant** Service 13:30-16:00, 21:00-23:00; menu 3,000Pts, also à la carte. Specialties: regional cooking. **Credit cards** All major. **Pets** Dogs not allowed. **Facilities** Swimming pool, garage. **Nearby** In Verín: Monterrey Castle - Church Santa Maria of Mijos - Church and Castle of Mezquita. **Open** Feb 1 - Nov 30.

Some four kilometers from the town, this parador profits from the isolation granted to a clientele seeking maximum peace and quiet. Of recent construction but respecting the style of the region, the building dominates the valley of the Tamega, covered with vineyards, and the chateau of Monterrey. The rooms all offer equal amenities in a traditional decor, but the prettiest are those looking onto the chateau, so be sure to ask for numbers 102, 104 and 106.

How to get there *(Map 2): 78km southeast of Orense via N525.*

Parador Conde de Gondomar

36300 Bayona (Pontevedra)
Tel. (9)86-35 50 00 - Fax (9)86-35 50 76
Sr Martín

Category ★★★★ **Rooms** 124 with telephone, bath, WC, satellite TV and minibar.
Price Double 15,000-20,000Pts. **Meals** Breakfast 1,400Pts, served 8:00-11.00.
Restaurant Service 13:30-16:00, 20:30-23:00, menu 3,800Pts, also à la carte.
Specialties: Fish - Sea food - Empanadas. **Credit cards** All major. **Pets** Dogs not
allowed. **Facilities** Swimming pool, tennis, garage, parking. **Nearby** Fortress (Monte
Real) - Monte Groba - Road from Bayona to La Guardia. **Open** All year.

The hotel rises like an incomparable watchtower on the Monte
Real peninsula, surrounded by a wall predating the Roman
colonization. It was here that the galley La Pinta touched shore with
the first Indians from America aboard. Its sheer size is impressive as
well as the space and installations (five lounges, three dining rooms).
The rooms all offer every amenity wished for. Its 18 hectares of land
and 3 kilometers of walls protect it from any tourist bustle, while its
sporting facilities allow one to avoid even leaving the hotel, which
can be very convenient with a family holiday.

How to get there *(Map 1): 20km southwest of Vigo via C550.*

Gran Hotel de la Toja

36991 Isla de la Toja (Pontevedra)
Tel. (9)86-73 00 25 – Fax (9)86-73 12 01
Sr Alvarez Cordero

Category ★★★★★ **Rooms** 197 with telephone, bath, WC, satellite TV, minibar; elevator. **Price** Single 16,000-21,750Pts, double 20,000-27,000Pts, suite 25,000-40,000Pts. **Meals** Breakfast 1,650Pts, served from 7:00; half board + 5,500Pts, full board + 10,000Pts (per pers.). **Restaurant** Service 13:30-15:00, 21:30-23:00; menu 5,500Pts, also à la carte. Specialties: Fish, sea food. **Credit cards** All major. **Pets** Dogs not allowed. **Facilities** Heated swimming pool, tennis, health center, golf course (9-Hole), parking. **Nearby** El Grove (Sell fish festival during the second week of Oct) - Salvora. **Open** All year.

There are the 'beach hotels' and the 'palaces on the coast', and the Gran Hotel de la Toja is certainly a 'palace on the coast'. Enjoying a privileged site on a small island of the Ria de Arosa, it has all the 'pluses' of a grand hotel: private beach, pine woods, swimming pool, tennis courts and golf. The public rooms are luxurious: vast ceremonial lounges, a more intimate bar, a welcoming dining room. The rooms are very comfortable, though they have more charm in the older part of the building. There is also a casino and a spa close to the hotel, which should please more than one visitor!

How to get there *(Map 1): 73km southwest of Santiago via N550 to Puente Cesures, then signs for La Toja; the hotel is located on the island.*

Parador Casa del Barón

36002 Pontevedra
Barón, 19
Tel. (9)86-85 58 00 – Fax (9)86-85 21 95
Sr Basso Puga

Category ★★★ **Rooms** 47 with telephone, bath, WC, TV, and minibar; elevator. **Price** Double 11,500-15,000Pts. **Meals** Breakfast 1,300Pts, served 8:00-11:00. **Restaurant** Service 13:00-16:00, 20:30-23:30; menu 3,200Pts, also à la carte. Specialties: fish, sea food. **Credit cards** All major. **Pets** Dogs not allowed. **Facilities** Parking. **Nearby** Monastery of Lérez - Castle of Sotomayor - Mirador of Coto Redondo. **Open** All year.

The Parador Casa del Barón occupies the 'pazo' of Maceda. A 'pazo' was an ancient Galician manor house, which abandoned the military character of the Middle Age chateaux, to be inspired more by monastic or rural architecture. When in 1955 this one became a hotel, it was insisted that the original style of this aged 'pazo' should be conserved and restored. The curious kitchen (now a lounge) and the elegant staircase of the entry testify to this. The other rooms of the house are also very agreeable. The dining room opens onto the terrace and an abundantly flowered garden, while all the bedrooms are very refined. The Casa del Barón is situated in the ancient 'Barrio' (quarter) of Pontevedra, a very attractive area in this town whose surroundings are rather disappointing.

How to get there *(Map 1): 57km south of Santiago via N550; in the old part of the town.*

Parador San Telmo

36700 Túy (Pontevedra)
Avenida de Portugal
Tel. (9)86-60 03 09 - Fax (9)86-60 21 63
Sr Baños Rodriguez

Category ★★★ **Rooms** 30 with telephone, bath, WC, TV, and minibar. **Price** Double 11,500-15,500Pts. **Meals** Breakfast 1,300Pts, served 8.00-11:00. **Restaurant** Service 13:00-16:00, 21:00-23:00; menu 3,500Pts, also à la carte. Specialties: Pulpea Feire - Lacon con grelos. **Credit cards** All major. **Pets** Dogs not allowed. **Facilities** Swimming pool, tennis, parking. **Nearby** In Tuy: Cathedral - Romanesque church of Pexegueiro - Mirador de Aloya - Salvaterra de Miño. **Open** All year.

Built on the model of Galician houses, the hotel rises on a small promontory on the right bank of the Miño in a quiet and green countryside evoking an Irish landscape. The atmosphere reflects the environment: serene and peaceful. The bedrooms are very attractive but number 22 also has the 'extra' of a small gallery furnished in cane rattan, while the suite has a large balcony. One should note that this is also a good hotel for sampling regional specialties.

How to get there *(Map 1): 34km south of Vigo via N550, towards Portugal.*

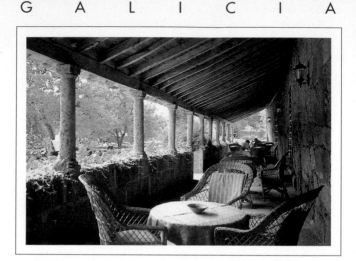

Hotel Pazo El Revel

36990 Villalonga (Pontevedra)
Tel. (9)86-74 30 00 - Fax (9)86-74 30 90
Sr Ansorena Garret

Category ★★★ **Rooms** 22 with telephone, bath, WC and TV. **Price** Single 6,850-7,500Pts, double 10,700-12,000Pts. **Meals** Breakfast included, served 9:00-11:00. **No restaurant** See p. 247. **Credit cards** Visa, Eurocard, MasterCard. **Pets** Dogs not allowed. **Facilities** Swimming pool, tennis, parking. **Nearby** Monastery of Lérez - Castillo de Sotomayor - Mirador de Coto Redondo - Pontevedra - El Grove - Beaches. **Open** June 1 - Sept 30.

This elegant 17th-century Galician residence has 22 simply appointed rooms: tiling, white walls and furniture limited to the strictly necessary, but nonetheless offering all the comfort required. The character of the house is shown more by the pretty garden with its swimming pool and tennis court, while on the covered terrace wicker armchairs await you. This place is quiet and one can listen to the birds singing, while the beaches nearby and the Romanesque churches of the region well deserve a visit.

How to get there *(Map 1): 23km north of Pontevedra via A9, exit Caldas or Pontevedra; 9km from Cambados.*

La Posada de Alameda.

28749 Alameda del Valle (Madrid)
Grande, 34
Tel. (9)1 869 13 37/869 00 17 - Fax (9)1 869 01 63
Isabel Carles Bohijas

Category ★★★★ **Rooms** 22 with air-conditioning, telephone, bath, WC, satellite TV, minibar. **Price** Double 10,500Pts, suite 12,000Pts. **Meals** Breakfast 750Pts, served 8:00-10:00; full board + 6,970Pts (per pers.). **Restaurant** Service 13:00-15:30, 21:00-23:00; also à la carte. Specialties: Castilian cooking. **Credit cards** All major. **Pets** Dogs not allowed. **Facilities** Parking and garage. **Nearby** Valley of Lozoya - Ségovia - Madrid. **Open** All year.

Some fifty kilometers from Segovia, you come across the Lozoya Valley, a place with ever-changing landscapes. The mountaintops are snow-covered in winter, and below them lie almond groves, lakes and rivers. It was in this peaceful setting that this wholly traditional inn was built a few years ago. It is, however, totally modern in spirit with excellent contemporary Spanish paintings on its walls. The rooms all look out on the countryside; they are spacious and identically furnished with attractive furniture, either lacquered white or in natural wood. Rooms 101, 102 and 103 are the largest. The Alameda is a particular favorite of Madrileños in quest of a pleasant weekend.

How to get there *(Map 13): 52km east of Segovia, 90km north of Madrid via N1. After 69km, take C604 to Rascafria, then to Alameda.*

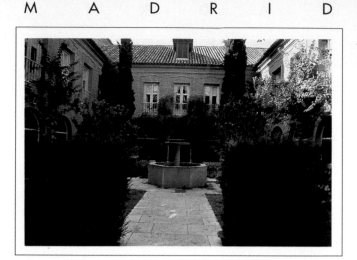

Parador de Chinchón

28370 Chinchón (Madrid)
Avenida Generalísimo, 1
Tel. (9)1-894 08 36 – Fax (9)1-894 09 08
Sr Bertolin

Category ★★★★ **Rooms** 38 with air-conditioning, telephone, bath, WC, TV and minibar. **Price** Double 17,500Pts. **Meals** Breakfast 1,300Pts, served 8:00-11:00. **Restaurant** Service 13:30-16:00, 20:30-23:00; menu 3,500Pts, also à la carte. Specialties: Castilian cooking. **Credit cards** All major. **Pets** Dogs not allowed. **Facilities** Swimming pool, garage (900Pts). **Nearby** Colmenar de Oreja - Nuevo Baztàn - Alcalà de Henares - Aranjuez - Madrid. **Open** All year.

Chinchón has a main square ('Plaza Mayor') which alone deserves a visit, and the parador is not far from it. A serene atmosphere pervades this ancient convent founded by the Augustinians in the 15th century. The main staircase ceiling has retained its original frescoes and the chapel of Santa Maria del Rosario is well conserved. The simplicity of the decoration, where white and the 'azulejos' reign, gives much elegance to the lounges, dining room and bedrooms. Choose for preference suite number 8 with its terrace. The decor also lends charm to the green and flowered patios. Hidden at the bottom of the garden, where the kitchen garden used to be, there is an attractive swimming pool and bar, both inviting relaxation, as with the little corners under the trees and bamboos, among the flowers and fountains.

How to get there *(Map 13): 42km southeast of Madrid via N3 to Puente de Azganda, then C300; close to the Plaza Mayor.*

Ritz Hotel

28014 Madrid
Plaza de la Lealtad, 5
Tel. (9)1-521 28 57 - Fax (9)1-532 87 76 - Sr Jordàn
E-mail: reservas@ritz.es - Web: http://www.ritz.es

Category ★★★★★ **Rooms** 156 with air-conditioning, telephone, bath, WC, satellite TV, safe and minibar; elevator. **Price** Single 40,000Pts, double 53,000-62,000Pts, suite 95,000-181,000Pts. **Meals** Breakfast 2,950Pts, served 8:00-11:00. **Restaurant** Service 13:30-16:00, 20:30-24:00; menu 5,900Pts, also à la carte. Specialties: Cocido madrileño - Paella Ritz. **Credit cards** All major. **Pets** Dogs allowed (extra charge). **Nearby** Palacio del Prado - Castillo de los duques de l'Infantado in Manzanares el Real - El Paular Monastery - Villages of the Sierra Pobre - Valle de los Caídos - Monastery of the Escorial - Valle de los Caìdos; Puerta de Hierro golf course (18-Hole). **Open** All year.

Bearing the name that has become the symbol of 'grand luxe' hotels, the Ritz of Madrid was built on the initiative of Alfonso XIII. Totally renovated but more faithful than ever to its initial decoration, the result is striking: the sumptuous carpets from the Real Fábrica that cover all the floors are superb, and so precious that a full-time repairer is employed. The gardens and terrace have been reopened, while the menu and the cellars of the famous restaurant have been yet further improved. In the rooms one always finds those Ritz details: sumptuous bouquets of flowers, the initialed towels of the hotel (that make one doubt one's honesty !), and the baskets of exquisite fruits. Even if not staying at the Ritz you can always take tea in the Royal ('Real') Lounge, lunch in the garden, cocktail on the terrace, or dinner in the most beautiful restaurant in Madrid.

How to get there *(Map 13): facing the Prado Museum.*

Santo Mauro Hotel

28010 Madrid
Zurbano, 36
Tel. (9)1-319 69 00 – Fax (9)1-308 54 77

Category ★★★★★ **Rooms** 37 with air-conditioning, telephone, bath, WC, satellite TV, minibar, safe; elevator. **Price** Single 32,000Pts, double 44,000-52,000Pts. **Meals** Breakfast 2,300Pts, served 8:00-11:00. **Restaurant** Belagua. Service 13:30-16:00, 20:30-23:00. Closed Sunday, national holidays, and August; à la carte 7,000Pts. **Credit cards** All major. **Pets** Dogs allowed. **Facilities** Covered swimming pool, garage. **Nearby** Palacio del Prado -Castillo de los duques de l'Infantado in Manzanares el Real - El Paular Monastery - Villages of the Sierra pobre (Talamanca de Jarama, Torrelaguna, Patones, the Sierra Pobre de Torrelagana towards El Berrueco) - Valle de los Caidos - Monastery of the Escorial; Puerta de Hierro golf course (18-Hole). **Open** All year.

Intimate and luxurious, traditional and modern. These are the attributes that make the Santo Mauro one of the best hotels in Madrid. A palace designed by a French architect which, before becoming a hotel, has housed innumerable foreign embassies. Totally renovated, the Santo Mauro has retained all its classic qualities – period woodwork and stucco decoration – and yet enjoys a modern and subtle decor both elegant and refined. This comes notably from a sophisticated use of color and marvelously sober contemporary furniture in a skillfully designed interior which allows you to have you meals in the library, something we found quite unique. The rooms offer five-star comfort and charm that is the hallmark of this hotel. Here, a spirit of creativity has happily embraced the tradition of the luxury hotel.

How to get there (Map 13): near the Paseo de la Castellana.

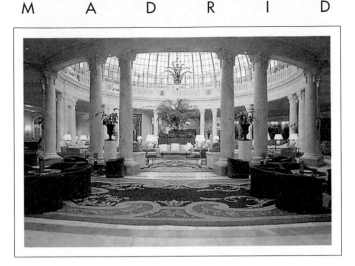

Palace Hotel

28014 Madrid
Plaza de las Cortes, 7
Tel. (9)1-360 80 00 - Fax (9)1-360 81 00

Category ★★★★★ **Rooms** 354 and 46 suites with air-conditioning, telephone, bath, WC, satellite TV, safe and minibar; elevator - Wheelchair access. **Price** Single 52,000Pts, double 59,000Pts, suite 90,000-150,000Pts. **Meals** Breakfast 3,100Pts, served 7:15-11:00; half board + 6,750Pts (per pers.). **Restaurant** Service 13:00-16:00, 20:15-23:30; closed Sat and Aug; menus 6,750-13,500Pts, also à la carte. **Credit cards** All major. **Pets** Dogs allowed (except in restaurant, with extra charge). **Facilities** Hairdresser, garage. **Nearby** Palacio del Prado - Castillo de los duques de l'Infantado in Manzanares el Real - El Paular Monastery - Villages of the Sierra Pobre (Talamanca de Jarama, Torrelaguna, Patones, the Sierra Pobre de Torrelagana towards El Berrueco) - Valle de los Caídos - Monastery of the Escorial - Valle de los Caìdos; Puerta de Hierro golf course (18-Hole). **Open** All year.

Admirably well situated, the Palace deploys its immense facade in the face of the square Canovas del Castillo, between the Prado Museum and the Congress. King Alfonso XIII opened it in 1912. Prestigious, it has been selected by many personalities of the century from Mata Hari to Richard Nixon, among many others. Its majestic hallway leads to one of the most beautiful lounges, 'La Rotonda', where a series of double neo-classical columns supports a magnificent cupola decorated with Art Nouveau tiles. A lamp with its palms of crystal hangs down from the ceiling to complete this superb 1900's decor. The bedrooms are perfect, while a luxury of good taste makes every space into an exceptional location. This hotel is for those refined friends who do not flinch at the prices!

How to get there *(Map 13): facing the Prado Museum.*

Villa Real

28014 Madrid
Plaza de las Cortes, 10
Tel. (9)1-420 37 67 - Fax (9)1-420 25 47 - Sr Garcia
E-mail: info.derbyhotels.es - Web: http://www.derbyhotel.es

Category ★★★★ **Rooms** 115 with air-conditioning, telephone, bath, WC, satellite TV, safe and minibar; elevator. **Price** Single 19,500Pts (weekend)-26,400Pts, double 19,500 (weekend)-33,000Pts, suite 29,500Pts-65,000Pts. **Meals** Breakfast 2,000Pts (buffet), served 8:00-11:00. **Restaurant** Service 13:30-15:30, 20:30-23:30; menu 6,000Pts, also à la carte. **Credit cards** All major. **Pets** Dogs allowed. **Facilities** Garage (1,600Pts). **Nearby** Palacio del Prado - Castillo de los duques de l'Infantado in Manzanares el Real - El Paular Monastery - Villages of the Sierra Pobre (Talamanca de Jarama, Torrelaguna, Patones, the Sierra Pobre de Torrelagana towards El Berrueco) - Valle de los Caídos - Monastery of the Escorial - Valle de los Caìdos; Puerta de Hierro golf course (18-Hole). **Open** All year.

In default of any charming small hotel in Madrid, we have selected this recent four-star house. With its 1900s' decor, it is very well situated facing the Prado Museum at the very heart of the cultural and financial quarter of the capital. Inside there is the atmosphere of a grand hotel: vast lounges luxuriously decorated and a cosy bar. The huge and classical rooms are very attractive, with very well equiped bathrooms, and which still have that freshness so lacking in certain bedrooms of the 'palaces'. The service is attentive, the welcome friendly and not at all starchy.

How to get there *(Map 13): in the city center, facing the Prado Museum.*

Hotel Wellington

28001 Madrid
Velásquez, 8
Tel. (9)1-575 44 00 – Fax (9)1-576 41 64 – Sr Lobo

Category ★★★★★ **Rooms** 250 and 27 suites with air-conditioning, telephone, bath, WC, satellite TV, safe and minibar; elevator. **Price** Single 17,000Pts (weekend)-21,500Pts, double 17,500Pts (weekend)-34,250Pts, suite 49,500-93,500Pts. **Meals** Breakfast 2,200Pts, served 7:00-11:00. **Restaurant** "El Fogon" Service 13:30-16:00, 21:30-22:30; à la carte 5,300-6,000Pts. Specialties: International cooking. **Credit cards** All major. **Pets** Dogs not allowed. **Facilities** Swimming pool, garage (2,250Pts). **Nearby** Palacio del Prado - Castillo de los duques de l'Infantado in Manzanares el Real - El Paular Monastery - Villages of the Sierra Pobre (Talamanca de Jarama, Torrelaguna, Patones, the Sierra Pobre de Torrelagana towards El Berrueco) - Valle de los Caídos - Monastery of the Escorial - Valle de los Caídos; Puerta de Hierro golf course (18-Hole). **Open** All year.

The Wellington is a luxurious hotel where a calm and cosy atmosphere reigns. The rooms are spacious and well equiped, and have beautiful bathrooms in marble. Those with windows over the Via Velásquez are protected with double glazing to assure perfect quiet. Choose first those rooms overlooking the interior garden and swimming pool, or even better those on the top floor with their own small terraces. One will linger happily at the hotel bar with its English style: panelling, copper work and lamps make it a particularly warm corner. The rustic decor of the dining room is perhaps rather surprising in such surroundings: beams, white walls and hunting trophees, but it is nonetheless attractive.

How to get there (Map 13): near the Parque del Retiro.

Hotel Inglés

28014 Madrid
Echegaray, 8
Tel. (9)1-429 65 51 – Fax (9)1-420 24 23
Sr Antonio Marco

Category ★★★ **Rooms** 58 with telephone, bath or shower, WC, satellite TV; elevator. **Price** Single 7,500-9,000Pts, double 10,800Pts, triple 14,400Pts, 4 pers. 18,000Pts. **Meals** Breakfast 550Pts, served 7:30-11:00. **Restaurant** See pp. 253-254. **Credit cards** All major. **Pets** Dogs not allowed. **Facilities** Garage (1,200Pts). **Nearby** Palacio del Prado - Castillo de los duques de l'Infantado in Manzanares el Real - El Paular Monastery - Villages of the Sierra Pobre (Talamanca de Jarama, Torrelaguna, Patones, the Sierra Pobre de Torrelagana towards El Berrueco) - Valle de los Caídos - Monastery of the Escorial - Valle de los Caìdos; Puerta de Hierro golf course (18-Hole). **Open** All year.

In the heart of the city and only two paces from old Madrid, the Calle Echegaray is a very lively street full of small restaurants. It is here that the Hotel Inglés is to be found. All the bedrooms have been recently renovated and offer full amenities, although one rather regrets their somewhat clinic-like floors. The 'British' aspect evoked by the name of the hotel is found in the discreetly lit lounge where deep leather armchairs await you. Another advantage of the hotel is the parking, and when you know Madrid and its traffic, this is a huge 'plus'. Finally, with more than 100 years of age, the Hotel Inglés is professional and efficient, while the prices are reasonable for Madrid, where charm is to be found in the palaces above all.

How to get there *(Map 13): near the Puerta del Sol.*

El Tiempo Perdido

28189 Patones de Arriba (Madrid)
Travesia del Ayuntamiento, 7
Tel. (9)1-843 21 52 - Fax (9)1-843 21 48 - Sr Fournier

Category ★★★★ **Rooms** 5 mini-suites with air-conditioning, telephone, bath, WC, TV, video, minibar and safe. **Price** Single 20,000Pts, double 25,000Pts. **Meals** Breakfast 2,000Pts, served 8:00-12:00. **Restaurant** "El Poleo". Service from 14:00, 21:00; à la carte 4,500-5,000Pts. Specialties: Endivas caramelizadas - Cordero ala miel. **Credit cards** Amex, Visa, Eurocard, MasterCard. **Pets** Dogs allowed. **Facilities** Garage (1,200Pts). **Nearby** Madrid - Castillo de Uceda **Open** From Friday midday to Monday midday, previous day and public holidays (Spanish) - closed July 15 – Aug 31; Christmas – Jan 3.

The owner of "El Tiempo Perdido," Pierre Fournier, at once a decorator and an antique collector, has lived for many years in Spain. He has opened this attractive hotel in a particularly beautiful little Castillian village some fifty kilometers from Madrid. It is a typical valley house and close to the church. Its interior is a model of refinement with antique furniture, old engravings plus Provence-style fabrics, skillfully displayed in all the larger rooms, all of which have an intimate lounge. If this weren't enough, you may also enjoy croissants direct from the Hôtel du Palais in Biarritz. Just across the street are two excellent restaurants: There is El Poleo, a large and genuinely gastronomic restaurant, with its smaller version under the same management offering a large terrace and a superb panoramic view of the surrounding countryside. While "El Tiempo Perdido" may well translate literally into "Lost Time," a far better name would be "Happy Days".

How to get there *(Map 13): 50km of Madrid via N1, to Torrelaguna then follow the road to Patones de Arriba. Puting your car aside behind the church, the hotel is not very far away.*

Hotel Santa Maria del Paular

28741 Rascafria (Madrid)
Carret. de Cotos, km 26, 5
Tel. (9)1-869 10 11/12 - Fax (9)1-869 10 06 - Sr Iruela

Category ★★★★ **Rooms** 58 with air-conditioning, telephone, bath or shower, WC and satellite TV. **Price** Single 7,500-10,000Pts, double 12,500-15,000Pts, suite 18,500Pts. **Meals** Breakfast 1,875Pts, served 8:00-11:00, full board + 9,000Pts (per pers., 3 days min.). **Restaurant** Service 13:30-16:00, 21:00-23:30, menu 4,500Pts, also à la carte. Specialties: Judiones de la Granja con Matanza - Cordero Lechal - Asado al Horno de leña - Cochinillo frito - Buñuelos al bon - Pastelerìa. **Credit cards** All major. **Pets** Dogs not allowed. **Facilities** Heated swimming pool, tennis, bike, billiards, parking. **Nearby** Monastery del Paular - Skiing in Puerto de Navacerrada. **Open** All year.

At the foot of the Sierra de Guadarrama beside the River Lozoya, and scarcely 85 kilometers from Madrid, we find ourselves at the very picturesque site of Santa Maria del Paular. Even though classified as a historical monument, this ancient monastery of the Carthusians dating from 1390 was abandoned. It was only in 1948 that part of it became a parador, and in 1952 that some Benedictine monks installed themselves in the monastery, to give life back to this beautiful ensemble. In passing through the main archway, similar to a triumphal arch, one comes to the Ave Maria patio surrounded by a colonnade supporting the red-brick building. Inside the same sobriety and the same good taste are found, while behind a garden leads to the swimming pool and tennis court.

How to get there (Map 13): 85km north of Madrid via N1; at km 69 take C604.

216

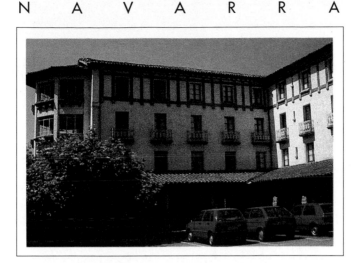

Hotel Ayestaran

31870 Lekumberri (Navarra)
Calle Aralarso
Tel. (9)48-50 41 27 – Fax (9)48-50 41 27
Sr Ayestaran Oquinena

Category ★ **Rooms** 90 (54 with bath or shower); 15 with bath and WC. **Price** Double 5,500-7,100Pts. **Meals** Breakfast 450Pts, served 8:30-11:00; half board + 4,700-5,200Pts, full board + 5,160-5,700Pts (per pers.). **Restaurant** Service 13:30-15:30, 21:00-22:30; menu 1,700Pts, also à la carte. Specialties: Alcachofas al jamòn - Meat. **Credit cards** Visa, Eurocard, MasterCard. **Pets** Dogs not allowed. **Facilities** Swimming pool, tennis. **Nearby** Fishing - Walking. **Open** Jan 20 - Dec 20.

Getting away from the coast and entering the real Basque country, the Hotel Ayestaran is lodged in two buildings, one residence for summer and a second for winter, on either side of the road. This latter is rather too busy at the moment, but within two years it will be diverted. In the meantime the hotel does not lack for charm, all white with red shutters in summertime, but all white with green shutters in winter. Its first hundred years have just been celebrated. The hotel corridors are filled with Basque furniture from the start of the century, while the bedrooms are simple and furnished with old beds from the region. Bathrooms have been renovated. Those rooms on the road are all double-glazed. The 100-year-old trees of the garden shade a swimming pool and tennis court. The winter hotel is more traditional with its typical dining room and open fireplace, its woodwork and furniture. Once again the bathrooms have been renovated. The welcome is among the most friendly.

How to get there *(Map 6): 56km south of San Sebastián via N1 to Tolosa, then N240.*

217

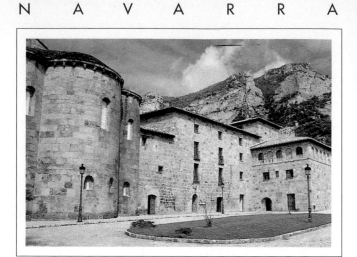

Hospederia de Leyre

31410 Monasterio de Leyre (Navarra)
Tel. (9)48-88 41 00 – Fax (9)48-88 41 37
Sr José Soteras

Category ★★ **Rooms** 32 with telephone, bath or shower and WC. **Price** Single 4,050-4400Pts, double 7,100-8,600Pts. **Meals** Breakfast 700Pts, served 8:30-10:00; half board + 2,200Pts, + 2,960Pts (per pers., 2 days min.). **Restaurant** With air-conditioning. Service 13:00-15:30, 20:00-22:00; menu 1,500Pts, also à la carte. Specialties: Regional cooking. **Credit cards** Amex, Visa, Eurocard, MasterCard. **Pets** Dogs not allowed. **Facilities** Parking. **Nearby** Monastery of Leyre - Pamplona. **Open** April – Dec 8.

In the Sierra de Leyre at the end of a winding and steep road, this ancient monastery rises up in the midst of a site of great beauty. The panorama over the artificial lake of Yesa and its environment of small hills is splendid. Considered in the 11th century as the great spiritual center of Navarre, and then abandoned in the 19th century, the monastery is now one of the most important historical monuments of the region. The hotel has been installed in the 17th- and 18th-century parts of the building, which have been renovated, and it offers 30 rooms, all simply furnished but comfortable. In the lounges you will appreciate the quiet that characterizes this establishment full of charm.

How to get there *(Map 6): 51km southeast of Pamplona via N240 to Yesa, then take small road to the left.*

Hotel Europa

31001 Pamplona (Navarra)
Espoz y Mina, 11
Tel. (9)48-22 18 00 - Fax (9)48-22 92 35 - Idoate Family

Category ★★★ **Rooms** 25 with air-conditioning, telephone, bath, WC, TV, and minibar; elevator. **Price** Double 7,850-9,850Pts. **Meals** Breakfast 875Pts, served 7:30-11.00; full board + 5,400Pts (per pers.). **Restaurant** Service 13:00-15:30, 21:00-23:00; closed Sun; à la carte 4,300-6,200Pts. Specialties: Dorada al sal con vinagreta de tomate y verduritas frescas - Manitas de cerdo crujientes y guiso de carrilleras de ternera en salsa con milhojas de patatas y foie. **Credit cards** All major. **Pets** Dogs not allowed. **Nearby** In Pamplona: Cathedral, Museum of Navarra - Feria (July) - Santiago de Compostella road in Navarra (Roncesvalles, Pamplona, Obanos, Puenta la Reina, Estella, Los Arcos, Torres del Rìo) - Ulzama golf course (9-Hole). **Open** All year.

Pamplona is famous for its festivals and notably its 'Encierro', when bulls are let loose in the streets of the town before the bullfights in the arenas on the same afternoon. Gourmet 'aficionados' know the Europa above all for its gastronomic restaurant preparing an excellent cuisine from the market - and for its wine cellar. This fully renovated hotel also makes you appreciate the 'know-how' of the family team. A classical but also modern decor which favors above all comfort and service : everything is impeccable, well thought-out, discreet, stylish - and also a little bit formal, as so often with the ambiance of any well-known restaurant. But one would be wrong to complain about too much perfection !

How to get there (Map 6): 80km south from San Sebasttián

Mesón del Peregrino

31100 Puente La Reina (Navarra)
Carretera de Pamplona, 11
Tel. (9)48-34 00 75 - Fax (9)48-34 11 90
Angel Combero - Nina Sedana

Category ★★ **Rooms** 14 and 1 suite with air-conditioning, telephone, bath, WC and TV. **Price** Single 7,000Pts, double 9,000-12,000Pts, suite 25,000Pts. **Meals** Breakfast 1,350Pts, served 8:00-10:30. **Restaurant** Service 13:30-15:30, 20:30-23:00; menu 3,500Pts, also à la carte. **Credit cards** Visa, Eurocard, MasterCard. **Pets** Dogs allowed. **Facilities** Swimming pool, parking. **Nearby** Pamplona - Feria of Pamplona (July) - Santiago de Compostella road in Navarra (Roncesvalles, Pamplona, Obanos, Puenta la Reina, Estella, Los Arcos, Torres del Rìo) - Ulzama golf course (9-Hole). **Open** All year except Christmas and New Year.

If you are rather fearful of the too lively nights of the Saint Firmin festival in Pamplona, then take refuge some twenty kilometers away at Puente La Reina, a strategic staging post on the road to Santiago de Compostela. At the Meson del Peregrino everything is done to attract you, and all is thought out to satisfy your well-being: reception, comfort, decor and gastronomy should create that harmony to satisfy all your senses. It is true that the old stone house is pretty, the large dining room opening onto the garden is welcoming and warm, the cuisine appetizing, the garden with its swimming pool restful. Nina and Angelo practise the art of receiving well admirably, and this is a very attractive address to seek out.

How to get there *(Map 6): 24km southwestfrom Pamplona.*

Parador Principe de Viana

31390 Olite (Navarra)
Plaza de los Teobaldos, 2
Tel. (9)48-74 00 00 - Fax (9)48-74 02 01
Sr Bertolin Blasco

Category ★★★ **Rooms** 43 with air-conditioning, telephone, bath, WC, TV and minibar; elevator. **Price** Double 14,500-17,500Pts. **Meals** Breakfast 1,300Pts, served 8:00-10:30. **Restaurant** Service 13:00-16:00, 20:30-23:00; menu 3,500Pts, also à la carte. Specialties: Regional cooking. **Credit cards** All major. **Pets** Dogs not allowed. **Nearby** In Olite: Castle, Church of Santa Maria la Real, Church of San Pedro - Monastery of Oliva - Pamplona. **Open** All year.

Installed in the residential part of the very beautiful chateau of the Kings of Navarre, the parador opens onto a small, quiet and sunny square planted with trees. The decor preserves the medieval character of the building and gives it all its charm. In addition, thanks to the stained glass windows, a soft and warm light gives the house an atmosphere of calm and meditation. The rooms have been installed in a recently rebuilt part of the building: they are sober and comfortable, but lack however the charm of the lounges.

How to get there *(Map 6): 43km south of Pamplona via N140, or via A15.*

Parador de Argómaniz

01192 Argómaniz-Vitoria (Alava)
Carretera N 1
Tel. (9)45-29 32 00 – Fax (9)45-29 32 87
Sr Jose Luis Rodriguez Gasco

Category ★★★ Rooms 54 with telephone, bath, WC, satellite TV and minibar; elevator. **Price** Double 15,000Pts. **Meals** Breakfast 1,300Pts, served 8:00-11:00. **Restaurant** Service 13:00-16:00, 20:30-23:00; menu 3,500Pts, also à la carte. Specialties: regional cooking **Credit cards** All major. **Pets** Dogs not allowed. **Facilities** Parking. **Nearby** In Vitoria: Church of Santa Maria and the museum - Salinas de Añana - Sanctuary of Estibaliz. **Open** All year.

Before giving battle to the Spanish and British at Vitoria, the Emperor Napoleon lodged in this 17th-century building. The earlier promenade with arcades has been transformed into the reception hall and one can still admire the original columns. The many lounges contribute to the hotel's comfortable ambiance, allowing you to enjoy the quiet of the building. On the top floor, under the eaves, the woodwork has been left uncovered, and here the dining room is to be found. The rooms are placed in the two modern wings, and are soberly decorated. Comfortable and very light, they also have small corner lounges. From the windows one can see the hill of Estibaliz with its monastery, and in the distance Vitoria, the capital of the province.

How to get there *(Map 5): 15km east of Vitoria via N1.*

Hotel Lopez de Haro

48009 Bilbao
Obispo Orueta, 2 and 4
Tel. (9)4-423 55 00 – Fax (9)4-423 45 00 – Sr Javier Muñoz

Category ★★★★★ **Rooms** 53 with air-conditioning, telephone, bath, WC, satellite TV and minibar; elevator. **Price** Single 10,800-20,250Pts, double 15,800-27,250Pts, suite 18,500-33,000Pts. **Meals** Breakfast 1,500Pts, served 7:00-11.00. **Restaurant** "Club Nautico" service 13:00-15:30, 20:00-23:30; closed Sat lunch, Sun and National Holidays; buffet (lunch): 3,500-4,000Pts, menus 5,300-6,300Pts, also à la carte. **Credit cards** All major. **Pets** Small dogs allowed. **Facilities** Garage (2100Pts). **Nearby** In Bilbao: Guggenheim Museum - Fine Art Museum - Nuestra Señora de Begoña - Campo de la Bilbaina golf course and Neguri golf course (18-Hole). **Open** All year.

This superb hotel occupies the former headquarters of the republican newspaper, "El Liberal", but behind the very classical and almost austere facade, a real jewel is hidden. The reception hall is particularly attractive with marble alongside green ivy, which makes for a remarkable effect. The caisson ceilings of the restaurant, the dainty tables with their pink linen and lamps, the elevator with its sparkling brass, or the very English bar with its soft club armchairs—all the details are carefully thought out. But however luxurious it may be, the hotel still keeps its warm character. In the bedrooms the walls have been left bare of any decoration and the effect is very successful: very comfortable, along with their very beautiful bathrooms. In the kitchens a French chef is in charge, and on the tables one finds Limoges porcelain and Bohemian crystal glassware. The welcome is always attentive and stylish, to crown the overall effect. An excellent base from which to visit the magnificent new Guggenheim Museum designed by the very talented Frank Gehry.

How to get there (Map 5): in the town center.

Mendi Goikoa

48291 Axpe (Biskaia)
Barrio San Juan, 33
Tel. (9)4-682 08 33 – Fax (9)4-682 11 36
Sr Iñaki Ibarra

Rooms 12 with telephone, bath or shower, WC. **Price** Single 3,975-6,425Pts, double 6,470-8,850Pts, suite 8,175-11,775Pts, 4 pers. 9,700-14,300Pts. **Meals** Breakfast included, served 8:30-10:30; half board 4,325-8,625Pts, full board 5,575-10,125Pts. **Restaurant** Service 13:00-14:30, 20:30-22:00. Closed Sunday evening and Monday; à la carte 3,000-6,000Pts. Specialties: Basque cooking. **Credit cards** All major. **Pets** Dogs not allowed. **Facilities** Parking. **Nearby** In Bilbao: Guggenheim Museum - Fine Art Museum - Durango - Abadiano - Elorrio. **Open** Jan 6 - Dec 21.

You leave Bilbao on the coastal highway, and reaching Durango, you head inland for the green pastures of the Aixondo Valley. The village of Axpe is typical of this region and it is in two former sheep-folds dating from the 18th century that Iellent hotel fp his restaurant along with a few rooms. Here, a truly rural atmosphere reigns with thick interior walls of stone and very rustic floors. The rooms have solid wooden furniture and there are very attractive engravings of mountain plants and flowers. Each is spacious with a fine view, our favorites being 4, 7 and 11. The dining room overlooking the valley is rarely empty, and it offers excellent regional food. This is a simple hotel, one that is well worth leaving the beaten path to enjoy.

Hox to get there *(Map 5): 20km east of Bilbao via E 70 Durango exit, take the raod towards Ellorio.*

Hostería de Señorio de Biskaia

48130 Bakio (Vizcaya)
Calle Cirarda
Tel. (9)4-619 47 25 – Fax (9)4-619 47 25
Sr Felipe Izarra

Category ★★ **Rooms** 16 with telephone, bath or shower, WC and TV. **Price** Single 3,975-6,425Pts, double 6,470-8,850Pts, 3 pers. 8,175-11,775Pts, 4 pers. 9,700-14,300Pts. **Meals** Breakfast included, served 8:30-10:30; half board 4,325-8,625Pts, full board 5,575-10,125Pts (per pers.). **Restaurant** Service 13:00-14:30, 20:30-22:00; à la carte. Specialties: Spanish and Basque cooking. **Credit cards** Amex, Visa, Eurocard, MasterCard. **Pets** Dogs allowed. **Nearby** Bilbao - Bilbaina golf courses (18-Hole). **Open** All year except Jan 7 - Mar 1.

It is difficult not to succumb to the charm of this large house with its pink stone and white balconies, converted some years ago into a small hotel. A rare balance is found here between a respect for the authentic and comfort. Its thick walls shelter a small restaurant and convivial bar on the ground floor, where they will serve you a few pinchos, among other drinks. A wooden staircase leads to the very well-arranged rooms, bright and pretty with their white walls and clear parquet floors. The bathrooms are perfect, while the suite on the upper floor has a veranda-lounge. The ultimate of romanticism, in the hotel park there is a small and shaded island reached via an aging wooden bridge. We should add that there is a very friendly welcome as well. Proximity to the Bakio beach, a paradise for surfers, is yet another 'plus' for this little hotel of charm.

How to get there *(Map 5): 26km north of Bilbao.*

Hotel El Puerto

48360 Mundaka (Biskaia)
Portu Kalea, 1
Tel. (9)687-68 67 – Fax (9)687-67 26 – Sr Jaon Ercilia

Rooms 11 with telephone, bath, WC, TV, satellite TV, minibar; elevator. **Price** Single 3,500-5,500Pts, double 8,500-9,500Pts. **Meals** Breakfast 900Pts, served 8:00-10:00. **No restaurant**. **Credit cards** All major. **Pets** Dogs allowed. **Facility** Garage (500Pts). **Nearby** In Bilbao: Guggenheim Museum - Fine Art Museum - Nuestra Señora de Begoña - Campo de la Bilbaina golf course and Neguri golf course (18-Hole). **Open** All year.

Mundaka is one of the typical little seaports spread out along the Basque Coast. Only thirty minutes from Bilbao, the El Puerto is known to surfers from the world over. It should be no surprise, therefore, that in the summertime, its clientele is young and very much into sports. The hotel is part of a traditional old house on the port with a delightful little garden with plane-trees. The interior is tasteful and well kept up, and the rooms are altogether classical; the baths and showers are all excellent. It should be noted that the stairs leading to the rooms on the third floor are somewhat steep. The best of them are those overlooking the square. In addition, the hotel has a shady terrace where you can have lunch or a quiet drink and enjoy the life of the village from a very convenient and sheltered hide-away. This is an excellent hotel.

How to get there *(Map 5): in th town center.*

Hotel Arocena

20740 Cestona (Guipúzcoa)
Paseo de San Juan, 12
Tel. (9)43-14 70 40 – Fax (9)43-14 79 78
Sr Arocena

Category ★★★ **Rooms** 110 with telephone, bath, WC and satellite TV; elevator. **Price** Single 4,510-6,200Pts, double 7,500-10,400Pts, 4 pers. 13,100-16,300Pts. **Meals** Breakfast 800Pts, served 8:00-11:00; full board + 4,000Pts (per pers.). **Restaurant** Service 13:00-15:00, 21:00-23:00; menu 2,500Pts, also à la carte. Specialties: fish. **Credit cards** All major. **Pets** Dogs allowed in the rooms. **Facilities** Swimming pool, tennis, sauna, fitness club, garage (800Pts).**Nearby** Therms - Sanctuary of San Ignacio de Loyala; San Sebastián - San Sebastián and Jaizkibel golf courses (18-Hole). **Open** Jan 15 - Dec 15.

This old hotel from the last century is in a plain lined with gently sloping hills that have always attracted those taking the waters. In this hotel they also found the charm they had come in search of, and the benefits of the medicinal waters of Cestona. Huge gardens surround the swimming pool, tennis court and park. The hotel's entry is well done with its interior gallery all in wood. Sadly, many of the rooms have been over-renovated in order to offer more amenities, but some have been preserved from this. The dining room has also been preserved and is set on two levels, with the second particularly attractive with stone columns, grand piano and flowered curtains.

How to get there (Map 5): 34km southwest of San Sebastián.

Hotel Obispo

20280 Fuenterrabia – Hondarribia (Guipúzcoa)
Plaza del Obispo
Tel. (9)43-64 54 00 – Fax (9)43-64 23 86 – Sr Alza
Web: http://www.camerdata.es/bidasoa/obispo

Category ★★★ **Rooms** 14 with telephone, bath, WC, TV and minibar; 1 for disabled persons. **Price** Single 9,000-12,000Pts, double 11,000-17,000Pts, suite 13,000-15,000Pts. **Meals** Breakfast 1,000Pts, served 8:00-11:00. **No Restaurant** (See p. 255). **Credit cards** Amex, Visa, Eurocard, MasterCard. **Pets** Dogs allowed on request. **Nearby** Ermita de San Marcial (view) - Road from Fuenterrabia to San Juan via Jaizkibel (view) - San Sebastián; San Sebastián and Jaizkibel golf courses (18-Hole). **Open** All year except Dec 22 - Jan 17.

This new hotel is in one of the beautiful Renaissance houses that resisted the siege by the Prince de Condé in 1638. Indeed, Fuenterrabia does not lack for history and qualities, while this charming town, only some twenty kilometers from San Sebastián, no doubt profits from the proximity of the Basque coast to attract a clientele who prefer getting away from the tourist crowd in the summer months. Inside the hotel the austerity of the stone and wood, traditionally used in the regional architecture, has been well exploited. The decoration creates a warm and even snug atmosphere: everywhere the pale wood furniture, the flowery fabrics, parquet floors and large cord carpets form a rustic ambiance in good taste. The amenities have not been forgotten, while the welcome and service are professional.

How to get there *(Map 6): 18km southwest of St-Jean-de-Luz.*

PAIS VASCO

Hotel Pampinot

20280 Fuenterrabia - Hondarribia (Guipúzcoa)
Calle Mayor, 3
Tel. (9)43-64 06 00 – Fax (9)43-64 51 28
Sra Alvarez

Category ★★★ Rooms 8 with telephone, bath, WC and TV. **Price** Double 10,500-14,000Pts, suite 15,000-17,000Pts. **Meals** Breakfast 1,200Pts, served 8:00-11:00. **Restaurant** See p. 255. **Credit cards** All major. **Pets** Dogs allowed. **Nearby** Ermita de San Marcial (view) - Road from Fuenterrabia to San Juan via Jaizkibel (view) - San Sebastián; San Sebastián and Jaizkibel golf courses (18-Hole). **Open** Dec 1 - Oct 30.

This is a former private house from the 18th century, in the heart of the very pretty town of Hondarribia. The entry hall with its walls of bare stone displays carefully chosen antiques, while a beautiful columned staircase leads to the rooms upstairs. Decorated more simply but all personalized with taste, the rooms are attractive and offer all the amenities. A quiet hotel offering a friendly welcome, where the absence of a restaurant adds to the peaceful impression. Our only regret: the 'airport-lounge-style' background music !

How to get there *(Map 6): 18km southwest of St-Jean-de-Luz.*

Hotel Maria Cristina

20004 San Sebastián–Donostia (Guipúzcoa)
Paseo de la Republíca Argentina, 4
Tel. (9)43 42 49 00 – Fax (9)43 42 39 14

Category ★★★★★ **Rooms** 139 with air-conditioning, telephone, bath, WC, satellite TV and minibar; elevator. **Price** Single 18,000-23,000Pts, double 24,500-39,000Pts, suite 55,600-88,500Pts. **Meals** Breakfast 2,000Pts, served 7:00-11:00. **Restaurant** Service 13:30-15:30, 21:00-23:30; à la carte 5,700Pts. Specialties: Regional and international cooking. **Credit cards** All major. **Pets** Dogs not allowed. **Nearby** Monte Ulia - Monte Urgull - Monte Igueldo; San Sebastián and Jaizkibel golf courses (18-Hole). **Open** All year.

This hotel evokes all the charms of the 'Belle Epoque', but it has been entirely renovated to satisfy a wealthy and refined clientele who appreciate luxury and comfort. There is tradition in the pseudo-Louis XV and Empire decors of the lounges and bedrooms, but contemporary efficiency elsewhere, as witnessed by the quality of amenities in the bathrooms and the immense kitchens. Its situation in the heart of the city is not the least of advantages. From the rooms, each with its own small balcony, one looks over the River Urumea, and there is a fine view of the Victoria Eugénia Theater that hosts the International Cinema Festival each September.

How to get there *(Map 5): in the city center.*

Hotel Monte Igueldo

20008 San Sebastián–Donostia (Guipúzcoa)
Tel. (9)43-21 02 11 – Fax (9)43-21 50 28 – Sra Pascual
Web: http://www.la-concha.com/mercure

Category ★★★★ **Rooms** 125 with telephone, bath, WC, satellite TV; elevator. **Price** Single 12,800-14,000Pts, double 16,000-17,500Pts, triple 21,500-23,500Pts. **Meals** Breakfast 1,050Pts (buffet), served 7:30-11:00. **Restaurant** With air-conditioning, service 13:00-15:00, 20:30-23:00; menu 2,200-2,500Pts. Specialties: fish, chipirones. **Credit cards** All major. **Pets** Dogs allowed (+ 3,000Pts). **Facilities** Swimming pool, parking. **Nearby** Monte Ulia - Monte Urgull - Monte Igueldo; San Sebastián and Jaizkibel golf courses (18-Hole). **Open** All year.

Built in 1967 on the summit of a hill dominating San Sebastián, this hotel is above all appreciated for its exceptional site. One has taken advantage of its beauty by giving the lounge and dining room huge bay windows looking over both sea and city. One might wish the bedrooms decorated with more taste, but nearly all of them have balconies except those on the corners, but these are brighter and have better access to the panoramic view: San Sebastián, with in the background the first peaks of the Pyrenees and, on a fine day, Biarritz in the distance. It is all superb! On the large roof-terrace there is a beautiful swimming pool and self-service restaurant, much appreciated in summer. One does regret however that the peace of the site is sometimes disturbed by the small amusement park close by.

How to get there *(Map 5): 5km west of San Sebastián, towards Monte Igueldo; a funicular railway ascends from the 'Ondarreta' beach to the amusement park.*

Hotel de Londres y de Inglaterra

20007 San Sebastián-Donostia (Guipúzcoa)
Zubieta, 2
Tel. (9)43-42 69 89 – Fax (9)43-42 00 31
Sr Vriarte

Category ★★★★ **Rooms** 133 with air-conditioning, telephone, bath, WC, satellite TV, safe and minibar; elevator. **Price** Single 11,500-16,700Pts, double 16,800-20,800Pts, suite 21,000-28,000Pts. **Meals** Breakfast 1,350Pts (buffet), served 7:00-11:00; half board + 3,450 Pts, full board + 8,050Pts (per pers.). **Restaurant** Service 13:00-15:30, 20:45-23:15; menu 1,975Pts, also à la carte. Specialties: Basque cooking. **Credit cards** All major. **Pets** Dogs not allowed. **Nearby** Monte Ulia - Monte Urgull - Monte Igueldo; San Sebastián and Jaizkibel golf courses (18-Hole). **Open** All year.

This hotel enjoyed a glorious period when the royal family came to San Sebastián for the summer months. The hotel overlooks the La Concha beach (enclosed by rocks), which was then very much in fashion. If this same fashion has now rather forgotten it, the hotel has however lost nothing of its splendor. There is still something of pride in this historic edifice. The service cannot take too much care, while the bedrooms are those of the classical grand hotel. One can hire a small boat from the hotel to cross to the small island of Santa Clara, which is always amusing.

How to get there *(Map 5): in the city center.*

Hotel Jatetxen Urrutitxo

20400 Tolosa (Guipúzcoa)
Kondero Aldapa, 7
Tel. (9)43 67 38 22 - Fax (9) 43 67 34 28
Sr Blanco Gordo

Category ★ Rooms 7 with telephone, shower, WC and TV. **Price** Single 5,000-5,500Pts, double 8,000-8,500Pts. **Meals** Breakfast 675Pts served 8:00-10:00; full board + 3,500Pts (per pers.). **Restaurant** Service 13:00-14:30, 20:30-22:30, closed Sun; menu 1,750Pts, also à la carte. Specialties: Regional and international cooking. **Credit cards** All major. **Pets** Dogs allowed. **Facilities** Parking. **Nearby** Monte Ulia - Monte Urgull - Monte Igueldo; San Sebastián and Jaizkibel golf courses (18-Hole). **Open** All year (except Jan 1 – 5).

An all-white-and-red house, and all Basque in the midst of the country: such is the Hotel Jatetxen Urrutitxo. The house was built in 1920 and restructured into a hotel in 1987. Both decoration and atmosphere have a lot of charm, with a small touch of French style. The bedrooms lack any great embellishments but are all in good taste, while the bathrooms lack no amenities. The restaurant is also good and the welcome friendly. This is a good halting place when discovering the Basque country.

How to get there *(Map 5): 27km south of San Sebastián via N1.*

Andorra Park Hotel

Andorra la Vieja (Principality of Andorra)
Les Canals
Tel. 376/82 09 79 – Fax 376/82 09 83 – Sr Antoni Cruz
E-mail: hotels@hotansa.com – Web: http://www.hotansa.com

Category ★★★★ **Rooms** 40 with telephone, bath, WC, satellite TV and minibar; elevator. **Price** Single 10,500-20,450Pts, double 14,450-26,900Pts. **Meals** Breakfast 1,700-1,800Pts (buffet), served 8:00-11:30; half board + 11,325-24,800, full board + 13,725-27,350Pts (per pers.). **Restaurant** Service 13:30-15:30, 21:00-22:30; à la carte 4,350Pts. **Credit cards** All major. **Pets** Dogs not allowed. **Facilities** Swimming pool, tennis, golf practise, parking. **Nearby** Skiing - Walking - Seu d'Urgell. **Open** All year.

The Andorra Park Hotel is a real oasis in this city suburb recently converted into a vast commercial center. The hotel is an excellent staging post and address on the way to Barcelona, or if you want to ski in the small resorts of the Principality. The result of an attractive restoration, three types of rooms are offered, and prices vary as to whether they have terraces or views over the valley. The decor is classical of a grand hotel, but modern and luxurious. The park surrounding the hotel is magnificent: carefully mown lawns, an admirable swimming pool carved out of the rock itself and with the mountains as back-drop, tennis, practice range – everything is done so that you get to know this 'natural' side of the town. There is also the restaurant opening out wide and directly onto the long terrace and garden. But the 'unconditionals of modern consumption' can also be reassured – the hotel could not resist having its own direct access to the "Pyrenees" department store !

How to get there *(Map 8): 220km north of Barcelona.*

Hostal Sant Pere

El Tarter/Soldeu (Principality of Andorra)
Prat dels Nogués
Tel. 376/85 10 87 – Fax 376/85 10 87
E-mail: hstpere@andornet.ad – Web: http://www.hstpere.andornet.ad

Rooms 6 with telephone, bath and WC. **Price** Double 9,000-12,000Pts. **Meals** Breakfast included, served 8:00-10:00. **Restaurant** Service 13:00-16:00, 20:30-23:00; closed Sun night and Mon except in summer; à la carte 5,000Pts. Specialties: Meat. **Credit cards** All major. **Pets** Dogs allowed in the rooms. **Facilities** Parking. **Nearby** Skiing - Walking - Seu d'Urgell. **Open** All year (except May 3-31).

Half way between the French frontier at Pas de la Casa and Andorra la Vieja, the Hostal de San Pere is a genuine mountain address magnificently sited at the foot of the Tarter ski runs, while one can enjoy here the peace and quiet and view of the summits. The house has been well restored and provides many small corners for sitting undisturbed by the open fires, or even at the bar to enjoy the view over so much nature. Very rustic and very warm, the restaurant lets you discover the specialties of Andorra and more particularly its grilled meats. The rooms are in the same style: with beams, timbered, some with sloping ceilings – all are different and comfortable. This is a charming and welcoming inn.

How to get there *(Map 8): 220km north of Barcelona.*

Xalet Ritz Hotel

Sispony/La Massana (Principality of Andorra)
Prat dels Nogués
Tel. 376/83 78 77– Fax 376/83 77 20
Sr Joan Fernández

Rooms 50 with telephone, bath, WC and TV; elevator. **Price** Single 7,500-14,000Pts,
double 11,400-19,000Pts. **Meals** Breakfast included, served 7:30-11:00; half board
8,200-12,000Pts (per pers.). **Restaurant** Service 13:30-15:30, 21:00-22:30; menu
3,500Pts. Specialties: Regional cooking. **Credit cards** All major. **Pets** Dogs allowed
(except in restaurant). **Facilities** Swimming pool, paddle-pool, garage, parking.
Nearby Skiing - Walking - Seu d'Urgell. **Open** All year.

One should forget the fair-time ambiance of the streets of the
'capital' of the Principality, to discover the snow-covered
summits of the Pyrenees, the woods and paths alongside the
mountain torrents. Just a few minutes away from all such frenzy, the
Xalet Ritz is found at the entry of the valley of the Valerà, on an
ideal site to profit from the mountain environment. It is a stone
building typical of the region, and offering many possibilities for
relaxation more or less sporting : from the hotel itself one can follow
the high mountain trails, reach the ski slopes in less than a quarter of
an hour, or enjoy the swimming pool and large garden in the warmer
season. The rooms offer all the comforts with the snug decor of an
alpine style. This is a good alternative staging post at more reasonable
prices.

How to get there *(Map 8): 220km north of Barcelona.*

El Elefante

03730 Jávea (Alicante)
Carretera de 3 Cabanes, 19
Tel. (9)6-646 00 09 – Fax (9)6-579 50 08/646 00 09 – Sra Frith

Category ★★ **Rooms** 5 with bath. **Price** Double 6,000Pts, suite 8,000Pts. **Meals** Breakfast included, served 8:30-10:30. **Restaurant** Service 19:30-23:00; menu 1,895Pts, also à la carte. Specialties: Regional and international cooking. **Credit cards** Visa, Eurocard, MasterCard. **Pets** Dogs not allowed. **Facilities** Parking. **Nearby** Cabo de San Antonio - Cabo de la Nao - Costa de Azahar to Valencia - Tosalet golf course (9-Hole). **Open** All year.

After spending fifteen years in the Middle East, John and Nadia Frith bought this house, which had the privilege of receiving Alfonso XIII when it was the only lodging house in the region. But why the Elephant ? Because in front of it there is a small mountain that looks strangely like such animal, and also because the owner has for a long time collected elephant-like objects, now scattered around the house. The greatest activity comes from the restaurant, while on the second floor five pleasant rooms, including that of the King with its private terrace, await you with their reasonable prices. Sun-tanning fanatics will delight in the large terrace-solarium on the roof, and will then refresh themselves in the swimming pool just close by which is surrounded by lawns. The cosy restaurant and bar have witnessed many an evening that finished far too late, for this place is much appreciated. This is a hotel without pretention but with a very warm welcome.

How to get there *(Map 22): 87km north of Alicante on the coast; before Jàvea, turn right, then Benitachell and the first on the left towards Cabo de la Nao.*

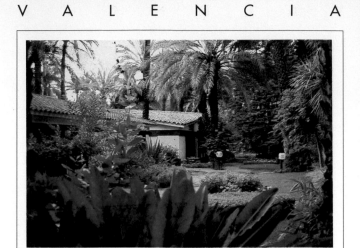

Huerto del Cura

03203 Elche (Alicante)
Porta de la Morera, 14
Tel. (9)6-545 80 40 - Fax (9)6-542 19 10 - Sr Orts

Category ★★★★ **Rooms** 80 with air-conditioning, telephone, bath, WC, satellite TV and minibar. **Price** Single 12,800Pts, double 18,000Pts, suite 19,000-40,000Pts. **Meals** Breakfast 1,500Pts, served 7:30-11:00; full board + 7,000Pts (per pers., 2 days min.). **Restaurant** Service 13:00-16:00, 20:30-23:00; à la carte. Specialties: fish. **Credit cards** All major. **Pets** Dogs not allowed. **Facilities** Swimming pool, tennis (1,000Pts), sauna (1,000Pts), parking. **Nearby** The palm forest of Elche - Church of Santiago in Novelda - Alicante. **Open** All year.

In the heart of Elche, a town known for its Paleolithic site and its celebrated 'Lady', the Huerto del Cura ('curé's garden') hotel will prove an agreeable staging post on the road to southern Spain. The garden is a real oasis, particularly luxuriant, and constitutes the main attraction of this parador built in the 'pavilion' style. The contemporary decor is without excess and the many services are appropriate to this type of establishment; all serve to create a relaxed atmosphere. The bedrooms are all quiet and well-equiped, and decorated with contemporary furniture, simple and in good taste. One may however regret certain details of the decor (hanging ceiling lights), that rather annoyingly recall collective institutes. Nevertheless, you will be sure to opt for a bungalow, but somewhat away from the swimming pool for greater quiet. The restaurant offers a rather jaded cuisine, said to be 'international', but this is compensated by the pleasure of lunching in the shade of the giant palm trees.

How to get there (*Map 21*): *19km southwest of Alicante.*

Hotel El Montiboli

03570 Villajoyosa (Alicante)
Tel. (9)6-589 02 50 - Fax (9)6-589 38 57
Sr José Manuel Castillo

Category ★★★★★ **Rooms** 53 with air-conditioning, telephone, bath, WC, satellite TV and minibar; elevator. **Price** Single 11,750-19,200Pts, double 17,000-25,700Pts, suite 21,950-35,200Pts, bungalow 23,950-37,200Pts. **Meals** Breakfast included, served 8:00-11:00; half board + 4,000Pts, full board + 6,800Pts (per pers., 3 days min.). **Restaurant** Service 13:00-15:30, 20:30-23:00; menu 3,650Pts, carte. Specialties: fish and regional cooking. **Credit cards** All major. **Pets** Dogs allowed (except in restaurant: 3,000Pts). **Facilities** 2 Swimming pools, tennis (900-1000Pts), fitness club, sauna, garage (2,500Pts). **Nearby** Alicante - Guadalest - Don Cayu de Setea golf course (9-Hole). **Open** All year.

Facing full on to the sea, the Montiboli is a hotel 'de luxe' on a promontory and enjoying a very lovely site. A pretty path in the stone itself leads down to a first panoramic swimming pool, and on to a second on the level of the semi-private beach itself. Near to this one, a small restaurant serves paellas and seafood at lunchtime. Spacious, very bright and with pretty bathrooms, the rooms all have terraces. Most attractive are the bungalows with private staircase, lounge and open fireplace facing the sea. In the main building a very 'cosy' lounge with its beams visible and very light colored furniture, is next door to a reading room. The reasonable number of rooms allows for an attentive welcome on the part of the hotel, and you will be very much at ease here. You will certainly appreciate the lifestyle as you wake up looking at the sea, then lunch on the beach, and go to sleep in peace having dined under the stars.

How to get there *(Map 22): 32km north of Alicante via A7, exit Villajoyosa.*

RESTAURANTS
SPAIN

ANDALUSIA

ARCOS DE LA FRONTERA

El Convento, Marqués de Torresoto 7, Tel. (956) 70 32 22. Pts 3,000.

CÓRDOBA

El Caballo Rojo, Cardenal Herrero 28, Tel. (957) 47 53 75 - Elegant and refined, traditional cuisine with specialties such as *rabo de toro* (bull's tail) and *salmorejo*. - **Almudaina**, Campo Santo de los Mártires, Tel. (957) 47 43 42 - Closed Sundays. Close to the Juderia and the Alcazar gardens. Pts 5,000. - **El Churrasco**, Romeno 16, Tel. (957) 29 08 19 - Closed Sunday evenings and Mondays in winter. Touristy with flamenco in the basement, a pleasant ambiance however. - **Mesón El Burladero,** Calleja la Hoguera 5, Tel. (957) 47 27 19 - A simple *Taverne* with a very correct *Manolete* menu. Some tables in the patio in summer.

BODEGAS AND MESONES NEAR THE PLAZA TENDILLAS

Bodegas Campos, near the Plaza del Potro. - Casa Rubio, Puerta de Almodóvar 5. - **Mesón de la Luna**, Calleja de la Luna.

CADIZ

El Faro, San Felix 15, Tel. (956) 21 10 68 - Welcoming decor, fish and seafood, Pts 4,000. - **Ventorrillo del Chato**, Playa de Cortadura - **Via Augusta Julia**, Tel. (956) 25 00 25 - Closed Sunday - Pts 3500.

GRANADA

Carmen de San Miguel, pl. de Torres Bermejas 3, Tel. (958) 22 67 23 - Closed Sunday, 15-30 August. In Alhambra, beautiful view on Grenade. – **Cunini**, Pescaderia 9 and Capuchinas 4, Tel. (958) 25 07 77 - Closed Mondays. The best fish restaurant in town. At the bar, a large variety of seafood tapas, Pts 3,500. - **Mesòn Andalus,** Elvira 17, Tel. (958) 25 86 61. Typical decoration - **Sevilla**, Oficios 12, Tel. (958) 22 12 23 - Correct cuisine, big tapas bar. Reservation needed. – **Ruta del Veleta**, road to Sierra Nevada (5km from Cenes de la Vega), Tel. (958) 48 61 34 - Closed Sunday evenings - Very good cuisine, grilled meat specialties, *carnes à la brasa*, and salted fish, Pts 4,000. – **Zoraya,** Panaderos 32, Tel. (958) 29 35 03. Beautifull terrace in Albaicin.

JAÉN

Los Maricos, Nuerva 2, Tel. (953) 25 32 06 - Delicious shellfish. - **Mesón Vicente**, Arco del Consuelo 1, Tel. (953) 26 28 16 - Closed Sundays evenings. Regional cuisine, tapas bar and friendly dining room.

JEREZ DE LA FRONTERA

Gaitán, Gaitán 3, Tel. (956) 34 58 59 - Closed Sunday evenings. Andalusian cuisine and some Basque specialties, Pts 3,300. - **Venta Antonio**, road to Sanlúcar, km 6, Tel. (956) 14 05 35 - Closed Mondays. Banal and functional decor but good and well-cooked fish specialties. - **Tendido 6**, Circo 10, Tel. (956) 34 48 35 - Closed Sunday evenings. Beautiful andalous patio. Pts 3500.

TABASCOS AND MESONES IN THE SAN MARCOS QUARTER

Maypa, near the Plaza des Angustias - The best known. - **Venenzia-Faustino,** near the Place de l'Arenale.

MÁLAGA

Café de Paris, Paseo Maritimo, Tel. (95) 222 50 43 - Closed Sunday evening in winter. Good cooking. Pts 3500-5000. − **Antonio Martín**, Paseo Maritimo 4, Tel. (952) 22 21 13 - Closed Sunday evenings. One of the oldest restaurants of Málaga. Fish, paella, on a beautiful terrace over the sea. - **La**

Taberna del Pintor, Maestranza 6, Tel. (95) 221 53 15 - Speciaties: Meats - Pts 3000-4000. - **El Boquerón de la Plata**, Alarcón Luyán 6 - the best bar for tapas and *gambas*.

FLAMENCO

Teatro Cervantes, a breeding ground of flamenco.

MARBELLA

La Fonda, Plaza del Santo Cristo 9, Tel. (95) 277 25 12 - On one of the prettiest squares in town, in an 18th century house, one dines on a marvellous patio. Very chic, Pts 6,000. - **Mesón del Pasaje**, Pasaje 5, Tel. (95) 277 12 61 - Closed at midday in summer. Victorian decor in the small dining rooms, international cuisine. Attractive and not very expensive. - **La Tricycleta**, Buitrago 14, Tel. (95) 277 78 00 - Closed Sundays and from January 15 to February 15. One of the best known restaurants in Marbella. Specialty, *Tricycleta brochettes*. - **Casa Eladio**, Plaza Naranjos 6 - Small and pretty ceramics-decorated patio.

TAPAS BARS

Bar Ana Maria, Plaza Santo Cristo - Closed Mondays. If not afraid of noise and a crowd.

MIJAS

El Padrasto, Paseo del Compás, Tel. (95) 248 50 00 - Beautiful view of Fuengirola and the coast.

Classic Spanish cuisine. Pts 3,500.

Pepe Rico, Almirante Ferandis 28, Tel. (95) 252 02 47 - Very pleasant in summer - Pts 2500-3000. - **De Miguel**, Pintada 2, Tel. (95) 252 29 96. Open the night Oct to Mar.

FLAMENCO

El Colono, Granada 6 - Flamenco in a typical Andalusian house. One can also dine here.

RONDA

Don Miguel, Pl. de España 4, Tel. (95) 287 10 90 - Closed Sundays from June to September. The restaurant is rather expensive but an attractive bar for having a glass and tapas, Pts 2,500. - **Pedro Romero**, Virgen de la Paz 18, Tel. (95) 287 11 10 - 'Bullfighter chic' ambiance, specialty *tocino del cielo al coco*, Pts 3,000. - **Mesón Santiago**, Marina 3 - Pleasant *taverne* in Andalusian style.

SANLUCAR DE BARRAMEDA

Mirador Doñana, Bajo de Guia, Tel. (956) 36 42 05. Fish and seafood. Pts 3,000. - **Bigote,** Tel. (956) 36 29 96 - Fish, on the Bajo de Guia beach.

SEVILLE

El Burladero, Canalejas, Tel. (95) 422 29 00 - Closed in Aug. The favorite restaurant of the bullfighters, Pts 3,500. - **La Albahaca**, Plaza Santa Cruz 12, Tel. (95) 422 07 14. Closed Sun. Beautiful Andalusian house of the famous architect Juan Talavera. Spanish and French cuisine, Pts 4,500. - **Egaña Oriza**, San Fernando 41, Tel. (95) 422 72 11 - Closed Sat middays, Sun and in Aug. Well situated above the Murillo gardens, a new restaurant appreciated by the Sevillians. Modern decor, gastronomic cuisine, Pts 5,000.

Hosteria del Laurel, Plaza Venerables 5, Tel. (95) 422 02 95 - Very touristic but well situated in the Barrio Santa Cruz. One dines on a terrace on the square, pretty house. - **Taberna del Alabardero,** Zaragosa 20, Tel. (95) 456 06 37 - In a old Palais- Pts 4000-7000. By reservation. – **La Dehesa,** Luis Morales 2, Tel. (95) 457 94 00 - Specialties: Meals. – **Rio Grande**, Betis, Tel. (95) 44 27 39 56. Big terrace on the river. **Enrique Becerra**, Gamazo 2, Tel. (95) 421 30 49 -

Closed Sundays. Pts 3,500. - **Rincòn de Casana**, Santo Domingo de la Calzada 13, Tel. (95) 453 17 10 - Closed Sunday in July, August, Pts 3500-4500. – **El Mero**, Betis 1, Tel. (95) 433 42 52 - Closed Tuesday. Shell fish, Pts 3500.

TAPAS BARS

Alhucema, Carlo Canal 20 A. - **Cerveceriá Giralda**, Mateos Gago 1. - **La Estella**, corner of Calles Estrella and Pajarito. Savory tapas and not expensive. - **El Jovcm Costalcro**, Torneo 18. - **Casa Román**, Plaza de los Venerables. - **Cas Robles**, Alvarez Quintero 50.

Casa Morales, García de Vinuesa 11 - Unchanged since 1850, ideal for taking a *fino* (sherry). - **La Taquilla**, ideal for the bullfight days, facing the arena. - **Rincón San Eloy**, San Eloy 24. - **El Rinconcillo**, Calle

Gerona 40 - The oldest bar in Seville (1670), tapas and *tortillas de bacalaó*. - **Tremendo**, just next door, Calle San Felipe - Good beer accompanied by codfish and dried *mohama* (tunnyfish). - **Carboneria**, Plaza de las Marcedarias - Rustic, pleasant patio. - **Bar Garlochi**, corner of Calles Boteros and Alhondiga - Kitsch *'Semana Santa'* decor. Visit in the evening.
MORE CHIC: **Abades**, Calle Abades, for cocktails. - **Bar of Hotel Alfonso XIII**, for tea.

FLAMENCO

El Arenal, Dos de Mayo 26, Tel. (95) 421 30 75. - **Los Gallos**, Plaza Santa Cruza 11, Tel. (95) 421 69 81 - One of the best known spots, in the heart of the Barrio Santa Cruz. - **El Patio Sevillano**, Paeso de Colón, Tel. (95) 421 41 20 - Vcry, and too touristy.

A S T U R I A S
C A N T A B R I A

GIJON

Casa Victor, Carmen 11, Tel. (98) 534 83 10 - Closed Sunday evenings, Thursdays and in November. 'Nouvelle cuisine' fish restaurant. Friendly welcome.

OVIEDO

Casa Fermin, San Francisco 8,

Tel. (98) 521 64 52 - Closed Sunday evenings. Sophisticated decor. Refined traditional cuisine, Pts 4,000. - **El Raitàn**, Plaza Trascorrales 6, Tel. (985) 21 42 18 - Closed Sundays in summer. Ideal for sampling regional specialties. No menu but 9 dishes regularly served, Pts 3,500. - **Del Arco**, Pl. de America, Tel. (98) 525 55 22 - Closed Sunday and August, Pts 3500-5000. – **Cabo Peñas,** Meaquiades Alvarez 24, Tel. (98) 522 03 20 - Typical restaurant, Pts 2500-3500.

BILBAO

El Asador de Aranda, Egaña 27, Tel. (94) 443 06 64 - Closed Sun evenings, July 25 to Aug 14. Pts 3,500. - **Goizeko Kabi**, Particular de Estraunza 4, Tel. (94) 441 50 04 - Closed Sundays from July 25 to Aug 14. The grand, good and elegant fsih restaurant of the town. Pts 6,000.

B A L E A R I C I S L A N D S

MALLORCA

PALMA DE MALLORCA

Honoris, Camino Viejo de Bunyola 76, Tel. (971) 29 00 07 - Closed Saturday midday and Sundays. Pts 3,950. - **Es Parlament**, Conquistador 11, Tel. (971) 72 60 26. Chic clientele with politicians that coming for the *paella del ciego* - Closed Sunday and in August. 3000-5000 Pts – **Porto Pi**, Joan Miró 182, Tel. (971) 40 00 87. Closed Saturday middays and Sundays. Old Mallorcan house. Basque 'nouvelle cuisine'. Pts 4,000. - **Abaco**, C/ San Juan 1. Baroque ambiance in a Manor-bar where you can drink cocktails with an atmospheric classical music. «in» - **Bar Celler S'Antiquari**, Plaza Santa Cataline Tomás - Local clientele.

DEYA

Ca'n Quet, Carret. de Valldemosa, km 1.2, Tel. (971) 63 91 96 - Closed from October to April, and Mondays. Pretty view of the mountains. Pts 4,000.

IBIZA

IBIZA

S'Oficina, Avenuda de España 6, Tel. (971) 30 00 16 - Closed Sundays. The entrance is not very elegant but pleasant interior with patio. Basque cuisine. Pts 4,000. - **Bar San Juan**, Calle Montgri 8, Tel. (971) 31 07 66 - Bistro style. Good fish. - **La Masia d'En Sord**, Carret. de San Miguel, km 6.5, Apartado 897, Tel. (971) 31 02 28 - Open from Easter till October. Old house, art gallery. Pts 4,000.

SANTA EULALIA

Cás Pages, Carret. de San Carlos, km 10, (Pont de

S'Argentara) - Closed Tuesdays and in February. Savory cuisine in this rustic old farmhouse.

SAN JOSÉ

Cana Joana, road Ibiza-San José, km 10, Tel. (971) 80 01 58 - Closed Sunday evenings, Mondays except in summer, from October 15 to December 29. Very pleasant setting in this old country house. Try the *riscalos* (mushrooms) and the *escallopinos de pato* (minced duck). Reservation advisable. Pts 4,000-6,000.

CASTILLA-LEON

AVILA

El Molino de la Losa, Bajada de la Losa 12, Tel. (920) 21 11 01 - Closed on Mondays in winter. Former 15th century mill in the middle of the River Adaja. Service in the garden on fine days. - **Mesón del Rastro**, Plaza Rastro 1, Tel. (920) 21 12 18 - In the wing of a medieval palace. Specialties: *El barco*, lamb and beans. Pts 3000-4000.

BURGOS

Mesón del Cid, Plaza Santa Maria 8, Tel. (947) 20 59 71 - Closed Sunday evenings. Well situated in a 15th century house. From the dining room on the upper floors, superb view of the cathedral. Good traditional cuisine. Pts 3,500.

LÉON

Casa Pozo, Plaza San Marcelo 15, Tel. (987) 22 30 39 - Closed Sunday evenings, from July 1 to 15. Simple and welcoming atmosphere under the attentive eye of Pin, the patron, who keeps his house well run. Pts 3,500-4,000. - **Adonias**, Santa Nonia 16, Tel. (987) 20 67 68 - Closed Sundays, 15 days in August. Regional cuisine in a rustic and lively setting. Pts 3,000-5,000.

BAR
Prada a Tope Bar, on corner of the Plaza San Martin - Tasting of regional wine from Bierzo.

SALAMANCA

Río de la Plata, Pl. del Peso 1, Tel. (923) 21 90 05 - Closed Mondays and in July. Small attractive restaurant serving a simple and quality cuisine. Pts 3,500-4,500. - **Chapeau**, Gran Via 20, Tel. (923) 27 18 33 - Closed August 15-31. Pts 3,500.

BAR
Café Las Torres, Plaza Mayor 26 - One of the best known bars on the square.

SEGOVIA

Mesón de Cándido, Mesón de Cándido, Tel. (921) 42 59 11 - Closed in November. All the personalities come here. An institution in Spain. Pts 3,000-4,000. - **Mesón de José Maria**, Cronista Lecea 11, Tel. (921) 43 44 84 - Closed in November.

Equal with, and some say better than, its historical competitor. Pts 3,000-4,000. - **Mesón Duque**, Cervantes 12, Tel. (921) 43 05 37 - Intimate decoration and atmosphere for this other good restaurant of the town.

BAR

La Conceptión, Plaza Mayor 15, close to the cathedral - The ideal halt for lunch.

SORIA

Mesón Castellano, Plaza Mayor 2, Tel. (975) 21 30 45 - Closed January 15 to 31 - Traditional restaurant. Specialties: *Chuletón de ternera, migas.* Pts 2,500-4,500.

VALLADOLID

Mesón la Fragua, Paseo Zorrilla 10, Tel. (983) 33 87 85 - Closed Sunday evenings, Mondays, in August. Luxurious, very expensive, frequented by the royal family. One of the best known restaurants of Castille. Pts 3,500-5,000.

CASTILLA - MANCHA

TOLEDO

Assador Adolfo, Granada 6 and Hombre de Palo 7, Tel. (925) 22 73 21 - Closed Sunday evenings. Major classic regional specialties such as *perdiz estofada toledana* and *delicias de màzapan.* Good wines selection. Pts 4,000-5,500. - **Venta de Aires,** Circo Romano 35, Tel. (925) 22 05 45 - On the outskirts of town - Good meats and generous Rioja wines. Pts 3,000-4,000.

BAR

In one of the small lanes south of the Plaza Zocodover, you will find numerous bars and small restaurants open on the sidewalks: these were used as decor in 'Tristana' by Luis Buñuel.

CUENCA

Figón de Pedro, Cervantes 15, Tel. (966) 22 45 11 - Closed Sunday evening, Mondays. One of the best known restaurants in Spain. Excellent regional cuisine. Pts 3,000.
Mesòn Casa Colgadas, Canònigos, Tel. (969) 22 35 09, Pts 4000. Very beautiful view on the valley.

PUERTO LAPICE

Venta del Quijote, El Molina 4. - Closed Thursdays and in September. Facing the church. Products of La Mancha in an ancient inn. Pleasant atmosphere, traditional and family cuisine. Pts 3,000-4,500.

G A L I C I A

LA CORUNA

El Rápido, La Estrella 7, Tel. (948) 22 42 21 - Closed Sunday evenings except in summer and December 15 to 31. The shellfish are magnificent. Regular and elegant clientele. Reservation advised. – **Coral,** La Estrella 2, Tel. (981) 22 10 82 - Closed Sunday except in summer, Pts 2500-4500.

SANTIAGO DE COMPOSTELA

Anexo Vilas, Avenida Villagarcia 21, Tel. (981) 59 86 37. - Closed Mondays. Moncho Vilas is proud of having prepared the menu for Jean-Paul II's visit to St.-Jacques-de-Compastela in 1989. Good recipes from Galicia. Pts 4,000-5,500. - **San Clemente,** San Clemente 6, Tel. (981) 58 08 82 - Very good fish. Choose the more comfortable dining room. - **Bodega Abrigadoiro,** Carretera del Conde 5 - In the old town. Perfect for a lunch break (*chorizo* and *tortillas*).

PONTEVEDRA

Doña Antonia, Soportale de la Herreria 4, Tel. (986) 84 72 74 - Closed Sunday, Pts 3000-4000. – **Casa Solla**, in San Salvador, Carretera de la Toja, 2 km, Tel. (986) 85 26 78 - Closed Thursdays and for Christmas. The two best addresses in Pontevedra.

C A T A L O N I A

BARCELONA

In the town center.

La Cuineta, Paradis 4, Tel. (93) 315 01 11 - Typical restaurant in a bodega (17th-century). 3500-6000Pts.
Los Caracoles, Escudillers 14, Tel. (93) 302 31 85 - Opened in 1835, success has never left it.

Specialties: *Los Caracoles* (snails) of course, and *paella de mariscos*. The hot quarter in the evening. It's better to have a reservation
Can Ramonet, Maquinista 17, Tel. (93) 319 30 64 - Closed August. Pts 3500-4500
Ca La Maria, Tallers 76 bis, Tel. (93) 318 89 93. Closed Sunday

evening, Monday, August. Pts 2500.

Agut d'Avignon, Trinitat 3, Tel. (93) 302 60 34 - Pts 4000-6000.

Agut, Gignas 16, Tel. (93) 315 17 09 - Closed Sunday evenings, Mondays and in July. In the Gothic quarter, an old house (since 1924) always offering well cooked Catalan specialties. Good wines selection.

15 Nits, on the Plaza Real. One of the most charming place in Barcelona, very busy, it's better to go late for avoided to stand in line.

Egipte, Jerusalem 12, Tel. (93) 317 74 80 - Behind the Boqueria market. Small restaurant on several floors serving regional cuisine at very affordable prices. 'Plat du jour' at midday.

South

Ca l'Isidre, Les Flors 12, Tel. (93) 441 11 39 - Closed Sundays and July 15 to August 15. A classic of Barcelona, Catalan cuisine, chic ambiance. Go there by cab in the evening, the hot quarter. Pts 4,600-5,600. - **El Tragaluz**, 1 passage de la Concepciò 5, Tel. (93) 487 01 96

- Closed Sunday. Pts 5500. Design decoration, at the first floor Japanese-grill, at the second floor traditionnel cooking under a beautiful glass roof. Fashion and society ambiance. – **La Tramoia**, Rambla de Catalunya, 15, Tel. (93) 412 36 34 - "in", tapas and catalonian cooking – **Els Pescadors**, plaza Prim 1, Tel (93) 309 20 18 - Closed Easter, Chrismas, New Year. Shell fish. Pts 5000. – **Rias de Galicia**, Lleida 7, Tel. (93) 424 81 52 - Fish. Pts 4000-5000. – **Font del Gat,** passeig Santa madona Montjuic, Tel. (93) 424 02 24 - Closed Monday. Pts 4500. – **El Cellar de Casa Jordi**, Rita Bonnat 3, Tel. (93) 430 10 45 - Closed Sunday and August. Pts 2000-3000.

North

Botafumeiro, av. Gan de Gracia 8, Tel. (93) 218 42 30 - Closed in August. Specialties fish and sea food. Pts 4000-6500. – **El Asador de Aranda,** Avenida Tibidabo 31, Tel. (93) 417 01 15 - Closed Sunday evenings. Traditional atmosphere, decoration and cuisine. Pts 4,000. - **La Venta,** Plaza Doctor Andreu (at Tibidabo, served by the blue tramway) - Closed Sundays. Good fish and superb view of the city and sea. Pts 4,200-5,000. - **A la Menta**, passeig Manuel Girona 50, Tel. (93) 204 15 49 - Closed Saturday evening, Sunday in Juni to September. Pts 3000-4000.

Port Vell and La Barceloneta

Les Set Portes, Passage Isabel II 14, Tel. (93) 319 30 33 - The 7 doors in fact total 11 ! Paellas, rice in cuttlefish ink. Always lots of people. Pts 3,000-4,500.

Salmonete, Playa de San Miguel 34, Tel. (93) 319 50 32.

L'Arrosejat, Playa de San Miguel 38 - It is a Barcelona institution to go and eat paella and seafood on the Barceloneta beach.

Merendero dei Mari, Palau de Mar du port Vell, plaça Vila 1,

Tel. (93) 221 31 41. Tapas with fish. When you leaving, stop at the café Magatzem just near.

Barceloneta, L' Escar 22, Moll del Pescador, Port Vell, Tell. (93) 221 21 11. Gastronomic address, managed by the famous Mey Hofmann in a wonderful liner decor by Estrella Salietti. She have also decorated the Merendero dei Mari. Not to be missed - **Casa Costa-Cal Pinxo,** beach of Barceloneta Baluard 124, Tel. (93) 221 50 28. A good

cooking (fish) served in a very pleasant dining room or terrace.

'XAMPANYERIAS'
Tapas bar Basque, often closed Sunday evenings and Monday.

La Cava del Palau, Verdaguer i Callis 10 - Closed Sundays. Near to the Palau de la Música. Large choice of wines, champagnes and cocktails with sampling of patés and cheeses. - **El Xampanyet,** Montoada 22 - Closed Mondays. A lot of atmosphere in this 'xampanyeria', certainly one of the nicest in Barcelona, close to the Picasso Museum. - **Euskal Etxea** (opposite) Placete Moncada. Pintxos, cider, keep your small stick for the addition – **Café du Musée du Textile**, Montoada 28. Drinks and snacks available in the delightful courtyard of the museum.

Tapas bars

Bar Rodrigo, L'Argeneria 67 - Closed Wednesday evenings and Thursdays. Near to Santa Maria de Canaletas church. One samples tapas with *vermut*, house specialty. - **Cervecería Baviera,** Ramblas 127 - Sampling of tapas and seafood, at table or standing at the counter. - **Can Paixano**, Reina Christina, after the Plaça de Palau - Famous for its good 'cave' and tapas. Very modest prices.

Cafes

Café de l'Académie, Lledo 1 - Closed evenings. Near the Generalitat. Clientele of politicians taking a *bocadillo*.
Els Quatre Gats, Carrer. Montsio - Closed Sundays. Very famous café in a building (1896) of Josep Puig i Cadafalch, where Picasso had his first exhibition. Careful ! - a modern version is next to the old bar.

Cafeteria de l'Opera, Rambla dels Caputxins - Beautiful café from the 'Belle Epoque' which has conserved its decor. Very

good 'café au lait' (*cortado*). - **Bar del Pí,** Plaça del Pí - Very popular 'Art-Deco' bar. Large outside terrace. - **La Fira**, Provenza 171, decored with slot machines, bumper cars... "in" - **Marsella**, San Pau 65 - One of the most famous night bar in the town. - **La Torre de Avila**, Poble Espanyol - Open the weekend from midnight to 4 a.m. Ouvert en fin de semaine de minuit à 4 heures du matin. The favorite nightclub of the yuppies in a Mariscal decor – **La Paloma,** Carret. del Tigre 27 - Open Thurdays to Sundays from 9Pm. Vast rococo dance hall, surrounded by two tiers of seating where one finds all generations and social classes mixed together, rock and tango dancers. - **Bar Mundial**, Plaça Santa Agusti Vell 11 - Closed Mondays. Very popular local bar for evening tapas. The back room serves *zarzuelas* and welcomes a more 'with it' clientele. Other specialty: peach liqueur (*melocotón*).

Ramblas 83. Specialties: cakes with pine nut.

Vincon, passeig de Gracia 96, near Pedrera.

LA BOQUERIA

On the Ramblas, 89, don't forget to go for a stroll at the Boqueria market. - Just by side, the **Casa Guinart** for the salt specialties.

The famous pastrymaking-tea room of **Christian Escriba**,

NEAR TO BARCELONA

MONTSERRAT

Montserrat, Plaça Apostols - Open only at lunchtime.

SITGES

Vivero, Paseo Balmins, Tel. (93) 894 21 49 - Seafood. Pts 2,300-4,500.

GERONA

Albereda, Albereda 7, Tel. (972) 22 60 02 - Closed Sundays. Pts 3,500-5,400. - **Isaac el Sec**, beside the museum - Tapas.

FIGUERAS

Ampurdán, Carretera de Olot, km 1.5, Tel. (972) 50 05 62 - Very good Franco-Catalan cuisine. Pts 4,500-6,000.

CADAQUÉS

Galiota, Narcis Monturiol 9, Tel. (972) 25 81 87 - One comes here for the fish and the Dali drawings on the walls - **Casa Anita**, Carrer Miguel Roset, Tel. 25 81 71. This address is the must of Cadaqués she's stornm in summer between 8 and 10 p.m.

CAFES
Cafe de la Habana, Carrer Bartomeus, it's a chic café for have a drink the evening - **L'Hostal**, Rambla, a bar-disco, "in".

TORTOSA

San Carlos, Rambla Felip Pedrell 19, Tel. (977) 44 10 48 - The decor is without interest but do not be put off. The fish specialties such as *rosseyat*, fish from the Ebro delta, or *romasco de rape*, are excellent. - **Raco de Mig-Cami**, route Simpatica, 2.5 km, Tel. (977) 44 31 48 - Closed Sunday evenings, Mondays. Pts 2,550-3,500.

PUIGCERDÀ

La Vila, Alfons I. 134, Tel. (972) 14 05 04 - Closed Mondays. Very good cuisine. Pts 3,500. - **Madrigal**, Alfons I. 1, Tel. (972) 88 08 60 - Bar-restaurant serving tapas and some house specialties: snails, cuttlefish.

LLIVIA

(6km from Puigcerdá)
Can Ventura, Plaça Mayor, Tel. (972) 89 61 78 - Closed Sunday evenings, Tuesdays, in October. One of the good restaurants in the Puigcerdá area for its decor and cuisine. Reservation necessary.

MARTINET

(on the road 26km from Puigcerdá)
Can Boix, Tel. (973) 51 50 50 - Gastronomic restaurant with French and Catalan specialties. Good and expensive. Pts 5,000.

E X T R E M A D U R A

CACERES

El Figón de Eustaquio, Plaza San Juan 12, Tel. (927) 24 81 94 - Small restaurant very popular at lunchtime (reservation), well prepared traditional cuisine, one of the best addresses in the region. Pts 2,500-3,300.

TRUJILLO

Hostal Pizarro, Plaza Mayor 13, Tel. (927) 32 02 55 - Convivial atmosphere in this small restaurant; Two sisters have taken over this family business. Keen to promote regional specialties such as stuffed chicken (*gallina truffada*). – **Mesòn La Troya**, plaza Mayor 10, Tel. (927) 32 13 64 - Tipical restaurant. Pts 1800.

N A V A R R E

ARISCUN

Etxeverria, near to Frontón, Tel. (948) 58 70 13 - Pretty little inn in a former farm. Regional cuisine. Some pretty rooms.

PAMPLONA

Josexto, Principe de Viana 1,

Tel. (948) 22 20 97 - Closed Sunday except in May and for the Saint-Fermin. Pts 6000-8000.

M A D R I D

MADRID

El Cenador del Prado, Prado 4, Tel. (91) 429 15 61 - Closed Saturday luncht, Sunday, 2 weeks in August. Pts 3000-4000.

Posada de la Villa, Cava baja 9, Tel. (91) 366 18 80 - Metro: Latina - Closed Sunday evening, 24 July to 24 August. In a old posada. Pts 6000-3000.

El Mentidero de la Villa, Santo Tomé 6, Tel. (91) 308 12 85 - Closed Saturday lunch, Sunday, August. Pts 4000-5000.

Las Cuevas de Luis Candelas, Cuchilleros 1, Tel. (91) 366 54 28. Pts 3500-5000.

La Dorada, Orense 64, Tel. (91) 270 20 40 - Closed 3 weeks in August. The best for seafood and salted fish.

Café de Oriente, Plaza de Oriente 2, Tel. (91) 541 39 74 - Closed Saturday middays, Sundays and in August. Chic. In summer the most elegant terrace in Madrid to take a glass. One dines inside. Catalan cuisine. Basque cuisine on reservation. Pts 5,000.

La Bola, Bola 5, Tel. (91) 547 69 30 - Closed Saturday evenings, Sundays and in July and August. Cosy atmosphere.

Traditional cuisine. Pts 3,000-4,200.

Botín, Arco de Cuchilleros 17, Tel. (91) 266 42 17 - The Guiness Book of Records names it the oldest restaurant in the world, made famous by Hemingway. Specialties: *cochonillo* and *cordero asado*. Reservation necessary. Pts 3,000-5,000.

Casa Lucio, Cava Baya 35, Tel. (91) 365 32 52 - Closed in August. 'Taverne' freqented by artists, intellectuals, bullfighters. Traditional cuisine, very good Jabujo ham, reasonable prices. -

Casa Mingo, Paeso de la Florida 2 - Closed Saturdays. In an old 'taverne' decor. Dinner outside in summer. Grilled chicken and Asturian cider. Ideal for lunch. Pts 800.

Casa Paco, Puerta Cerrada 11, Tel. (91) 266 31 66 - Closed Sundays and in August. Atmosphere of a real *'mesón'* (Catalan 'taverne'). Steakhouse specialties. Pts 2,000-4,000.

Salvador, Barbieri 12, Tel. (91) 521 45 24 - Closed Sundays and in August. Bullfighting restaurant decorated with photos and trophies. Family cuisine.

Taberna Carmencita, Libertad 16, Tel. (91) 531 66 12 - Metro: Chueca - Closed in August. Pts 4000.

El Pescador, José Ortega y Gasset 75, Tel. (91) 402 12 90 - Closed Sundays. Delicious fish specialties. Pts 5,000.

TAPAS BARS

Bocaíto, Libertad 6 - Reputed to serve the best tapas in Madrid.

Las Bravas, Alvarez Gato 6 - For its *papatas bravas*.

Casa Alberto, Huerta 8 - Tapas eaten standing at the bar in beautiful wine cellar.

La Chuleta, Echegaray 20 - Bullfighting atmosphere.

La Dolores, Plaza de Jésus 4 - In a noisy ambiance, the best beer in Madrid accompanies the tapas. A few tables.

Mesón Gallego, León 4 - For its *caldo gallego*.

The Reporter, Fúcar 6 - For its trellised terrace.

La Trucha, Manuel Fernandez y Gonzales 3 - The tapas are delicious.

BARS

Café Gijon, Paeso de Recoletos 24 - One of the best known cafés of the capital.

Chicote, Gran Via 12 - Immortalized in Hemingway works.

Los Gabrieles, Echegara 17 - Little known by tourists.

Cervecería Alemana, Plaza Santa Ana 6 - Closed Tuesdays. Another Hemingway refuge. Tapas.

Hermanos Muniz, Huerta 29 -

Typically Spanish.

Café Commercial, Glorietta de Bilbao 10 - Superb, go and have a *café solo o cortado* (black or with milk).

Bar Cock, Calle Reina 16 (corner Alcala and Gran Via) - Kitsch, to the glory of the famous Madrid barman, Don Chicote.

Viva Madrid, Calle Manuel González y Fernandez 7 - Old 'azuleros', tapas.

Circulo's, Alcala 42 - Magnificent 19th century café, base of the 'Cercle des Beaux-Arts' club. Frequented by artists and intellectuals.

FLAMENCO

EL Andalus, Capitan Hayas 19 - **Café de Chinitas,** Torija 7, Tel. (91) 248 51 35 - One of the best known and most touristy. Dinner served.

Corral de la Pacheca, Juan Ramon Jiménez 26, Tel. (91) 458 11 13 - Less touristy, more reasonable prices.

NIGHT BARS

Teatrix, hermosilla 15. Open night and day. Decor by Starck for this old theater. A lot of ambiance in this bar-restaurant – **Joy Eslava**, Arenal 11, an another theater changed in a nightclub, open until 5 a.m. – **Viva Madrid**, Manuel Fernandez y Gonzalez 17 (near plaza Santa Ana), tapas-bar very frequented until 2 a.m. – **Chocolateria San Gines**, at the end of Joy Eslava, the appointment of the reveller for the breakfast.

BASQUE COUNTRY

SAN SEBASTIÃN

Arzak, Alto de Miracruz 2, Tel. (943) 27 84 65 - Closed 3 weeks in June and 3 weeks in September. The reputation of the cuisine of Juan Mari Arzah has gone beyond the frontiers. Delicious Basque cuisine, delicious pastries. - **Salduba,** Pescaderia 6, Tel. (943) 42 56 27 - Closed Sundays and June 10 to July 10. Pts 3,000-4,000. - **Bodegon Alejandro,** Fermin Calbeton 22, Tel. (943) 42 11 58 - Closed Sunday evenings, Mondays, November 15-30, in February. Pts 2,800-4,600.

FUENTARRABIA

Ramón Roteta, Villa Ainara Irun, Tel. (943) 64 16 93 - Closed Thursdays and Sunday evenings except in summer. Very good cuisine served in summer in the garden of this beautiful old villa.– **Zeria,** San Pedro 23, Tel. (943) 64 27 80 - Closed Sunday evening, Thursday (except in summer), November. Pts 3500-4000. – **Kupela,** Zuloaga 4, Tel. (943) 64 40 25.

SANTANDER

Posada del Mar, Juan de la Cosa 3, Tel. (942) 21 56 56 - Closed Sunday, 10 September to 10 October. Pts 4000. – **Bodega del**

Riojano, Rio de la Pila 5, Tel. (942) 21 67 50 - Closed Sunday evenings. Lots of charm and atmosphere in this former wine cellar. Seasonal and market cuisine. - **La Sardina,** Dr Fleming 3, Tel. (942) 27 10 35 - **Au Sardinero,** closed Sunday evenings, Tuesdays except in summer. Pts 3,700-5,600.

V A L E N C I A

VALENCIA

La Hacienda, Navarro Reverter 12, Tel. (96) 373 18 59 - Closed Saturday middays, Sundays and in Holy Week. The chic restaurant of Valencia. Good classical cuisine. Reservation advised. Pts 4,500-5,800. - **Civera,** Lerida 11, Tel. (96) 347 59 17 - Closed Sunday evenings, Mondays and in August. Great specialist in grilled, poached and salted fish. Delicious but expensive. Reservation advised. Pts 4,500. - **El Timonel,** Felix

Pizcueta 13, Tel. (96) 352 63 00 -
Closed Mondays, Holy Week and
in August. Very good fish cooked
simply. Pts 3,500-5,000.

MORELLA

Mesón del Pastor, Cuesta Jovani
3, Tel. (964) 16 02 49 - Closed
Wednesdays. Savory cuisine.

INDEX

INDEX

M

N

O

P

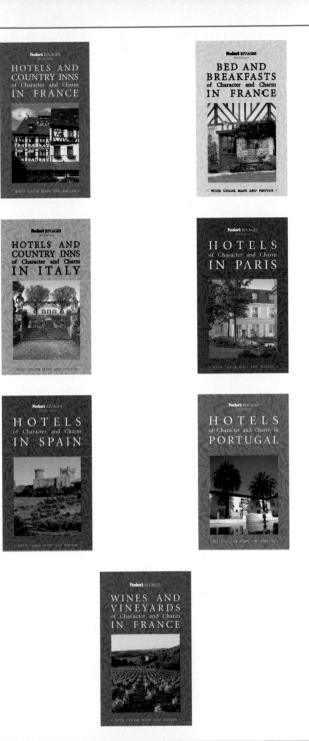

NOTES

NOTES

NOTES

NOTES

NOTES

NOTES

NOTES

NOTES